WHISTLING IN THE DARK

WHISTLING IN THE DARK

TWENTY-ONE QUEER INTERVIEWS

Edited by
R. RAJ RAO
DIBYAJYOTI SARMA

SAGE Los Angeles • London • New Delhi • Singapore • Washington DC
www.sagepublications.com

First published in 2009 by

 SAGE Publications India Pvt Ltd
B1/I-1 Mohan Cooperative Industrial Area
Mathura Road, New Delhi 110 044, India
www.sagepub.in

SAGE Publications Inc
2455 Teller Road
Thousand Oaks
California 91320, USA

SAGE Publications Ltd
1 Oliver's Yard
55 City Road
London EC1Y 1SP, United Kingdom

SAGE Publications Asia-Pacific Pte Ltd
33 Pekin Street
#02-01 Far East Square
Singapore 048763

Published by Vivek Mehra for SAGE Publications India Pvt Ltd, typeset in 10.5/14 Garamond by Diligent Typesetter, Delhi and printed at Chaman Enterprises, New Delhi.

Library of Congress Cataloging-in-Publication Data

Whistling in the dark: twenty-one queer interviews/edited by R. Raj Rao,
    Dibyajyoti Sarma.
        p. cm.
    Includes bibliographical references.
    1. Homosexuality.   2. Gays—Interviews.   I. Rao, R. Raj.   II. Sarma,
Dibyajyoti.

HQ76.25.W4775   306.76'60954—dc22   2009   2008048925
ISBN: 978-81-7829-921-1 (PB)

The SAGE Team: Rekha Natarajan, Prashant Gupta and Trinankur Banerjee

Cover: A still from BomGay (1996) directed by Riyad Wadia.

To
Ashok Row Kavi

CONTENTS

INTRODUCTION

R. RAJ RAO

I

In 1999, a few former students and I got together to form the Queer Studies Circle (QSC), a support group that was concerned with the intellectual, cultural, social and political aspects of being gay in India, rather than with issues like AIDS.[1] We felt that most support groups in the country had come to acquire a one-point agenda: HIV and AIDS. It was a funding matter—there was big money in AIDS coming from wealthy NGOs abroad, so everyone wanted to milk the AIDS cow. This, of course, was not to undermine the excellent work that some of these support groups were doing. Yet, to our way of thinking, it made the issue of gayness rather grim. A stage had come, thanks to worldwide propaganda, when homosexuality came to be seen as synonymous with AIDS. Was there none left who wanted to celebrate gayness? we asked ourselves.

At meetings, which were held in my office in the Department of English, University of Pune, we encouraged people to talk. We wanted them to acquaint us with their personal histories, perhaps even jot them down in writing. In order to do so, we provided them with pointers. There are multiple queer sex identities in India: gay, bi, MSM (men who have sex with men), *hijra* (eunuch), *koti* (effeminate men, usually passive in the sex act), etc. How did they view themselves? Since several members were married to women, who, according to them, did not have an inkling of their interest in other men, did that not, in a way, endorse patriarchy and male chauvinism from a feminist point of view? In short, were they not cheating on their wives?

The idea for this book took shape during those meetings. Most—though by no means all—interviewees here are those who have come to QSC at some stage in its nine-year existence. These include people not just from India, but also from countries like Canada, Spain, Sri Lanka, Mauritius and even Iran. However, one of the highlights of the book is that it also features interviews with several MSMs from plebeian society, such as auto-rickshaw drivers and masseurs. Two of our respondents have been imprisoned for sex-based crimes, and speak to us of their experiences in jails, notorious for the kinds of things that go on there. Such interviews were surreptitiously conducted in the manner of a Tehelka-type sting operation. We realised that if we revealed to our respondents that we were interviewing them for a book of this kind, and switched on a tape-recorder or took notes as they spoke, they would never open up to the fullest and speak from the depth of their hearts. So we employed different strategies to get them to talk, which included partying with them and taking them on overnight jaunts to nearby hill stations like Matheran and Lonavla.[2] Some interviews were conducted not in one sitting but over a period of time. As such, the majority of interviews in the book appear under assumed names, which makes it impossible for readers to identify the people about whom we write. If this seems controversial or politically incorrect to some, we accept the blame for it in all humility. Our aim was to present the life stories, nay testimonies of queer men and women, as they actually exist, without vetting or editing them in the interest of propriety. To us, the experiences and personal histories were as important as the issues arising out of queerness, since to artificially separate the two in the manner of most academic books smacked of prudishness. In any case, we were not aiming at a hard-core academic book, but wanted to produce a work of non-fiction that, like fiction, was able to sustain the interest of the general reader, even as it educated him about an aspect of life about which he knew very little or virtually nothing. What we ended up securing, then, is a range of thought, with the ideas of Michel Foucault at one end of the spectrum, and voyeuristic street sex at the other; the 'respectable' interview, needless to say, would preclude the latter. Also, we, the editors, were not putting ourselves on a pedestal and adopting a holier-than-thou attitude. Most respondents spoke to us with a frankness that is unusual precisely because they knew us well as out gay men, icons even, and took us to be one of them. If they had experiences and encounters, so did we. It is this that enabled us to win their confidence. Undoubtedly, we did not come across to them as cats among the pigeons.

My university went autonomous around the turn of the century. Soon after the formation of QSC, I formulated a course on gay and lesbian literature to be taught to fourth semester M.A. students. The Board of Studies in English (BSE), an academic body made up of politically rather than academically minded individuals, promptly singled it out and rejected it, remarking that Indian students did not need such a course! Matters really got ugly when the local English language press reported this on the front page, quoting both the statements of the chairman of the BSE as well as my statements made in defence of the course, as a sort of rejoinder. The newspaper, a leading English daily, seemed to be entirely on our side, for ours, after all, was the progressive side, but this did not cut ice with the BSE. In questioning the need for such a course to be taught in an Indian university, the BSE was really reinforcing the familiar stereotype of gayness and lesbianism as corrupt Western imports, alien to the sanitised culture of India. Nothing could be further from the truth. India is not just the land of Khajuraho and the *Kamasutra* and the *ghazal* as a lyric form that celebrated homosexual love, but there are a whole host of myths pertaining to same-sex love that surround our very gods and goddesses (Pattanaik 2008, Vanita and Kidwai 2000). Thus, the attitude and the approach of the BSE were parochial. But the BSE was not unique in its hostility towards the course. As Ruth Vanita and Saleem Kidwai point out, there is a

> ...studied silence maintained by the Indian academy on the subject of homo-
> sexuality. While avidly picking up other kinds of critical theory generated in
> the Western academy, such as Marxism, feminism, deconstruction and post-
> colonial theory, the Indian academy has by and large avoided lesbian and gay
> studies. (Vanita and Kidwai 2000: 205)

When I conceived the idea of such a course, which was already being taught by my friend Dr Hoshang Merchant at the University of Hyderabad, my idea was to bring QSC members and students who opted for the course together on a common platform to brainstorm issues. Unfortunately, the resistance displayed by the BSE towards initiating change, abruptly put an end to that dream. For a number of years, the course continued to be listed in the prospectus of my department, but ironically, students could not opt for it, even if they wanted to. The QSC was in possession of its own resource centre, but the course simply couldn't be taught because of BSE's embargo.

Then, sometime in 2006, I was invited by my university's Canadian Studies Programme to organise a three-day international conference on queer-related issues the following year. This reflected openness on the university's part, a willingness to break taboos, which was heartening. I immediately accepted the offer and got to work, enlisting the support of my very close friend Thomas Waugh, Film Studies professor at the Mel Hoppenheim School of Cinema, Concordia University, Montreal. Together, we zeroed in on a theme for the conference and drew up a tentative list of participants from both Canada and India. For a whole year, we sent out invitations, received both acceptances and rejections, and discussed conference budgets.

The conference finally took place in February 2007. We called it 'Queer Literature and Cinema: The Canadian and Indian Experience'. A galaxy of luminaries attended it, comprising both writers and filmmakers. These included Shani Mootoo, Saleem Kidwai, John Palmer, James Miller, Ruth Vanita, Ashok Row Kavi, Etienne Desrosiers, Hoshang Merchant, Sridhar Rangayan, Parmesh Shahani, Sarah Stanley, Richard Fung, Onir, the director of the critically acclaimed film *My Brother Nikhil*, which was screened at the conference, and of course Thomas Waugh and myself. For the first time in India had so many distinguished queer men and women gathered under a single roof and that too in an academic institution. The sessions went off superbly, despite Pune's ludicrous power cuts, each presentation being something to write home about. However, I had two regrets. The first was that student presence at the conference was minimal, and the reason for this, according to me, was that many students had mistakenly assumed that anyone and everyone who attended the conference had to be gay and lesbian themselves! In other words, being seen at the conference amounted to being 'outed', to declaring one's sexuality, and this none of them wished to risk, regardless of their own sexual orientation. If this betrayed a sort of homophobia on their part, my other observation was much worse. I discovered to my consternation that several members of the general public, though educated and English-speaking, had found their way to the conference, widely publicised in the press, only to network for the explicit purpose of sexual activity! This was unfortunate. Yet, one of biggest surprises in store was the mammoth audience that turned up on the last day of the conference for a theatrical presentation of 'Off Beat' in Marathi and English by Zameer Kamble and his friends. The sheer numbers in the auditorium compelled me to reconsider my earlier view that students shied away from the conference fearing the queer label. Perhaps it was something else not known to me.

In the next academic year, June 2007, the ban on the gay and lesbian literature course was finally revoked. A change in the nomenclature was all it took to convince the powers that be that a course of this kind was in order. Earlier, we simply called the course Lesbian and Gay Literature in India, or some such thing, whereas we now prefixed that with 'Alternative Literature II', so that the full title of the course was Alternative Literature II: Lesbian, Gay, Bisexual and Transgender (LGBT) Writing in India. But the change in the nomenclature was not just cosmetic. We offer a course called Alternative Literature I: Dalit Writing in India, and by calling our course Alternative Literature II, we were emphasising the underlying connection between both these forms of marginal literature or literature of protest: we were suggesting that coalitions of oppressed groups was the need of the hour.

I nervously introduced the course to fourth semester M.A. (English) students, who would be opting for it, at a meeting of students and faculty. I found myself ending my introduction with a disclaimer: opting for the course did not mean that those who took it were lesbian or gay.

There were titters among the students. When the polling was over and the votes were counted, I discovered that there were well over the mandatory five students—the minimum number required to start a course—who had signed up for it. The number was actually closer to fifteen or twenty, though this included some students who chose to audit but not take up the course. My joy knew no bounds. Of course, it is not easy to please everyone, and a couple of students from conservative countries like Iran had to quit the course merely because the university authorities insisted on printing both parts of the course title (Alternative Literature II: Lesbian, Gay, Bisexual and Transgender Literature in India) on the certificates. These students argued that the explicit use of the words lesbian, gay, bisexual and transgender would land them in trouble with the government of their country, once they received their degrees and went back.

II

The mainstreaming of queer identity entails treating lesbians, gays, bisexuals, transgender persons, and so on, on par with heterosexuals. Urvashi Vaid speaks of the goals of such mainstreaming as 'civil rights for lesbian and gay people and our integration into the mainstream of politics, law and society' (Vaid 1995). Thus, gay marriages, which are currently legalised only in a handful of countries like Canada, Spain, the Netherlands, South Africa and a couple of states in the USA, must gain worldwide recognition and support. In India, archaic 19th century laws such as Section 377 of the Indian Penal Code (IPC), authored by T.B. Macaulay, the very man who introduced English education in this country in 1835, must be abolished. Queer activists lobby for the same personal rights and privileges as enjoyed by heterosexuals, ideally wanting nothing to be different except the gender of one of the partners. Needless to say, global capitalism gives a fillip to such a viewpoint. It is well known that queer men and women have higher disposable incomes than heterosexuals, and now the market forces want that money, which can only be had by brainwashing queer people into spending on consumer durables and the like. One of the dubious ways in which this is achieved is by co-opting queers into heteronormativity, so that they live under the perpetual illusion that they are a family, and even start spending like a heteropatriarchal family. Advancements in science such as sex reassignment surgeries and test-tube babies, and changes in adoption laws that permit queer people to adopt children, all lend their tacit support. The seduction is also engineered by the media, advertising, fashion designing and even mainstream literature—witness, for example, J.K. Rowling making Dumbledore, one of the characters in her Harry Potter series of novels, gay. Similarly, in February 2008, Bombay's prestigious Kala Ghoda Arts Festival, a *Times of India* event, included for the first time a panel discussion on lesbian and gay literature, entitled 'Queering the Pitch', moderated by Vikram Doctor, the founder of Gay Bombay, in which I was one of the panellists.

The AIDS endemic has played a major role in the appropriation of queerness by heteronormativity. In the absence, as yet, of a foolproof cure for HIV/AIDS, the least complicated way of tackling the disease is to implore gay men to forfeit their supposedly promiscuous lifestyles and embrace monogamy. This perpetuates the myth that a gay couple is no different form a straight couple, for the former, like the latter, remain faithful and committed to each other till death does them apart.

What such a myopic point of view overlooks is the intrinsic quality of resistance built into queerness that is now being traded for political correctness. Thus, Barbara Ryan's notion of political lesbianism is a form of resistance to heteropatriarchy. Similarly, in an interactive session in my department in December 2007, Professor Gayatri Spivak said, in response to a question on the subject put to her by the audience that 'gay marriage is writing back into heteronormativity'.

Indeed, the metaphoric implications of queerness are lost when one begins to see things from a purely pragmatic perspective. One such implication is that queer culture is counter culture, and must challenge mainstream assumptions exactly as, say, the Beat generation in the 1950s or the hippies in the 1960s did, opposing the values of the majority, should the need arise, even for their own sake. The Beats

...dressed in sweatshirts or sweaters or boat-neck fisherman shirts, sandals, dungarees, dark glasses and berets, lived in garage apartments, North Beach walk-ups, little cottages, and storefronts, listened to jazz records, drank wine and smoked marijuana and ingested Benzedrine to stay up all night and be startled at their revelations, rejoiced in sex, painted and admired paintings, wrote poetry and admired poetry, and—most of all—they were young, even if sometimes in a morose, bored but intense and intellectual way. (Dalzell 1996)

Based on Jonathan Dollimore's readings of Oscar Wilde's life and work (Dollimore 1991), one speculates that queer sexuality, when genuinely subversive or transgressive, among other things, inverts the notions of sameness and difference. What is *same/similar* in non-transgressive sexuality is *different* here, for example, age and class. On the other hand, what is *different* in non-transgressive sexuality is *same* here, for example, gender. Naturally, it does not, a priori, follow that all gay sex is transgressive, while all straight sex is non-transgressive. In truth, there is a spectrum of possibilities. Two midway positions would be (*i*) a gay couple of the same age and social status, and (*ii*) a straight couple from different social strata and/ or with a significant age difference between them. One of the implications of subversive or transgressive sexuality is that one is not looking for sexual compatibility and intellectual compatibility in the same partner.

Hence, subversive or transgressive sexuality rejects the twin myths of monogamy and fidelity. It endorses the idea of multiple partners and celebrates promiscuity, which it does not view as infidelity. Perhaps it even recognises that 'adultery' incorporates the word 'adult', so that faithfulness is puerile. It defers judgement on paid sex and sex tourism, and questions the validity of received terminology like 'prostitution' (for what is heteronormative marriage if not a form of prostitution?). The mantra of subversive, transgressive sexuality may be said to be 'more the merrier at whatever cost', while its methods might include hooking, seduction, the roving eye and sexual favours. Subversive, transgressive sexuality also pits lust against love, only to abjure the latter. Accordingly, it approves of flings, affairs and one-night stands, but not of relationships that are anathema to it. Similarly, it recommends all forms of sexual activity other than vaginal intercourse, which is capable of leading to pregnancy and childbirth. These would include anal sex, oral sex and masturbation. In queer theory, the anus is not just an orifice in the body for the discharge of excrement. Like the vagina in feminism, it is a political site, with all its implications of entry, exit, surrender and feminisation of the male body.

Given its radicalism, the onus of a transgressive aesthetic rests on the arts—literature, theatre, cinema and painting. The real world is too self-righteous to experiment with true alterity and frequently, what passes off for transgression is only an eyewash. But contemporary literature, theatre, cinema and painting, through a paradigm shift in their very idiom and ideology, become invested with a power to dismantle structures. This, I would say, is the pioneering contribution, in India, of painters like the late Bhupen Khakhar, filmmakers like the late Riyad Wadia, and of writers like Suniti Namjoshi, Hoshang Merchant, Mahesh Dattani and I. In any case, metaphor as a device, strategy and figure of speech bears a connection to the imagined rather than to reality, though a few like the bearded poet Hoshang Merchant (a latter day Walt Whitman or Allen Ginsberg) may have attempted to make it a part of their highly idiosyncratic lifestyle.

A gay writer is not one who merely writes on gay themes: it is imperative for him to have 'come out' as well. The mere presence of a gay character in Makarand Paranjape's *The Narrator* (1996) does not make Paranjape a gay writer. Again, Vikram Chandra's short story 'Artha' (1997) does not in itself suffice to define Chandra as a gay writer. For one thing, Chandra writes about his gay lovers exactly as if he were writing about a straight couple.[3] More significantly, however, Chandra, like Paranjape, does not identify himself as gay. The issue here, without intending to be essentialist or reductive, is whether one writes as an insider or as an outsider. For this reason, gay literature, like any alternative literature, must formulate its own critical tools and critical vocabulary by which it must be evaluated, in the absence of which it may emerge as aesthetically inferior. This is because gay writing is writing against the grain, often unabashedly autobiographical and confessional, cashing in on personal histories and underscoring the 'personal as political' principle. However, to the extent that gay writing is propaganda, what needs to be reiterated is that agendas are not necessarily at the expense of craft, and might be manifested at best in the fictional *point of view*, whereas aspects pertaining to craft, such as language, diction, imagery, plot, characterisation and narration, would, as in the case of mainstream literature, depend on the author's talent. In short, there can be both good and bad gay writing.

To a gay writer, art and activism are (or should be) two sides of the same coin. One cannot write from the point of view of a gay protagonist, and then shy away from, or feel squeamish about, responding to helpline calls from homosexuals in distress. This would amount to hypocrisy. On the other hand, to reject the 'gay writer' label is to be status quoist, for labels, however undesirable, are necessary in the short run. The long-term goal is, of course, revolutionary change, but in order to accomplish this, some ghettoisation is inevitable in the short run. A ghetto, thus, is not a place that smacks of claustrophobia, in-breeding and parochialism. Instead, a ghetto is like a trade union where the like-minded bond.

The French philosopher Michel Foucault says: 'One day the question, "Are you homosexual?" will be as natural as the question, "Are you a bachelor?"' (Lotringer 1996).

This is a utopian statement, the signfier 'one day' pointing to the idealised future. Also, 'bachelor', unlike homosexual, is a neutral construct that implies a deferring of judgement, as well as an expression of choice—the choice to stay single.

I said earlier that neither Makarand Paranjape nor Vikram Chandra identifies himself as gay. But what does gay identity mean? It means, for one, that though we possess multiple identities and are fragmented subjects, identity based on sexual orientation is not subsumed by previous categories of race, class and gender. If these identities intrude, so that a white gay man foregrounds skin colour in his dealings with a gay Asian or African, or a gay prince like Prince Manvendra, a contemporary Rajput prince from Rajpipla, Gujarat,[4] foregrounds class in his dealings with, say, a gay servant in his father's palace, then perhaps it is time for queerness to secede from the union of identity markers, and establish itself as an autonomous category (Raj Rao 2001).

III

Heterosexism is the fallacious belief that the prerequisite for sexual attraction is that the partners invariably be of opposite sexes, that is, male and female. However, heterosexism serves the interests of homoerotically inclined men in most Eastern cultures, including India, by allowing them to establish an alibi: it guarantees that a homosexual liaison arouses no suspicion in the minds of one's immediate kith and kin, and indeed, society at large, by making the association seem like friendship, or, to use a more resonant word, *yaari*. Two people of the same gender can never be lovers—they can only be friends. Conversely, two people of the opposite sex, when seen together, must inevitably be in a sexual relationship.

In India, heterosexism reinforces social and cultural taboos that insist on a segregation of the sexes until marriage. Boys and girls are not allowed to mingle before marriage, which is strictly arranged by parents and other family members, and this is manifested in the way, say, there are specially demarcated seats for women in trains and buses, or even separate queues for them in cinema halls and places of religious worship. Similarly, dorms and hostels in educational institutions are classified on lines of gender—there are men's hostels and women's hostels, but never any type of student accommodation in which men and women might live together! Several surveys and opinion polls conducted from time to time by newspapers and private television channels have revealed that a majority of Indians, including urban, educated, English-speaking Indians, prefer arranged marriages to love marriages. Needless to say, the conservatism fostered by global capitalism is responsible for this to a large extent, as an analysis of mainstream Indian cinema demonstrates.

The socialism of the 1970s and 1980s yielded a movie like *Ek Duje Ke Liye*, where the heroine, Rati Agnihotri, in order to defy her mother who sets fire to a photograph of her lover Kamal Hasan in her presence, drops the charred remains of the photo into a glass of milk and drinks it up. The global capitalism of the mid-1990s, by contrast, gave us a film like *Dilwale Dulhaniya Le Jayenge*, where the hero Shah Rukh Khan prefers being beaten up by the heroine Kajol's father, Amrish Puri, to eloping with her without his blessings. This movie, alarmingly, also betrays the conspiracy that exists between capitalism and its close ally, patriarchy, for the hero rejects a well-intentioned suggestion by the heroine's mother, Farida Jalal, that her husband being stubborn and unreasonable, he should run away with her daughter, and leave the consequences to her. We have every reason to conclude, on the basis of this scene, that Shah Rukh Khan, when he becomes a father himself, will be no different from the dictatorial Amrish Puri.

The fallout of all this is that homosexuality flourishes, albeit by default. It does not take institutions like the military or jails, where men are denied the company of women for extended periods, for them to turn to one another. All of India is like the army, or a prison, where men and women are sexually quarantined. Female sex workers, of course, who inhabit the red light district of most towns and cities, may provide an option, but many men prefer causal sex with other men to visits to female sex workers, because the former is free of cost and the chances of contracting VD or HIV are, in their view, less. This, in fact, is how an MSM community comes into being.

MSMs are those for whom sexual activity with persons of their own gender neither constitutes an identity nor a preference. At best, they see it as a tendency, something they have got addicted to like tobacco or alcohol, and find it hard to relinquish. Obviously, there is an implicit sense of denial in their stance, in their perception of themselves, that needs to be dealt with through counselling, and this is where support groups come into the picture. Yet, the large number of non-heteronormative male single-sex spaces that dot the socio-cultural landscape of India, nourishes the existence of MSMs. These homosocial spaces include the *nukkad* or street corner, the public urinal, the beer and country liquor bar, the *paan-beedi* (betel nut and cigarette) and *gutkha* (tobacco) stall, the hair-cutting saloon, the auto-rickshaw stand, the chai *tapri*, the second-class local-train compartment, and so on, where mischief rules, where the watchword is *masti* and the idiom macho. Ashok Row Kavi's over-generalised, unpublished view that a non-heteronormative male single-sex space like a beer bar cannot nevertheless become a cruising site without jeopardising the safety of a man who makes a pass at another man, is, in my experience, sometimes disproved by what goes on in actual practice.

It is the existence of male single-sex spaces and the alibi offered by the notion of *yaari*, that makes Amol Palekar's 2006 film *Quest* based on a story by his wife Sandhya Gokhale unconvincing. But first, what is *yaari*? Who is a *yaar*? Raj Ayar says, 'There is really no English equivalent of the concept, no word that approaches its breadth and depth. Friend is not enough. Buddy is superficial...' (Ayyar 1993).

Ayyar himself attempts a definition of the elusive term when he says, 'For me a *yaar* embodies elements of both a friend and a lover and I yearn for just such a connection with a man in my life' (Ayyar 1993: 167).

Elsewhere, I have pointed out that while a man may refer to a male friend as a *yaar*, a woman can also call her male lover her *yaar* (Raj Rao 2000). The word is thus enriched by its ambivalence, its greyness.

In *Quest*, the wife, Sai, unexpectedly returns home one morning to find her husband Aditya in bed with his best friend Uday. All hell breaks loose after that, and we are forced to suffer her hysterics for the rest the film (Gokhale 2006). In an interactive session at Open Space, Pune, after a special screening of the film, both Palekar and Gokhale pleaded ignorance about the existence of the buffer zone provided by male single-sex spaces in India, and by the notion of *yaari*. Their conception of the film, and of the character of Sai, seemed to me to be westernised in the extreme, borne out by the fact that Gokhale has been, for many years, a resident of New York City.

Although art house cinema in India has so far failed to treat the subject of alternative sexuality with sensitivity, mainstream cinema, ironically enough, especially the cinema of the 1970s and 1980s, featuring superstar Amitabh Bachchan, who disrupted the running-around-trees romantic flick of the 1960s through his sheer presence, is increasingly beginning to lend itself to queer interpretations. These films cash in on the idea of both male single-sex space and *yaari*, and were mostly scripted by the male writer duo Salim–Javed. Queer readings are possible not just of the films themselves, but also of the songs.[5] The 1975 blockbuster *Sholay*, set in the wilderness of the imaginary Ramgarh with two tramps and former jailbirds, Jai and Veeru, for protagonists, is one such film that finds an excellent parallel in the overtly gay, 2007 film *Brokeback Mountain* featuring two Wyoming cowboys, Ennis Del Mar and Jack Twist. *Brokeback Mountain* is in fact the other side of *Sholay*, its off-screen side. The *Yeh Dosti* number sung by Jai and Veeru on a motorbike emerges as a queer song when one scrutinises its lyrics and imagery.[6] If audiences are resistant to queer interpretations of the song, as my experience has repeatedly shown, it is merely because heterosexism interferes: there is nothing latent in the song to prove that it is not queer. In the end, however, I win by asking my audience, made up mostly of postgraduate students and college-level teachers, a simple question: if Amitabh Bachchan were to be replaced in the song by Hema Malini, the heroine, so that it became a regular duet between her and Dharmendra, would they still insist that the song was no more than a song of friendship? And the answer is a resounding NO.

Substituting Hema Malini for Amitabh Bachchan—an extraneous act—is enough to confer on the song the status of a love lyric! There we are! Heterosexim at work!

IV

Section 377 of the Indian Penal Code says:

> Whoever voluntarily has carnal intercourse against the order of the nature with any man, woman or animal, shall be punished with imprisonment for life, or with imprisonment of either description for a term which may extend to 10 years, and shall also be liable to fine.

> Explanation. Penetration is sufficient to constitute the carnal intercourse necessary to the offence described in this section.

This law, sometimes known as the anti-sodomy law, was introduced by T.B. Macaulay in October 1860, and continues to be in force even today. Macaulay's reasons for introducing it were Victorian, and bear a connection to his previous controversial document, *Minute on Education*, that, apart from gifting us the English language, had many uncharitable things to say about the indigenous systems of education of a civilisation 5,000 years old. In both cases, the aim was purism. Ronald Hyam speaks of the 'fanatical purity campaigns' (Hyam 1990)[7] that obsessed British imperialists in the 18th and 19th centuries. The English system of education, Macaulay felt, would put an end to the cultural decadence that had set in at the end of the 18th century. Similarly, a law that validated only 'natural' sex, that is, vaginal intercourse between a man and a woman, and made all other innovative forms of sexual activity illegal, would effectively terminate the licentiousness that was the legacy of medieval India. Britain itself scrapped the law in 1967, a little over a hundred years after it was introduced in India, but India continues to hold on to it for reasons best known to our politicians.

The law, technically, makes all gay men criminals. Lesbians are probably excluded from its purview, because the emphasis seems to be on penetration. Few convictions may have actually happened under Section 377, but that could be because the corrupt police have a vested interest in not letting the matter reach the courts: their bribes. The few convictions that *have* taken place mostly involve minors, and this lends credence to the official view that the law is needed in order to make child sexual abuse a punishable offence. However, there are other IPC laws that safeguard the interests of children.

Some years ago, the Naz Foundation, a Delhi-based NGO concerned with AIDS, filed a PIL in the Delhi High Court, asking for a reading down of Section 377 to exclude consensual sex between gay men above the age of 18. But, as Gautam Bhan argues,

> If we read down the law, we decriminalise same-sex sexual activity between consenting adults in private. What we do not do is challenge the idea of 'unnatural' sexual activity in the first place. At present, there is a clear and hierarchical division between natural/unnatural, public/private, heterosexual/homosexual sex in our legal code, and an understanding (given the government's response) that this hierarchy is reflective of the way Indian society thinks. Reading down the law would simply ensure that we do not

fall under the 'criminal' category anymore but it would not, in any way, challenge the very idea that the state, law and society has the right to decide that certain sexual acts are 'unnatural'. (Bhan 2005)

Be that as it may, the union government, not willing to take a stand, has been dithering on its decision to abolish or even read down the law. A recent intervention by the National Aids Control Organisation (NACO), also a government body, has put the union government in a spot. For NACO has endorsed the view of the Naz Foundation that Section 377 is in a way responsible for the spread of AIDS, because it encourages homosexual men—many of whom are married—to be in hiding and in denial, and not come forward for testing and for treatment, once they are infected, in fear of being 'outed', and then transmit the virus to their wives. However, far from embarrassing the union government, NACO's intervention seems to have made little difference to them, as they continue to vacillate, and the case continues to oscillate between the Delhi High Court and the Supreme Court, the latest being that the Delhi High Court has questioned the *locus standi* of the Naz Foundation to file the PIL, as it is not, in legal language, an interested party.

Progressive Indians are all in favour of repealing Section 377, which, fundamentally, is a violation of personal freedom. The English-language press and private television channels have frequently featured stories in support of gay rights, and no less a legal luminary than former Attorney General of India, Soli Sorabjee, seems to concur with their point of view, as his public utterances have often shown. Last year, writer Vikram Seth was one of the panellists on a 'We the People' show on NDTV 24×7, anchored by the redoubtable Barkha Dutt, and he used the opportunity to declare that he is 'gay or partly gay', even as he too called for a reading down of Section 377. But the presence of celebrities notwithstanding, India continues to be one of the few countries in the world where a draconian 19th century law rules the roost in the 21st century.

Law-enforcing agencies such as the police use Section 377 to harass homosexuals, unlike the West, not out of any genuine homophobic conviction, but merely to grease their palms. In truth, it matters not a farthing to them whether a man sleeps with women or with men. In a stage-managed act, I was once caught by cops in Bombay, who, after they had received their bribe, sang a completely different tune, saying homosexuality was fine by them as long as it was practised in private and not in public. 'You see, our seniors will pull us up if we turn a blind eye to homosexual acts practised in public', they had the temerity to say, after they had made me poorer by 5,000 bucks! These cops eventually got so friendly with me that they even offered to find me a place to make out, and partners too!

Not so long ago, the police, on the doubtful complaint of a local *maalishwallah* (masseur), raided the office of a gay support group in Lucknow and issued non-bailable warrants against several gay-rights activists who ran the NGO, besides destroying valuable literature. The activists had to spend close to a month in jail for no culpable crime. Identical incidents have been reported from cities like Bangalore. The lower echelons of the police in these instances are simply unable to differentiate between a sex club and a support group with seriousness of intent, and they receive little help from their superiors. What does one do in the face of such ignorance?

If the police hound homosexuals exactly as they hound, say, Maoist Naxalites, there are other parallels as well between these two outlawed, underground communities, that link ideology to violence, literal and figurative. Like Vikram Seth, I was once a panellist on a 'We the People' show, soon after the publication of my novel *The Boyfriend*, and found myself in the company of the late Nishit Saran's mother, who was another panellist. Earlier, I had seen and admired Nishit Saran's film *Summer in My Veins*, which is about how he invited his mother to the US for his graduation ceremony and came out to her, not disclosing as he did so, that there was a hidden camera in the room! The result? The movie catches the mother's spontaneous reactions to her son's declarations about his homosexuality for which she was completely unprepared. A brilliant piece of reality cinema! However, shortly after he made the movie and returned to India, Nishit Saran tragically died in a car crash in Delhi, as he and his friends were returning from a party one Saturday night. On the Barkha Dutt show, his mother, who, after the death of her son, took the trouble to read up everything she could lay her hands on, on the subject of gayness, was opening the doors of her home to the queer community of India, saying that even if the whole world was against us, she was one person we could count on for succour and for patronage. She was being no different here from the mother in Mahasweta Devi's Bengali novel *Mother of 1084* (filmed by Govind Nihalani as *Hazar Chaurasi Ki Ma*, starring Jaya Bhaduri Bachchan in the role of a lifetime). The story is about a mother who, upon the death of her Naxalite son in a police encounter, assiduously studies the Naxalite movement, and becomes one of its foremost supporters, though until the time of her son's death she knew nothing about Naxalism and certainly had no inkling that her son was a Naxalite!

V

A number of issues are triggered off by the interviews in this volume, and one of the foremost of these is masculinity. To auto driver Aslam Shaikh, men cannot be commodities like women, so male prostitution by its very definition is a contradiction in terms. There are no red-light areas where men can be picked up, argues Shaikh, in whose view a man cannot be with another man without one of them thinking of himself as a woman. A passive sexual role, by this formulation, is tantamount to being a *hijra*, a much-misunderstood and much-maligned queer category. Shaikh sees his same-sex activity as a male privilege that excludes the wife if one, like Shaikh, is married. His view here is affirmed by small-town college lecturer Sushil Patil, who, when asked if he would accept his wife if he discovered that she was a lesbian and had a female lover, said, 'Absolutely not, I will not accept it.'

Masculinity raises its head in other working-class interviews. To Satish Ranadive, passivity in the sex act can be damaging to the male psyche. Similarly, for jailbird Avinash Gaitonde, who stalked us as we researched this book, and later went to jail on a rape charge for which he was acquitted, 'I must be the one who screws. I would never let another man screw me. It would violate my manliness…' Only Manohar Shitole questions the validity of the top/bottom binary when he asks, 'What's the harm in being versatile and playing both roles in accordance with one's bodily responses?'

Like Aslam Shaikh, Ganesh Holay is resistant to the idea of male prostitution though he himself has, on occasion, charged older, wealthy upper-class men who have had sex with him.

Both patriarchy and heterosexism inform the statements of Aslam Shaikh, Ganesh Holay, Avinash Gaitonde, Satish Ranadive and Manohar Shitole. Three of them Shitole, Holay and Ranadive, have been victims of gay bashing and recount their testimonies to us. Gay bashing, which is a universal phenomenon all over the world, including the West, is a direct consequence of the homophobia that permeates all layers of society. In India, the prevalence of Section 377 gives gay bashers the upper hand and enables them to go scot-free for crimes that warrant punishment. But the paradox is that in the eyes of the law it is gay men who are criminals, while gay bashers may be seen as those who wish to cleanse society, and are therefore forgiven for abominable acts that cause grievous injury to people who seek sexual fulfilment, which, after all, is a human need. As suggested earlier, however, in a poor country like India, the reasons for gay bashing may not even be ideological. The two broad categories of gay bashers are (i) the police and (ii) hoodlums, and both indulge in gay bashing for money. Their modus operandi is to act as agent provocateurs at typical cruising hotspots such as public parks and public toilets, and lure unsuspecting homosexual men into sexual activity, only to make a complete volte-face afterwards and reveal their true identity and true intent.[8] Homosexual men give in to their demands for cash and valuables for fear of blackmail, for the culprits usually threaten to call the homes of their victims and spill the beans. If one is caught by the police, there is the additional worry of being thrown into the lock-up and of not being able to admit to family members what got them there, so that they may bail them out. This, precisely, is the story of Ganesh Holay, who preferred doing time to calling his parents to get him released.

The English language, the *mahabhasha*, plays a significant role in the Indian queer culture. Much of the terminology is English, for ideas pertaining to queerness are expressible mainly in that language. The vernacular word *samlingi* (for a homosexual man) has gained currency only recently, and it is only in the present time that serious books such as *Indradhanu: Samleingikteche Vividh Rang* (Khire 2008) in Marathi, authored by Bindumadhav Khire, have begun to see the light of day. Gay support groups like the Humsafar Trust in Bombay and Sangama in Bangalore have tried, on occasion, to circumvent the divisive role played by English, spoken chiefly by upper-class college-educated men, by conducting meetings bilingually, whereby a statement made in English is immediately translated into the regional language for the benefit of those who don't know the queen's language. Manish Pawar touches upon the issue in his interview, as he talks about how he felt alienated at Humsafar Trust meetings, because the proceedings were in English. Pawar is the son of a truck driver and a ward-boy by occupation. Two constructs merge here, language and class, and go on to show, among other things, how cross-class sex typifies same-sex activity (possibly because true romance necessitates the presence of the 'other' in the self/other binary). If this reasoning seems specious or exploitative from, say, a hardliner Marxist point of view, it is because, as explained earlier, class as a category subsumes sexual orientation. It can be negotiated by letting one kind of empowerment cancel out another, and by asking that if exploitation is mutual, does it still amount to exploitation?

Ruth Vanita, commenting on *The Boyfriend*, says:

> Thus, in cross-class relations, it is not always...the subordinate who is exploited. When the social superior is single and the subordinate married, heterosexual privilege may trump class privilege and result in a transaction that is mutually useful but that downgrades the gay person. (Vanita 2005)

Manish Pawar remains one of the few working-class respondents in the book who refers to his visits to gay support groups in Bombay and Pune. Most others consciously avoid associating with these groups, as they are publicity-shy. Some men approach a support group with the express purpose of finding sexual partners, but are soon disillusioned. Their stance, in a way, is summed up by the lesbian who said, 'I just want to be gay, I don't want to attend conferences about it.'[9]

This is a reactionary statement that forestalls change, for support groups play a yeoman role, both socially and psychologically, in eradicating the misery that characterises the life of an average gay person. Yet those who have devoted their lives to the cause of gay liberation sometimes find themselves lonely, with martyrdom thrust upon them against their will. When Dibyajyoti Sarma asked Bindumadhav Khire, as he interviewed him, if he had a lover, Khire's reply was that no one wanted to have an affair with an activist because that would be suicidal! This obsession with personal safety also drives a wedge between *kotis* and straight-acting gay men, with the latter wanting to have little to do with the former socially, as they are perceived as a threat. Developing countries like India are more apt to revel in such skin-saving tactics than the developed countries of the West, where most universities, for example, have an LGBT association. Again, in a book like Barbara Summerhawk's *Queer Japan* (Summerhawk et al. 1998) many of the men and women interviewed, speak in favour of support groups, and admit that they gave them a fresh lease of life.

In a scenario where homosexuality is criminalised by the law, where heterosexism thrives, and where society insists on marriage and procreation, gay love is but likely to rely on chance and casual encounters that do not blossom into permanent relationships on account of the odds. The heterosexual mainstream accuses homosexuals of not being committed to the idea of love, and of not taking the trouble to nurture relationships, without bothering to go into the reasons for such 'irresponsible' behaviour, attributable, naturally, to society's hostility towards gays. Sushil Patil and Manohar Shitole, both married, middle-class Maharashtrian men in white-collar jobs operating within the framework of heteronormativity, imply in their interviews that though they would like to have long-term relationships with their male partners, they see this as an impossibility. They represent here the viewpoint of the majority of gay men in India. This is what makes the joint interview of Christopher Benninger and

Ram Naidu, by contrast, unique. Benninger and Naidu are committed lovers who have been living together for over a decade. To all intents and purposes, theirs is a gay marriage, though it is Naidu, the Indian, more than Benninger, the American, who prefers to see it this way. If it is not a marriage in the technical sense, it is because Section 377 makes homosexuality illegal, and even if it were not so, same-sex marriage does not exist in India. Moreover, Benninger who is an accomplished architect was married to an Indian woman before he met Naidu and that marriage is still to be annulled. However, it is to the credit of Benninger and Naidu that in spite of the odds, they have made their relationship work. In this, they are paralleled by another distinguished couple, the fashion designer Wendell Rodricks and his partner Jerome Marrel, who also consider their relationship a marriage, and who have been living happily together for a quarter of a century. Says Wendell Rodricks in a first-person account:

> Even now, in India, it is frustrating that Jerome has to apply for a visa each year. When I see my model friends who marry foreigners and get a PIO card for their spouses, I wish the Indian government would be kind to our love. After all, it is 25 years this year. (Rodricks 2008)

The contentious issue of paedophilia comes up in the interview with Darius Ankleshwaria. A familiar stereotype in the gay world is that one turns gay because one was sexually abused in childhood, and at least one interviewee, Ganesh Holay, attempts to link his homosexual activity in adult life to an appalling incident that took place when he was a child. In the recent past, two important books on the subject, both by Indian women authors, have been published to critical acclaim. The first is Pinki Virani's *Bitter Chocolate: Child Sexual Abuse in India* (Penguin Books, 2000), a work of non-fiction, and the second is Meher Pestonji's *Sadak Chhaap* (Penguin Books, 2005), a novel. Both books castigate the paedophile in no uncertain terms. Then, there is the much-publicised case of Duncan Grant and Alan Waters, two British nationals who ran Anchorage, a shelter for destitute kids at Colaba, Bombay, and allegedly abused them. Grant and Waters were undertrials in Bombay but were recently acquitted by the Bombay High Court.

While child sexual abuse must be condemned in the harshest possible terms, there is also the other side, which is about the co-dependency of children on adults. Many homosexually inclined adolescents have troubled relationships with their biological fathers, and are subconsciously in search of substitute fathers, as the Sri Lankan writer Shyam Selvadurai's novel *Funny Boy* (Penguin Books, 1994) demonstrates. This is what leads to the phenomenon of the sugar daddy, a well-established trope in gay life. A US-based organisation, North American Man Boy Love Association (NAMBLA) actually advocates relationships between younger boys and older men, as they have the potential to fulfil a mutual need. In the US again, Michael Jackson, as we know, was acquitted on charges of child molestation at his Neverland ranch. However, in the Grant-Waters case, the Bombay High Court turned down an intervention by the government of the UK, requesting that its legal representatives be allowed to be present during the trial. The learned judges are believed to have sardonically remarked that India was no longer a colony of England.

Indeed, colonisation is an apt metaphor if we consider how wealthy white foreigners frequent the nations of the Third World as sex tourists looking for prey, be it Colombo, Bangkok or Goa. This is an issue that is highlighted in the interview with Sri Lankan national Raja Chandraratne.

Other issues that are discussed in the book are AIDS and the use of condoms, religion and sexuality, the use of aliases among gay men and lesbians, and homosexuality in prisons—something that received widespread media attention when Kiran Bedi was superintendent of the Tihar Jail in Delhi.

My co-editor Dibyajyoti Sarma and I wish to thank my Ph.D. student Vida Rahiminezhad for helping out with the typing of the manuscript (and apologise for shocking her in the process).

Endnotes

1. For a full account of the formation of Queer Studies Circle see Raj Rao (2006).
2. In his book, Shahani (2008) discusses the ethnographic issue of sexual involvement with one's research subjects, and cites the works of James Clifford, Mark J. McLelland and David Bell and Gill Valentine, all of whom appear to endorse such involvement (p. 155).

3. For a literary-critical analysis of the story 'Artha', see Raj Rao (1998).
4. For an interview with Prince Manvendra, see Kulkarni (2008).
5. For an English rendering of some of these songs see Raj Rao (2000: 299–306).
6. A queer reading of this song appears in my novel *Engineering College Hostel* (forthcoming).
7. Quoted in Bhaskaran (2002: 16).
8. See my poem, 'Underground,' and Riyad Wadia's filming of it in *BomGay* (1996).
9. Quoted in Sukhthankar (1999: Introduction, p. xxix).

References

Ayyar, Raj. 1993. 'Yaari', in Rakesh Ratti (ed.), *A Lotus of Another Color: An Unfolding of the South Asian Gay and Lesbian Experience*, pp. 168–69. Boston: Alyson Publications.

Bhan, Gautam. 2005. 'Challenging the Limits of Law: Queer Politics and Legal Reform in India', in Arvind Narrain and Gautam Bhan (eds), *Because I have a Voice: Queer Politics in India*, p. 45. New Delhi: Yoda Press.

Bhaskaran, Suparna. 2002. 'The Politics of Penetration: Section 377 of the Indian Penal Code', in Ruth Vanita (ed.), *Queering India: Same Sex Love and Eroticism in Indian Culture and Society*, pp. 15–29. London: Routledge.

Dalzell, Tom. 1996. *Flappers 2 Rappers: American Youth Slang*, p. 88. Springfield, MA: Merriam-Webster, Inc.

Dollimore, Jonathan. 1991. *Sexual Dissidence: Augustine to Wilde, Freud to Foucault* (esp. Chapters 1 and 4). Oxford: Clarendon Press.

Gokhale, Sandhya. 2006. *Quest: Story, Screenplay and Dialogues*. Bombay: Popular Prakashan.

Hyam, Ronald. 1990. *Empire and Sexuality: The British Experience*, p. 116. London: Manchester University Press.

Khire, Bindumadhav. 2008. *Indradhanu: Samleingikteche Vividh Rang*. Pune: Samapathik Trust.

Kulkarni, Vishwas. 2008. 'The Pink Prince', *Mumbai Mirror*, 24 February.

Lotringer, Sylvere (ed.). 1996. 'History and Homosexuality', in *Foucault Live: Interviews, 1961–1984*, p. 369. Trans. by Lysa Hochroth and John Johnston. New York: Semiotext(e).

Pattanaik, Devdutt. 2008. *The Pregnant King*. New Delhi: Penguin Books India.

Raj Rao, R. 1998. 'Nine to Five Straights', *Bombay Dost*, 6(2–3): 14–15.

———. 2000. 'Memories Pierce the Heart: Homoeroticism, Bollywood-Style', in Andrew Grossman (ed.), *Queer Asian Cinema: Shadows in the Shade*, p. 305. New York: The Hawroth Press.

———. 2006. 'Academic Outlaws in Pune', *Trikone*, March 2006.

———. Forthcoming. *Engineering College Hostel*. Penguin.

Rodricks, Wendell. 2008. 'What We Did for Love', *Indian Express*, Pune, 19 February.

Shahani, Parmesh. 2008. *Gay Bombay: Globalization, Love and (Be)longing in Contemporary India*. New Delhi: Sage Publications.

Sukhthankar, Ashwini (ed.). 1999. *Facing the Mirror: Lesbian Writing from India*. New Delhi: Penguin.

Summerhawk, Barbara, C. McMahill and D. McDonald (eds and trans.). 1998. *Queer Japan: Personal Stories of Japanese Lesbians, Gays, Bisexuals and Transsexuals*. Norwich: New Victoria Publishers.

Vaid, Urvashi. 1995. *Virtual Equality: The Mainstreaming of Gay and Lesbian Liberation*, p. 107. New York: Anchor Books.

Vanita, Ruth. 2005. *Love's Rite: Same Sex Marriage in India and the West*, p. 244. New Delhi: Penguin.

Vanita, Ruth and Saleem Kidwai (eds). 2000. *Same Sex Love in India: Readings from Literature and History*. New Delhi: Macmillan.

I

hoshangmerchant

Editors: You've been reading Susan Sontag on camp. What does she have to say?

Hoshang Merchant: 'Style is everything.' Genet's ideas are very camp. For instance, his statement that 'the only criterion of an act is its elegance', and Wilde said, 'In important matters it is not sincerity but style that matters' (Susan Sontag).

I am a Parsi. Some say we invented monotheism even before Abraham. For modern Europe, as Harold Bloom notes, there are two conflicting bases of civilisation—Jewish moral seriousness and Paganism. Camp neutralises moral indignation and sponsors playfulness, as Sontag says. Facetiousness of homosexuality is always tender. It loves the things it satirises. I'm not talking about the High Bitches of high camp. As Freud notes, too much irony hides an underlying hostility, especially towards women in gay culture.

Camp is daring, witty and hedonistic. If you think of Andy Warhol's seriographs of Campbell Soup Cans, Marilyn, Liz or even Mao, you can see that the attitude is not playful at all but hedonistic. It demolishes cultural icons while setting up ridiculous, trivial things unrelated to Western culture. If you are asking about the camp of the transsexual on the borders of which I have lived all my life, then I would call that camp of the queen, a whistling in the dark, if not a horrible grimace of the dark played out in full public glare.

Editors: Foucault in an interview says that for the ancient Greeks and Romans, being homosexual was not a problem, but being passive in the sex act with another man was. Because that made a free man a slave. In Foucault's words, 'It's immoral for a free man to be fucked.' Please comment.

Merchant: There are many ramifications of this question. Foucault lived in modern day France not in ancient Greece and Rome, which is obvious to us, but not to him. If you are talking of free men and slaves of ancient Rome and Greece and comparing it to the penetrator and penetrated in the gay sex act of the modern day, then what I can get from reading between the lines and from my own experience as a Parsi queen among old Muslim hunks in Hyderabad is that Foucault is just setting up a pseudo-historical, pseudo-philosophical veil or framework to justify male chauvinism and its worst excesses. Even the modern day feminists know that a man in a heterosexual act does not always have to be on top, and this is borne out by sensational instances like the longest serving speaker of the US senate getting handsome young senate pages to mount him in his chambers during afternoon breaks and senate recesses. I'm not ranting; I'm telling you what I know, and have read, as a fact. What I am saying is, love and power are two faces of the same coin, and this is what I learn from Foucault. But in his personal life, Foucault as a brilliant ageing sado-masochistic queen is neither able physically or willing mentally to powerfully penetrate an object of his love. Now, if you're talking about '*tendresse*' (French word) for young children, that opens up another can of worms—the debate on paedophilia. The boy in ancient Greece, modern Europe and contemporary Hyderabad is so delicious precisely because he can be parted like a peach and be eaten whole. No one wants to chew old stringy meats. Since I have put my foot into my mouth, and am wont to deliberately do so for provocation, let me tell you that I share with Foucault that status of an old queen minus the brilliance and the sado-masochism.

Editors: Foucault also talks about monosexual communities in ancient Greece and Rome, and also in modern day America. Would you say Indian society, with its emphasis on segregation of the sexes, is mono-sexual in that sense?

Merchant: I think there are many issues thrown up by your question. I know I was being unfair to Foucault in my previous answer when I said that modern day USA is not ancient Greece. I mean that it is so obvi-ous to everybody. What is less obvious is the fact that gay writers, art-ists, philosophers, editors, etc., are looking for historical bases for being gay in their own societies, like I do in Indian history to justify modern homosexuality that stems according to Anais Nin from 'polarity being lost'. That is, we have lost the women in us if we are men, and the men in us if we are women. As everybody knows, from the time of Plato's primal egg, we're all bisexual. But once that 'syzygy' is broken, we're all trying to go back to our original bisexuality.

Gay men and women will one day in their lives, or in a new epoch of civilisation, reach bisexuality by monosexual communities. That is, to put it in very crude terms, one has to play father, the other mother; one has to play wife, the other husband. And I personally think the man who plays female has already found his own bisexuality within himself. But since modern society does not care for bisexuality, societies being scien-tific, gay feminised men get lost in the dreaded wood of monocultural societies. I mean, bisexuality has been chic among Berlin's 'softies' since the 1970s, something poor, demented Shah Rukh and Shahid discovered only yesterday on the shores of Bombay by the name of metrosexuality, thanks to the coinage invented for India by Mahesh Dattani (or was it our dear Shobha De?). If lesbians are adopting children, after birthing them through artificial insemination, if intelligent, loving, committed elite gay men go out of the way to 'adopt' children of not quite their own class, then I see it as a triumph not of the wretched heterosexual nuclear family (based on property) as Makrand Paranjape would like to believe, but a heartfelt if even unspoken plea for people to see the bi-sexuality in a struggling soul that it has already discovered for itself.

Editors: Is India today a bit like Europe in the 17th and 18th centuries, where according to Foucault, 'A whole system of traps and threats [for gays] is set up, with cops and police spies...'

Merchant: I have lived in Khomeini's Iran. I marched in the streets for the Revolution and wept for its young martyrs. One week into the Revolution the first young gay man was killed. The story went that he had returned home from a liberal Western university to actually breathe the freedom in his own hometown, a freedom that the Iranian Revolution seemingly promised to all Iranians. He was trapped by the homoerotic and, consequently, homophobic guards, tricked into fellating them serially (all six of them—what a gay haven!). Then he was tried by a Kangaroo Court of these very same guards who were then both accomplices and accusers, taken out into the yard and shot summarily six times under the new laws of the new Republic. Gay gossip in Tehran had it that after death, the body was sodomised while it was still warm, *thanda gosht* (cold meat) being a delicacy from the plains of the Punjab to the Danube, from the times of Timor, Changez, Vlad of Transylvania, etc., even Nixon and Bush's America. What I am saying is, Khomeini's Iran is 20th century Asia. The Hyderabad I live in today is 21st century India, fully globalised. The Lebanese border where the Israeli soldiers get sodomised at night by the Fedayeen before turning their American machine guns on them the next morning, is 21st century West Asia. What I'm saying is, why compare the barbarism of medieval Europe to so-called modern societies, Eastern or Western, which are barbaric and medieval to all people—gay or straight—as long as they don't have the gumption to grab power either intellectually, as I hope I'm doing, or in groups, like the children currently in the Paris Banlieux or the Fedayeen of Palestine.

Editors: Then Foucault says: 'One day the question, "Are you a homosexual?" will be as natural as the question, "Are you a bachelor?" ' How would you interpret this?

Merchant: One has to have compassion. Even the Dalai Lama says that not all people are born equal. If a well-meaning young man or old woman asks a gay icon like myself in India, 'Are you married or are you a bachelor?', I should not blow up in their face because it is a polite way of asking if you're gay, or just plain innocence and dumbness, I vainly hope. At the same time, I should not make up elaborate stories about NRI wives, absconding children, married daughters, etc., to cover up for the loneliness of a gay, as I did in the train compartment, mostly for amusement, while coming to this interview, to my eternal shame. I promised never to do it again, even for fun. Probably nobody was fooled. Maybe they were just playing along with me. To bring in the Dalai Lama again, for advanced souls like myself, I say with some immodesty, Foucault's day has already come. But then I would be uncompassionate to throw my homosexuality in the faces of my interlocutors. I'm not endorsing Clinton's 'don't-ask-don't-tell' policy, which is so pervading even in Western academic circles, that you want to tear your own heart out, and slap the professors till the masks crack to reveal the true homophobia beneath. Impatient people like Foucault, and myself would just have to wait for the day when everybody catches up with the *Bodhi Satava* as the Dalai Lama would have us believe. (Incidentally, the Dalai Lama does not endorse homosexuality and neither of us is talking about the monosexual monastries.) In India, 'bachelor' is a loaded term and a circumlocution for the word homosexual. Of course, in Foucault's politicised Europe, 'gay' is a loaded term and 'bachelor' the more innocuous one. Dear reader, kindly note that Hoshang, though aware of Western queer theory, always insists on living in his own here-and-now where Western queer theory is of no avail. If it sounds autobiographical, so much the better.

Editors: Finally, to Foucault's cryptic remark: '...it is not necessary to be homosexual but it is necessary to be set on being gay.' What do we make of this?

Merchant: Thank God, this is the last question dealing with Foucault. I thought he was dead sometime back. The great conscience of Europe who gave AIDS to his boyfriend, who then went to court and got half of his estate. I'm not knocking Foucault's great intellectual achievement on which I dare to stand, but what amazes me is the sheer intellectual stupidity of the Western philosophers who merrily go to their death with the slogan 'I die as I lived' on their lips.

Coming back to the question, after all, I am the editor of *Yaraana*. The greatest intellectual prize I have received in my life is the phone call I got from one Ganesh of Hibbagoddi, who told me, 'Sir, *Yaraana*, saved my life.' What this means is that in being set on my way of being homosexual against the homophobic tyranny of my Parsi family, my Christian schools, the Bombay police force, the Hyderabadi gossip mongers, the Purdue sissy-beaters and malicious legacy-grabbing relatives, I have given the unaided Ganeshes of the small towns the courage to live rather than to die, from the armchair comfort of my metropolitan academic sinecure. That is to say, Foucault and little people like me after him give an intellectual *raison d'être* and ballast to an individual's decision to lead an alternative life in the face of traditional society's great opposition. This is what all the little support cells in the gullies of Hyderabad are doing for the closet-queers and the married gays passing for bisexuals. I am too old, and again too comfortable, to receive innocent entreaties from 16-year-olds asking me how to come out to their parents. I did that millions of years ago, and I could not be bothered now. But the fact remains I had done it for myself and they have to do it for themselves, and I have written *Yaraana* to help them along, which is more than all those gays who criticise me have done.

Editors: You have edited *Yaraana*, India's first anthology of gay writing. What was the experience like?

Merchant: Because I have partly answered your question already, I will take my reader through the dramatic experience of what kind of panic I felt when invited by my intelligent woman-editor at Penguin, who also happens to be my first student ever at Hyderabad. I protested, I cut off the phone; I fled to my sympathetic boss asking what they would do to me, and would I lose my job. My dear, liberal, *Tambrahm* (Tamil Brahmin) teacher said, like a good resident of Mylapore, 'This is an intellectual activity. You are here to do it.' So you see, there are some bright spots in the dark scenario, even in India. Being the cowardly Parsi I am, forever shirking my responsibilities, I decided that my sweet little acolyte, then writing the first-ever thesis on the gay Indian poet Sultan Padamsee, would be a better choice than me to write the book. I rationalised, after all, homosexuality is the way of the future. 'No', said my *Tambrahm* friend, '*You* have been asked to do it.' Then started the tedious process of getting the families of dead Indian English writers to accede that someone like Padamsee was indeed gay. (I got the news elliptically from a venerable old Parsi gentleman, who, after years of teaching Padamsee, I suspected of being Padamsee's lover till the day he [Padamsee] killed himself.) But this is not academic discourse. This is an intuition of a lived life, of an intellect living as a poet and a gay. So then you come up with what proof you do have. Then there were living gays, bright luminaries, who refused to state publicly in India that they were gay, while living deliciously gay lives in the West. As you can see, the first enemy is always within. Now that Aga Shahid Ali is dead, a person whose poetry I teach as if he were Shakespeare, I can briefly sketch for you the heartbreaking pleading correspondence I had with a totally evasive man—no, it was not the fear of losing an inheritance, nor the fear of an *outing*, nor the fear of paining one's devout parents, nor incriminating one's friends, nor falling in the eyes of the holier than thou *bhadralok* heterosexist so-called literary critics. No, it was something quite else. Amitav Ghosh, in an obituary for Shahid Ali said, 'Ali wanted to be the first poet laureate of a free Kashmir.' Which means, Ali was already courting the Indian nation's displeasure once. And he did not want to do it twice over—also as a gay. Not only earn the ire of the Indian nation, but also of the Islamic Fedayeens on both sides of the border.

Yaraana was conceived at Penguin in 1995. I birthed it in 1999. Now, it's 2008. Read my essay 'Aga Shahid Ali, Kashmir and the Gay Nation', in *The Phobic and the Erotic*, edited by Brinda Bose and Subhabrata Bhattacharyya, and published by Seagull Books in 2007. This is only the story of Indian writing in English. The water gets murkier when the scene shifts to the Indian languages in the linguistically determined states of India. To my knowledge, Konark, not Khajuroho, is the only temple in India, which depicts homosexual and heterosexual oral and anal sex. In the land of Konark, in the year 2000, I am expected to believe that there is no homosexual in the state of Orissa. My Oriya students brought to my attention the first and only Oriya gay novel, whose title can be roughly translated as *Root and Fruit*. The poor author was set upon physically, all the copies of his published book burned in his *aangan* on the very day of its publication, and belaboured till he was made to burn with his own hands the only extant manuscript of his book in his possession. What is my trouble as compared to his trouble? But I remember the Cuban gay writer, Reynaldo Arenas, who in the jails of Castro, the darling of the liberal communists, East and West, re-writing *When Night Falls* seven times from memory, when finally freed went to New York to die of a 'capitalist' disease called AIDS. We namby–pamby intellectuals (and I include myself here) neither have the gumption nor the guts to do what Arenas has done.

Editors: How would you define a gay anthology? Would it not mean that all those who are included in it are gay themselves? Yet in *Yaraana*, you have included the work of a Dalit writer like Namdeo Dhasal, who might not agree to being called gay or even homosexual. I mean, it's the whole insider–outsider syndrome, this business of voice appropriation. I've said somewhere that Makarand Paranjpe may have a gay character in his novel *The Narrator*, but that doesn't make him a gay writer.

Merchant: There are three questions rolled into one here, and I will answer each one of them by turn.

One, for India's first gay anthology, there were slim pickings. Please remember that you are dealing with people who are alone, who may be having thoroughly comfortable private lives in a very traditional society that respects privacy (read social hypocrisy) above all else. Now, in USA or UK, we have volume upon volume of the series *Men on Men* year upon year, where gay men richly tell their rich stories of heartbreak and fulfilment in a social framework where homosexuality is legalised, but where the minds and hearts of sexualised beings hold the terms of a savage interior. So I had to include stories by heterosexual men and women dealing with fictionalised or real gay characters. I also included a story satirising heterosexuality from the gay perspective. But Penguin dropped it. About Makrand's *The Narrator*, a rival company published it and we could not afford the copyright royalties. There were other Penguin books, but the author was either Sri Lankan or had foreign publishers, which meant paying copyright fees in dollars and pounds. There were Indian gay authors published by Penguin and that would be a duplication of effort. By which I mean, who would read the entire novel if they get all the salacious bits in *Yaraana* for Rs 200? These are commercial considerations beyond my control. Everywhere else, it's the marketing division and not the editorial division which calls the shots.

Two, about Namdeo Dhasal, who was introduced to me by Professor Jahagirdar, whose son I taught in 1996. The professor kindly lent me, for one month, his own rare first edition of Namdeo's Marathi anthology carrying a poem called *Gandu Bagicha*. (Saleem Peeradina had told me of Dhasal creating a sensation reciting the same poem at Bharat Bhawan in 1984.) In 1996, there was yet no English translation of the poem. So I created one from my rudimentary *kaamwali* (housemaid) Parsi–Marathi. Namdeo was kind enough to send word through the professor's son that he liked my translation. Not a question was raised as to what he was doing in a gay anthology. Namdeo was then going through a political crisis of conscience and had quit

Ambedkar's Republican Party, which, according to him, was leaderless, and had joined the Shiv Sena, which shows the kind of shifting sands passions, commitments, lies, writings, etc., are built on, which India's academia doesn't have the wit to address. Please note that someone as gossipy as me had not learnt the biography, until literally yesterday, that Namdeo's mother was a sex-worker in Kamatipura, that against all odds, she sent him to the Brihanmumbai Municipal Corporation (BMC) schools where he learnt the grammar to write the stories of the Kamatipura prostitutes in the language of their clients, their pimps, their police exploiters and about sexuality: Kamatipura offers sexualities of every kind imaginable and unimaginable to the mind of a little son of a female sex worker. Hence, no question arose about the poet's sexuality, by the poet who knows better than the *bhadralok*.

Three, as for Makarand, he was my office-mate and was at continuous loggerheads with me when he actually wrote *The Narrator*. Now he is my soulmate, which shows that he was only trying to give a very puzzled and vulnerable individual like me some of his karmic insights that he got by way of his Brahman karma. When I read the prologue to *The Narrator*, I had a frisson, that is, goosebumps all over my body, with a feeling of déjà vu. Where have I experienced that before? I went to Makarand's house once and only once when he was all alone by himself. The doors were open and I moved through those *satvik* rooms without permission, something Makarand in meditation would have sensed in the other room. So, the encounter between the narrator and the gay persona introduced in the book is given as a frisson felt by the writer, the reader and the character. Of course that afternoon when we were watching an Indian English movie on TV, I had no way of knowing all this. But I do remember Makarand keeping on telling me to watch silently, to not jabber unnecessarily as was my wont, because he was probably still in the throes of or prolonging the frisson to write about it later. Makarand did tell me he had based a character in his gay novel on me. But at that time, both of us were young, so Makarand's gay character turns out to be evil, and I characteristically, was thankless and un-understanding. He did offer Penguin a lesbian story published in

Femina, which they rejected, since *Facing the Mirror*, a lesbian anthology was concurrently being published.

Editors: Yes. Around the time *Yaraana* was published (in 1999), Penguin also brought out this anthology of lesbian writing edited by Ashwini Sukthankar. How would you compare your book to hers? Although in your book all contributors have written under their own names, in hers many have used pseudonyms. Is this because it's harder to be openly lesbian than to be openly gay?

Merchant: As Shakespeare's Bottom would say, 'All comparisons are odorous.' I cannot judge, but I can tell you that the parameters of the two books were as different as the personalities of their editors. Ashwini, I imagine, is a middle class, liberal, left-leaning, non-conformist woman, then physically situated in the US. I was the elitist, Western returned, literature professor. Hers was the lived life, mine the life crystallised in literature, as the future gay canon to be taught. The demands on us as editors were vastly different. Even so, courageous literary reviewers, men and women, naively said that there was no Dalit experience in Hoshang, while Ashwini's was the unspoken sexual suffering of lower-class lesbian women. Hers were a series of interviews interspersed with narratives. Mine were published, and unpublished or unpublishable stories, crystallised in high prose in all kinds of languages, dealing with all strata of society, for example, a carpenter, a lorry driver and his gay sidekick, the cleaner, albeit written by upper-class men like myself. They had nothing to say about Dhasal or about my own autobiography of a 12-year-old elite child being sodomised on the beaches of Bombay till the age of sixteen or eighteen, on his way to and from school, by people of all classes. What do the Marxists have to say to that? What could they say? For it's outside their experience.

As for names, it is not as easy as you make it out to be. I agree that a woman, straight or gay, has it harder than a man, straight or gay, in our chauvinistic society. I see this subterfuge even in elite lesbians of my acquaintance, for reasons of family, honour and so on. I am not making a social revolution. I am interested in literature effecting a change of conscience at one remove, which means, in another generation, not my own. It also means, that even when I write a so-called autobiography, it is not the lived life, but writing about the lived life, which is to say, fiction. Nietzsche knew a hundred years ago that there are no facts, only interpretations, something which our middle-class professors have not caught up with yet. Which brings me to the question of pornography in *Yaraana*. Pornography, traditionally, over the centuries in all parts of the world, has always been anonymous. I put my name to the pornography I wrote not because it sells (that too!), but because I am a writer who believes in all kinds of writing having equal valency, and also because I am a teacher and gay sex, like all sex, has to be taught because it's a social construct, my included autobiography amply showing that there was no one to teach me when I began. I also wanted to break stereotypes and myths about my sexuality by having a versatile and fictitious I. If there is too much of autobiography creeping in here, it's because, in the early stages, the Dalits and gays will get a theory only out of autobiography, as women and blacks did in the nascence of their respective movements.

Editors: You are a university teacher in Hyderabad. Given the traditional image of a teacher in India (as a spiritual guru and so on), is it easy for you to be openly gay? Have you ever faced discrimination and hostility from students, administration and faculty? Even in America, a gay professor is, at the end of the day, an aberration, as William Tierney establishes in his book *Academic Outlaws*.

Merchant: I am a creative person. Creativity means not being this and that, homo or hetero, but both, or a third thing which Aurobindo calls 'the birth of a musical being' and Shakespeare 'to make thirds', which means to make harmony and concord within yourself and without. This is a literary ideal my Shakespeare teacher taught me. That does not mean that there is not a reality of discrimination. I have had fourteen teaching jobs in seven years of bumming around the world, job hunting. And in the city of my first permanent job, which I got at forty, I had to change eleven homes in seven months. I am not complaining, I faced it and it made me what I am today—a person with authority of what Foucault meant by the phrase 'being set on being gay'. My enemy in the teaching establishment is the un-understanding student, colleague, intriguing careerist, using prejudice against gays to his own advantage to get ahead. Remember a gay has to work twice as hard to get where he's got, but the first enemy and usually the only enemy of anyone is himself. I found that when I accepted myself, others accepted me, at work and play. But it took a lot of doing, coming as I do from heterosexist family, school, church, work establishment, etc., and even my own circle of friends.

Things have changed in the West considerably since the late 1990s. In India too, things are changing, slowly but surely, even at the work place. I am happy that in my own small way I have become an agent of that change.

Editors: Is it true that when you joined the University of Hyderabad, you were refused campus accommodation (unlike the others) on account of your sexual orientation?

Merchant: What you are referring to is an unthinking comment made by a colleague who said, 'You cannot live on campus because you will seduce our children.' To which, my riposte was, 'What makes you think I won't seduce you?' In any case, campus accommodation is usually given to married rather than unmarried faculty. So I had to go to the Gulf to earn money to buy a flat. I started my job at the University of Hyderabad in 1989 on a salary of Rs 1,200!

Editors: But you have successfully been running a course on gay literature in your department. My university (University of Pune) had not allowed me to start a similar course.

Merchant: That is because we have a departmental board of studies, unlike yours, which approves of courses. Like any other optional course,

I get up to ten students for the course. But they're not the best students. None of the students are gay. I do it as a tokenism and they allow me to. But it isn't having the kind of impact it would have in a metropolitan setting.

Editors: Before you joined the University of Hyderabad, you were briefly with the University of Pune (in the mid 1980s). I know it for a fact that you faced a lot of prejudice here. Can you tell us what exactly happened?

Merchant: My appointment was for three months. It was the third bid to fill a reserved post. It was only later that they found out I was gay—a letter to me from the US was opened, and that's how they got to know. To keep a job in India, I had gone back to the closet. I used to have nightmares about the phone ringing and a detective picking up the phone. I've always had a good equation with my women students—interacting socially with them after the class, in the canteen, etc. But with men I'm circumspect. Anyway, the head of the Department of English wilfully misconstrued this as seduction of female students by a male teacher. They started a whispering campaign against me. Also, in a letter-writing campaign in a Marathi daily, they referred to me indirectly. They even took in hand one of the members of the selection committee at the University of Hyderabad. They asked me at the interview if I was married or single! Is that the kind of question you ask at an interview for a teaching post? But then, I'm not the only one. Straight women too have suffered at the hands of such chauvinists.

Editors: You did your Ph.D. from Purdue in the US in the early 1980s. What was it like to be gay in America then at the start of the AIDS epidemic?

Merchant: I was in America from 1969 to 1976. I was beaten up by a Redneck faggot-hating sissy-beater and left for dead on the street. That radicalised me. I became one of the founders of Gay Liberation in

Purdue. That movement has now collapsed in the neo-conservative Bush regime. I was lucky to leave America just before the start of the AIDS epidemic.

Editors: Then you went to the Middle East. Is there ambivalence towards gayness there?

Merchant: In Islamic societies, where woman is property, and bloodline of family goes from father to son, female virginity is highly prized. Therefore, adolescent male homosexuality (and also female) is tolerated socially, though the Quran and the Saudi state have the strictest punishment for sodomy. In short, they turn a blind eye towards it. I must say that they don't mind boys of the same age group having sex with each other, but they mind older men going for younger boys. Which is of course contrary to the ancient Persian etiquette and education, where the older lover teaches the young boy the culture of the nation.

Editors: Why did you choose to do your Ph.D. on the work of Anais Nin?

Merchant: When I wanted to write on gay topics, there were no openly gay writers. Everyone knew or suspected that the great Victorians were also greatly gay. But there were no authoritative studies on the topic because such research was not encouraged then (a lacuna which has since then been filled, thanks to the feminist and gay movement). One suspected Whitman and one knew about Ginsberg, but he wasn't taken seriously in the academy. Anais Nin in her dairy talked openly about her one lesbian affair, and more importantly about her friendship with young gay men whom she counselled, who later went on to be Truman Capote, Gore Vidal and Robert Duncan. Anais Nin also made me a poet—I learnt to write poetry from her, so to speak.

Editors: You have over fifteen collections of gay poetry, most of them published by P. Lal's Writers Workshop in Calcutta. Has your work enabled you to arrive at a sort of definition of gay literature? Or, say, a gay aesthetic?

Merchant: I evolved as I wrote and I wrote as I evolved. It is not that a poet makes a poem, but a poem makes the poet. As I happened to be gay, my aesthetics were gay. But not having any Indian model, I had first to rely on Western ones stated earlier and then evolve my own Indian style. I don't think of it as a division between gay and straight literature, but as the division between literature and popular culture.

My preceptor in this is Ezra Pound. Not Eliot or Yeats, but Pound, who is a heroic, broken man who wrote as complete a work as possible for his bad life, in his Cantos. I understand the talking of sex, as women and gays do, makes literature slip into the realm of popular romance. But again, as Pound said, if high literature is really high, then pop culture will not be so low. The depiction of gays in Indian films is obnoxious—something that young gay people get their cues from—because feminist, gay, Dalit literatures in India have failed to set an example for popular culture.

Editors: You know, you combine in yourself male and female characteristics to a degree that few gays do. You have a thick manly beard, and yet your gait is so feminine. You also have a high-pitched voice. Moreover, you always refer to yourself in the feminine gender. Does that create an identity crisis? Do you see yourself as a direct descendant of *Ardhanareshwara* (half-man, half-woman; one of the avatars of Lord Shiva, where he assumes the form of half-man, half-woman)?

Merchant: I failed to answer an earlier question where you said that in India gurus cannot be gay. But the fact of the matter is that modern psychology and research into religion has proven the link between eroticism and spirituality in all religious traditions. Jeffery Kripal from Chicago has dared to prove that Ramakrishna had a homosexual longing not only towards a male Krishna, but also towards his disciple Vivekananda. He has done this at the expense of his career. So now, it is easy for me to be a gay guru or a bisexual poet. In India, our answers are spiritual. In the West, they have material answers to even spiritual questions. I don't have to go for a sex change operation. I can be Ardhanareshwara in my poems and play Krishna in my bed with my lovers. I refer to myself as 'she' because both hyper-masculinity and hyper-femininity of Indian society and films repel me. With one word, I can demolish both fake men and fake women, while holding up my psychic femininity as the true norm for all people, straight and gay.

Editors: You are often abusive in your speech. Isn't that deliberate—a form of political subversion of refined behaviour?

Merchant: Yes, it is political subversion, but it is also pent-up anger at injustice directed towards me from prejudice based on false intellectual and moral premises. These are know-nothings abusing a one-in-a-million person. Phallic superiority is no superiority. It's of the most fragile kind. Male chauvinism is so repressive precisely because it's based on such slim premises—the accident of being born male. No amount of abuse is too little for such people. Offence is the best form of self-defence. It is also an aristocratic privilege to offend the masses. However, unlike you [R. Raj Rao], I'm not abusive in my writing. It's not scatological though my everyday speech may be. It's linguistic violence I practise against enemies.

Editors: We believe, you had a sad childhood and were treated shabbily by your father on account of your sexuality. He even disinherited you. Would you like to talk about this?

Merchant: Whatever I know of male chauvinism, I learnt in nursery from the abuse heaped on the women and children of the house by an all-powerful father. It was only too convenient for him that the only other male in this nuclear family, viz., myself, also happened to be gay. I was deprived of my patrimony on moral grounds, not so much by my father as by the machinations of my step mother—herself an immoral woman hiding under the cloak of bourgeois respectability. I am not angered by the loss of property because I am a saintly and a self-made man. But it is injustice towards my siblings and myself that angers me.

However, compassion is the other side of anger, and my writing has now become more compassionate. It is only after reading Ashish Nandy's *Intimate Enemy* that I realised the need of my father's generation, abused outside the home by a foreign master, to try and recapture lost male pre-eminence at home by bossing, bullying, abusing and torturing. I don't condone it, but I can understand it. Violent victims learn sadism from violent masters. Sweet people learn sacrifice from being subjected to violence. That is the difference between *himsa* (violence) and *ahimsa* (non-violence). Though I was a very violent child, and am still linguistically violent, as I said, I have tried to learn *ahimsa* from my mother.

Editors: You have never been in a committed relationship with another man. Why?

Merchant: I am too much of a perfectionist to share my life with imperfect people, having put love on a pedestal, thanks to the psychological idealisation of the mother that makes me gay, I suppose. Coming from the abusive marriage of my parents, I'm too emotionally broken to go into a relationship, and am too kind a person to inflict my trauma on my partners. Not that my partners are averse to inflicting their traumas on me—from which I got fifteen books of poetry. This does not mean that I've stopped trying for a loving relationship with whomever possible at whatever age. The Sufis say, 'Life is given for a moment with a friend.' It is not for how long, but how deeply you've known love.

2

sushilpatil

Editors: Please introduce yourself to us.

Sushil Patil: I am a most common middle-class Maharashtrian person, born and brought up in a *taluka* (administrative sub-division within a district) in Marathwada (one of Maharashtra's most backward zones). By profession, I am a lecturer in a college. I live with my parents, my brother, my wife and two children.

Editors: That is the briefest introduction we have heard. Would you like to elaborate on it a bit?

Patil: Well, what do I say? Did I call myself 'common'? Probably, I am not. People say I have feminine traits in my personality. They are right. I also have leukoderma, with white patch marks all over my body. No, I was not born with it, nor is it hereditary. In childhood, while learning to ride a bicycle, I fell and bruised my leg. It started from then and is increasing day by day. I love men, as opposed to women. Do I see any connection between leukoderma and effeminacy? Yes, both make me an outsider, a marginal person, a victim. That is the connection. Both exclude me.

Editors: Obviously, you view the fact that you love men and not women as an issue.

Patil: I was always attracted to boys as long as I can remember. I never felt any warmth for women. In the ninth and tenth standards, I liked to sit among the good-looking boys of the class. However, the process of realising my own orientation was difficult. I could not figure out what I was—hetero or homo. No doubt, there *was* some attraction for the opposite sex. But it was much less than that for men. In short, I was confused, conflicted. I was also curious. My feeling for other boys was not reciprocated. It was a one-way street. I could perceive how different I was from the others. In college, my friends would forever talk about girls. I liked boys, but could not discuss it with them for fear of being misunderstood. Nor could I speak my mind out to my teachers or family members.

Editors: When did you have your first sexual experience?

Patil: It was very late that I experienced puberty. I never learnt how to masturbate because I did not have friends who could teach me. When I realised I was different, I grew terrified of fellows who loved women. Of course, I used to dream about boys kissing and embracing. I was aroused by these fantasies, and I would discharge naturally, without having to use my hands. Other than this, nothing happened during my school and college days. My real sexual experience came when I was about twenty or twenty-one—as late as that. The year was 1982 or 1983. I was in my final year of B.A. and not in my hometown, but in

Solapur, Maharashtra, where I had come for my graduation. I also had a job. I worked at a movie theatre as a full-time administrative officer. In truth, however, I was everything from booking clerk to manager. I had to take up this job for economic reasons. There was a gatekeeper at the theatre with whom I grew friendly. In the beginning, it was just a passing friendship. He was uneducated, so I had to help him count coupons and ensure that they tallied with the number of patrons whom came to the show. Counting always confused him, so I had to help him. One day when I finished helping him, he came forward and kissed me as a way of saying thank you. No, he did not kiss me on the cheeks, but on my lips. I loved it, but I also wondered why he did it. I mean, he did not look effeminate or anything; he looked normal. Yet, I did not give it much thought.

Editors: Did this initial experience, though superficial, lead to something deeper afterwards? Did you wish it would?

Patil: The kissing sessions went on for several months. They usually happened in the manager's office, so we did not have privacy. The chap did not spare any opportunity to kiss me, and I enjoyed his kisses. But socially, I did not feel good. So I began to avoid him. My inner being longed for him, and yet when he was there, I tried to avoid him. Finally, I confronted him and asked him to put an end to our 'affaire', as I was afraid of losing my job if I was caught, and this I could not afford to do. I continued to think of him as a friend, but in a social context alone. In fact, I was always waiting for him to talk to me, to take him out to tea. Talking to him was a kind of solace. I liked my theatre job, not just because of him, but also because it gave me a chance to watch the crowd coming into and going out of the cinema. I especially liked to watch the men, the rustic muscular men. They were the ultimate turn-on. However, I was not comfortable with myself. I thought I had a problem.

Editors: So did you try to seek a cure?

Patil: Yes. It happened in Kolhapur, another town in southern Maharashtra. I went to see a doctor, a general practitioner. I told him that I was attracted to men. The doctor tried to scare me. He gave me some pills and tablets and told me that my problem was psychological. He said that logically, all men were heterosexual. He tried to be friendly and provided reasons as to why I should abstain from thinking about men. I took the pills and tablets religiously but nothing happened. Then I went to Belgaum in Karnataka to see a psychiatrist. He performed a narco-analytical test on me, which as you know is a neurological test. He gave me an injection and I began to speak to him about my sexual orientation even without realising it. He told me later that under the influence of the injection, I revealed everything about the gatekeeper in the movie theatre in Solapur, and how I was desperately in love with him. He said, he understood my 'problem' and gave me hopes that I would soon be okay. Like the quack doctor in Kolhapur, he too prescribed a course of tablets, which I was supposed to take for three months. I took the tablets hoping I would be cured and become normal. Three months later, I was exactly where I was. I stopped all treatment. I felt helpless. There was no friend I could confide in. Actually, there was a special reason why I went to see all these doctors. My parents were looking for a bride for me. I did not want to get married. But I had to. I did not have any other option. But before getting married, I wanted to 'cure' myself.

Editors: Before you went to see doctors, did you not have any idea that homosexuality has no cure?

Patil: No. I really had no clue that there were no medicines that could cure me. I took the tablets given by those doctors in good faith, believing, as one of them said, that mine was a psychological problem, an aberration even, that the pills would take care of. And one of the doctors was my own uncle! It was only a couple of months later when nothing changed, that I realised that they had taken me for a ride.

Editors: Did you get married immediately after that?

Patil: No, after my failure with doctors, I went to see a priest. He was actually a *jyotishi*, an astrologer. I told him about my problem. And what does he do? He molests me—shakes my hand, strokes my shoulders and touches me all over. Then he encourages me, in typical Marathi fashion, to visit him whenever I am hassled. I escaped from his clutches and never visited him again.

Editors: You say you had no option other than getting married. Why is that?

Patil: In middle-class families, our parents decide about our lives. I had no choice. I did not consider rebelling or walking out on them because of my mother, who is a heart patient. I thought that if I did so, I would be responsible for giving her a heart attack, even taking her life. Then again, my elder brother had cancer and was told by doctors that he should not marry. The next male member of the family was me, and I had to fulfil that obligation.

Editors: How was it after marriage?

Patil: Initially, it was okay. I was married and I had a lecturer's job with which to support my wife. Inside, though, I was restless, uneasy. My confusion about my personality, my sexuality and my physical needs intensified. True, I did not give my wife a chance to complain. But I was really craving for another kind of sexual union. It was then that I realised that though I was married, I would not be able to suppress my feelings. I had to give way somewhere. So I began to look for male partners regardless of the fact that I was married. Clearly, I was unhappy with the sex that marriage to a woman provides. Also, my view that my problem, my disorder—for that is how I continued to view my sexuality—would be solved after marriage was wrong. It was silly of me to anxiously await marriage, thinking it would make me normal. But it was now too late to regret it. Where did this belief originate? Well it was my own view, not that of the doctors. Maybe it was they who led me on by telling me that the problem was psychological, not physical. So I thought sleeping with a woman on a regular basis would be the solution.

Editors: Does your wife know that women do not turn you on?

Patil: I am quite sure that to this day my wife does not know about my homosexuality. And we have been married long. We got married in 1989, which makes it seventeen years, and we have two children. Nor do I suspect that she will get to know about it in the future. But that is because I have a good sexual life with her. In my place, I am a proper heterosexual householder—a good husband, father, brother and son. But maybe I can carry off my homosexuality because my wife, though educated, is from a small town, where awareness of these issues is non-existent. Actually, by any standard, she is highly educated. She has three degrees—B.Com., M.A. and B.Ed. She assists me in running a coaching class in my town. When I go out to meet my male friends, I lie to her. I tell her I am going out on duty assigned to me by the college, and she does not suspect that I am fibbing. Sometimes she does wonder about my 'chirpy' voice, laughs at it even. But I am quite sure she does not know anything about my same-sex relationships to be able to put two and two together. Yes, sometimes I do feel guilty about deceiving her, but can I help it? Would I accept her if she had a woman lover? Absolutely not. I will not accept it. I agree this amounts to double standards. I also agree that this is a sort of male prerogative I am exercising—being very male, for all that I say about being passive in bed and so on [later]. But that is how it is. Of course, sometimes I do worry that some day my wife would come to know about me. But only sometimes.

Editors: Men continued to pursue you, even after you were married. Was it because of your body language?

Patil: I am inclined to think so. It has to be on account of the signals I involuntarily give off, like my lady-like voice and manner of speech, perhaps even my walking style, though no one has told me about this yet, so I guess it is okay. The well-built middle-aged man who deliberately put his hand on my crotch in a night bus in which we were travelling—why did he choose me and no one else? I was tempted, but I did not encourage him, for we were in public transport. Or the teacher from my college, who, drunk, made a pass at me at a party, pissing me off no end, and compelling me to rudely tell him to behave himself. Why did he single me out over everybody else? It has to be because of the way I come across to these men—as a womanly man.

Editors: One stereotype about gay men is that where heterosexuals are generally monogamous, we are promiscuous. Would you say that if you are not monogamous, it is entirely on account of the circumstances?

Patil: You know, I have a monogamous bent of mind. I am guilty of cheating on my wife. But the matter ends there. It has never been difficult for me to find a partner. If I do not succumb to the temptation of sleeping around, it is because I live in a small town where everyone knows everyone else, and nothing can be done without arousing suspicion. Everyone in my town knows me. I am supposed to be the best teacher of my subject. I do not have a vehicle, and whenever I walk on the road, someone or other comes up to me to offer me a lift. No, no, out of respect, not for sexual reasons. How can I have multiple partners in such a scenario? Given a chance, I will not like to change partners. I prefer one partner. Like everyone else, I need physical, social and mental security. I like to move about in familiar company, with a group of people who know and trust each other completely. In relationships, we do not just share our bodies, but also our emotions. Bodies we can get a dime a dozen, but not the soul, which matters much more. Sex is for a few years; love is for life. So I do not like promiscuity. In a way, I am monogamous. As long as my friend is with me, I will not think of having sex with anyone else.

Sometime back, I met this man, who is my type, strong, muscular, and well built, very much like my friend himself. He wanted to date me, but I refused, telling him I had a partner to whom I was committed.

He persevered. 'It's only a matter of an evening', he said. 'Your friend won't come to know.' I told him it was not about my friend, it was about me. 'Leave your name and address with me', I said to him, 'and I promise to contact you as soon as my friend leaves me.' He turned his face and went away, though we did have a cup of tea together. At the same time, I feel guilty of two-timing. When I am with my partner, I feel I am deceiving my wife, and when I am with my wife, I feel this is not what I should be doing. As I said earlier, my body language proclaims to the world that I am gay. This upsets me. I see it as a disadvantage. I am a college teacher. Sometimes, I am made the butt of jokes. I remember a fishpond that I received in my college at the annual gathering. It said, '*Jo bhi ho khuda ki kasam la jawab ho...*' (whoever you are, by God, you are incomparable...).

Editors: Does that mean your students know about you?

Patil: I do not know. But once, in Pune, a young guy cruised me outside a public loo. His face seemed familiar, but I could not place him. We got talking and, as is my wont, I invited him for a cup of tea at a nearby restaurant. This is my habit, for it helps break the ice. As soon as we settled down in the restaurant, he asked me what my preference was, that is, whether I was active or passive in the sex act. I smelled a rat. I asked him if we had met before, but he evaded the question. It was not that important, he said. It was only when I persisted that he disclosed that he was from the same town as me, and was once even my student! Imagine how upset I was. Luckily, the fellow took it sportingly and did not out me. He now runs a tea stall at my place, and whenever our paths cross, we greet each other. He recently offered to procure someone for me, an offer I flatly refused. Then there's this other student who keeps shaking my hand. To me, it clearly comes across as a sexual handshake, and I've spent many hours wondering why he does it. Do they do it for money? Yes, that's quite likely. With so much rampant unemployment, I'm not surprised that boys in their teens and early twenties have to resort to selling their bodies to keep body and soul together. Especially in towns such as mine, where chances of landing a decent job are bleak. However, I don't believe in sex for money. I may be starved, but I will never pay money to gratify my desires.

Editors: You make much about the class issue in same-sex encounters. Why?

Patil: You will agree that Indian society is highly stratified. And as I told you earlier, I am a typical middle-class person. If people of my own class find out whom I'm consorting with, they'll shun me. They may even blackmail me. I have to protect my status as a college lecturer, think of my family background. I have not made my sexuality public, and I don't want to be treated as an outcaste. However, I am equally uncomfortable with people from the upper class. There was a time when I tried to mix with them, in cities like Pune. I was not at all comfortable. At meetings of the QSC, I tried mingling with others, but it was a fiasco. I would sit there all by myself, and no one would talk to me. I don't hold it against them, though. There's much difference between their living standards and mine, their lifestyle and mine. And above all, they are open or semi-open about their sexuality, while I'm completely closeted. So much so, that some people have questioned my closeness to you [R. Raj Rao]. But I must confess that my meeting with you was a great eye opener. I think you are doing great work, which I respect. After talking to you, I have been able to sort out some of my own confusions. I think more people like me should meet you. But I am not sure you are accessible to middle-class people. Middle-class people don't find it comfortable to approach you and talk to you.

Editors: Do you firmly believe in this active–passive dichotomy? Or do you think sexual activity among gay men is fluid?

Patil: You know, most gay men are passive. This is evidence I have garnered on the basis of what goes on in the public toilets. Most people there are waiting to *see* others' dicks, rather than show their own. To me this indicates that they are passive. You will be surprised that some very macho looking men, like army personnel, are also passive. Some people can be both, active and passive, but not everyone.

I'm passive too. Though married, I see myself as a homosexual, not an MSM or anything else. Given a chance, I won't have sex with a woman, except, of course, my wife. I am a female acting as a male in marriage, and a male acting as a female in my homosexual life. I agree this may cause an identity crisis. To balance both these sides is difficult. Maybe it amounts to playing a role? Our Hindu gods had multiple gender identities—they switched from one to another with ease. There's the obvious example of Ardhanareshwara.

As a homosexual, I need active partners only. I hate it when someone insists that I be active. That's why I like my current friend—because he's always active. At the same time, though I have feminine traits in my personality, I don't believe in flaunting them. That's why I don't like the members of Udaan (a support group for *kotis*). They are overtly feminine, they give themselves feminine names, and behave like women, ending up looking like *hijras*. They even refer to themselves as 'she'. Except when I'm with my partner, I don't want the whole world to think of me as a female. Men should behave like men. Why these add-ons? I remember, once, when I was working as a coordinator for a cultural programme in my college, a student came up to me and said he would like to do a *lavni* (Maharashtrian folk dance) dance wearing a sari. I admonished him strongly. I didn't mind the *lavni*, but wearing a sari in public? But he was adamant. Finally, another teacher intervened and the boy got to dance in a sari.

Editors: You say you are put off by the behaviour of Udaan members. But has it occurred to you that they behave so for political reasons?

Patil: Maybe it's my own conservatism that makes me react to them in this way. Like I say again and again, I'm from the middle class. Maybe their feminine mannerisms amount to a sort of political subversion. But for me, I'm against the very idea of politicising sexuality. That's why I can't see eye to eye with the Udaan guys. There could also be an unconscious reason for my dislike of them—the fear of being outed if I act like them, or am seen in their company.

Editors: Have you ever thought of divorcing your wife?

Patil: No. Because in normal life, a man is expected to be a married man. And besides, now that you ask, let me also say that I love her. I think one can love two people, but no more than two. I'm aware that the scales are tipped in my favour, if that's the right phrase. For my friend knows about my wife, but my wife does not know about him. Probably I love her because she does not know about me. I'm not implying that I'd stop loving her if she found out about me.

Editors: You've been referring to this friend of yours all through the interview. Evidently, you have found happiness. Tell us about it.

Patil: He's a security guard and we met in a city bus. We knew from the look in each other's eyes that we wanted each other. And that's how we came together. It's all very romantic. Now, I'm deeply in love with him and committed to him. So is he. Like me, he too is a married man, but his wife and kids are away in another town. He lives by himself, and whenever I come to the city, I stay with him. We're a couple, man and wife. I'm so lucky to have him. We keep in touch everyday, and I think of him as my life partner. When he's ill, I'm so restless. Recently, he had some financial troubles and was depressed. I offered him money, but he refused to accept it. I forced it on him with the promise that he would return it as soon as he could. Unlike me, my friend is *bindaas* (without a care) about his sexual orientation. He holds my hand everywhere, and once he even kissed me on the cheek in a crowded bus. When I affectionately reprimanded him, he said, what's the harm if one friend kisses another? You know, he's everything that I always dreamt about in a partner. Since he's married, we can't think of living together. Moreover, we have jobs in different towns. Yet, it's brilliant the way we keep in touch. Finally I'm in love.

Still, after going through so much in life, I'm sceptical enough to realise that a relationship of this kind cannot last long. In a way, I'm waiting for the day when my friend will leave me. But this does not deter me from making hay while the sun shines. I believe only in the present, like the yogis. If my friend ever leaves me, I'm confident of finding another. After all these years, I have learnt the tricks of the trade.

Though I am not a member of any support group other than the QSC, after meeting my friend, I have come to know a lot of gay people, all of whom are good friends. We constantly stay in touch. I once went to a wedding reception with my friend. A boy stared at the two of us for a long time, and after a while, approached me and asked me about myself. I told him I was a college lecturer. Then he asked me about my friend and I replied that he was a watchman. The boy was shocked; how can a lecturer be friends with a mere watchman, he wondered. I said, 'why not?' I told him he was my best friend in the whole world. So you see, I've even transcended the class issue.

Editors: Sushil Patil, is there anything else you would like to say?

Patil: Yes. I would like to get a job outside my backwater, in a city. This will automatically ensure that I don't have to live 24×7 with my wife—who shall continue to remain in our town with the kids. I would like to reverse my timetable—stay permanently with my friend and see my wife only once in a week, rather than the other way round, as I do now. What I'm also saying, I guess, is that the two towns, that of my wife and friend, should be closer to each other than they are at present. This is my only wish.

3

manishpawar

Editors: Hi Manish Pawar, please introduce yourself to us.

Manish Pawar: You already know my name—Manish Pawar. I'm about twenty-five years of age. I was born and brought up in Kopargaon and have lived here all my life. Heard of Kopargaon? It's a *taluka* in the Ahmednagar district of Maharashtra. It's very close to Shirdi, world famous [sic] for its Sai Baba temple, and basks in the reflected glory of Shirdi. But I've rarely been out of Kopargoan, and even when I have, it's strictly within the state of Maharashtra. I speak Marathi and Hindi well, but I do not speak English. I've studied up to class twelve. I'm unmarried and work as a ward boy in a private hospital in Kopargoan. No, it's not a permanent job—I can lose it at any time. There are the usual tensions at home. I am the only son, and therefore my parents' only support in their old age. I have two sisters, both of whom are married.

I live with my parents. Our family isn't well off. My father works as a contract driver, driving TATA trucks rolled out of the Telco factory in Pune to different destinations in India. What else do you want to know? I'm reticent and deep-seated by nature.

Editors: When and how did you first realise that you were sexually attracted to people of your own sex?

Pawar: I realised it pretty early, say when I was a teenager, but did not admit it to myself till I read an article in the Marathi newspaper *Sakal*. It was called 'Sister's Advice' and was a sort of an agony aunt column where someone asked a question about his homosexuality—said it made him feel guilty. His story matched mine. I was also initially guilty and confused, but eventually I would read books on the subject in Marathi, meet activists and openly-gay men in support group meetings in Bombay and Pune, and thus come to terms with my own sexuality and begin to accept it.

Editors: You call yourself a *koti*. Any connection between this and the job you've chosen for yourself—a ward boy?

Pawar: Maybe some *kotis* become ward boys because the nature of their job allows them to strip male patients. But no, it wasn't so in my case. I took up the job because it was the only one easily available. Beggars can't be choosers, can they? Besides, none of the patients at the clinic where I work have ever made a pass, or any such thing, at me. Nor have I tried to get fresh or intimate with them, though there are the usual opportunities. The word *koti* is unknown to most people in a small town like Kopargaon. So I suppose I'm relatively safe.

Editors: So what is it like to live a homosexual life in Kopargaon?

Pawar: A small town like Kopargaon doesn't offer much opportunity for any kind of sexual activity outside marriage, let alone same-sex activity.

Even for heterosexual men. There is precisely one narrow street, not far from the State Transport (ST) bus stand, that serves as its red-light district. People in small towns tend to be conservative and narrow-minded. Also, they're hypocrites. However, those like me who are in search of same-sex partners know where to find them. The public loos at the ST bus stand and on the highway are hot cruising spots. Kopargaon is bang on the Ahmednagar–Manmad state highway. Trucks frequent it at night, and truck drivers often seek out men when women are not readily available. They don't have to pay men the same rates that they pay women. It's quite likely that they get away without paying the men anything at all. Shridi, too, has a major role to play in all this. Since Bombayites (or Mumbaikars) continually visit Shirdi, they've infected it with their morals. There's a lot of anonymous sex between men that goes on at Shirdi, and some of it rubs off on Kopargoan. So though I'm not really promiscuous, I don't have to live a sexually starved life in the place where I am.

Editors: You live in a small *taluka* town like Kopargaon, which is not even a district headquarter, and you don't speak English. It seems to us you are brave in your determination to live your life (sexually) on your own terms.

Pawar: No, I'm not extraordinary. Kopargaon is a small town, no doubt, and I frequently think of leaving it and settling down in Bombay or Pune. In fact, I'm pretty determined to do so some day. I know I have a job here, but like I said, it's temporary. So I don't lose much if I chuck it and migrate to Bombay or Pune. Right now, however, Bombay is only a fantasy to me. I can't think of leaving Kopargaon at this point. Speaking of Bombay, it is said that a lot of Bollywood movie stars are homosexual. Is that true? Do you have any idea which of them in particular is? Is it Jackie Shroff? Akshay Kumar? I've been to Bombay only a couple of times. I actually want to resume my studies, and that perhaps is one way of getting to Bombay. I can do my college there. And then of course there are the gay support groups. I'm sure they won't see me high and dry.

Editors: How do you relate to your parents? Does your family know about your being homosexual? If so, what is their reaction? Do you plan to seriously come out to them some day?

Pawar: My mother knows about me, but not my father. How did I come out to my mother who's not educated? I sat down with her one day and gave her a detailed explanation of words like homo, hetero, etc., [in English] and the categories they represent. Her reaction, predictably, was negative. She felt that what I said/did was wrong. She thought I was possessed and that one day the evil spirit would be exorcised. That was a couple of years ago, and it was soon after I returned from my first visit to the Humsafar Trust in Bombay. Now, my mom's a bit more reconciled, but the topic keeps coming up from time to time. She says in resignation, 'Well son, live with me till I'm dead.' She has stopped referring to her would-be daughter-in-law, which Indian mothers love to talk about.

As for my father, I'm not going to tell him at all. There's no need to. In any case I don't speak to him much—I'm scared of him. If my dad knows, he might even beat me up. He's hardly bothered about me, so I don't think it'll concern him if I'm married or not. He has bigger worries than my marriage—like how to feed his family. My sisters and their husbands? If the topic ever comes up—it hasn't to this day—I'll openly tell them I'm homosexual. At my work place I've told all my colleagues about my sexual identity. They did not react in any particular way. Just had deadpan expressions on their faces, as if what I was saying was totally incomprehensible to them. To a lot of these people, I guess I come across as a sort of *hijra*, because they don't know the difference between a homosexual man and a eunuch, who is often castrated.

Editors: Have you ever had sex with a woman?

Pawar: No, never. Women don't attract me at all. I'm not bisexual.

Editors: You say you plan to stay single. But in India men marry for reasons of social security. A man also needs a wife to cook and keep house for him, and he needs kids to look after him in old age. How do you plan to deal with these aspects of your life? You are still young. Is it possible you may change your views on marriage some day? Is sex that important?

Pawar: No, sex is not that important. But I need to at least feel emotionally close to the person I'm married to. And I can't feel emotionally close to a woman—any woman. As to the first part of your question, let me tell you that I don't like kids. Even if I were straight and married, I wouldn't have kids—it's too much of a responsibility. Food, I can cook on my own. Don't men cook their own food? For example, there's a Rajasthani guy in my neighbourhood, whose wife is away in the village. He cooks his own food, keeps his own house. And then there's always my mother to cook for me. What will happen when she's no longer there? Frankly, I haven't given it a thought. In old age, maybe I'll have to live alone. I'm prepared for that. Or maybe I'll find a male partner to move in with. Or perhaps join a gay rights group, and then the entire community will be there for me.

Editors: Have you ever thought of moving in with a man and living together with him—not in old age, but now? What are your views on gay marriage?

Pawar: In reality, I don't have any long-term relationship or friendship with another man. I'm not even looking for one because I know it's impossible to find. I just do my work, and so what if I'm lonely?

Ideally, however, I'd love to move in with the man of my dreams. And I'm going to do my best to turn this dream into reality. And when that happens, I'll be happy to play the feminine role of keeping house and cooking, while my man goes out to work. These are family duties that mustn't be taken lightly. I am on the lookout for such a man, and I hope I find him one day. True, the role I would like to play in the relationship makes me out to be the 'wife'. But this doesn't bother me at all. Of course, I don't consider myself to be a woman entirely—a woman trapped in a man's body. I'm 50 per cent woman and 50 per cent man. Which is what most *kotis* are, I guess. In bed, however, I am entirely passive, though anal sex scares me because it is painful, and I prefer oral sex for that reason. Oh yes, I do insist on a condom. I do not want to die of AIDS. I do not have any views on gay marriage. I do not think it will ever come to India.

Editors: Elucidate the role that gay support groups have played in your life.

Pawar: It was a friend of mine in Pune who took me to the Humsafar Trust in Bombay for the first time. I begged him to do so after I had read the article in *Sakal* (referred to earlier). At their office in Vakola, I picked up a copy of *Bombay Dost* and enjoyed reading it, especially the article in the Marathi section of the newsletter. I also read an article by you [R. Raj Rao] and asked my friend to translate it for me. After that, we went to Pune where there is another support group, Samapathik Trust, run by Bindumadhav Khire. In the beginning, I was not particularly impressed by these support groups and felt that they were of little use to people like me. Why do I need them, I thought to myself. One thing, in particular, that put me off was that in places like the Humsafar Trust, all the discussions were in English. I felt alienated. At that point, I did not know that there were working-class gay groups too, like Udaan for example, where members talk to each other in Marathi and Hindi. It is this kind of support group that I like. However, I now realise that all my earlier view vis-à-vis gay support groups were founded on ignorance. I now realise that gay support groups are a *must*, without which homosexual men like me would be lost. Because of the existence of these groups, I do not think of myself as alone any more. They have succeeded in reducing my sense of isolation and instilling self-confidence. I now know that there are others like myself in India, and together we can form a community. I have also become aware of the need to change unsympathetic laws, like Section 377 of the IPC. The two gay support groups I have visited are the Humsafar Trust in Bombay and

Samapathik Trust in Pune. I like the nature of their work—distribution of condoms and so on. Bindumadhav Khire of Samapthik Trust, especially, has been a true friend to me. He has loaned me a lot of books and magazines in Marathi, which have enabled me to understand the issue of same-sex love in a scientific way. Besides, he is an excellent counsellor. Whenever I have been down in the dumps, he has given me time and discussed my problem with me patiently and this always makes me feel better. So, three cheers to gay support groups and to the gay movement in India.

Editors: Manish Pawar, is there anything else you'd like to say by way of conclusion?

Pawar: You know, when you first approached me for this interview, I was not quite willing to do it. But you were insistent. I thought to myself then, if they are hell bent on interviewing me, let them go ahead and do it. Let them write what they want. Who cares? What difference does it make to me or anyone else in the world? How will the world know if they are telling the truth, or lies? No, it was not about my being ousted after the interview is published. I am not scared of that. In fact, you need not even use a disguised name. Go ahead and use my real name. That was not the point. The point was, I just did not wish to be interviewed, and did not wish to provide any reason either. Nor is it that I was reclaimed. No, it was not that I was suddenly ashamed of being different. It is just that at that point I did not wish to talk, not just to you, to anyone. I was lonely, but I felt it was not due to my sexuality alone. There were family problems and tensions. There still are. True, I did not have a single friend. But I did not think then that gay activists made good friends. And that is how I saw you—as mere gay activists. And I resolved not to take down the addresses and telephone number of any gay activists. I just wished to be left alone. Now, however, my perceptions have changed. I am not disillusioned anymore. I have a more positive outlook towards these things. I realise that a book like the one you are doing is a form of gay activism that can bring hope to the lives of many young people like me in godforsaken places in India. What brought about the change? It may be the gay fiction and non-fiction, I have been reading in Marathi. And other stuff too, like the Marathi novel *Krishna* by Sumed Wadawala Riswud, which is not a gay novel, but has a good style. Movies have also brought a degree of cheer into my life. I love seeing movies, especially art movies [sic]. I see them on cable TV. My favourite Bollywood heroes are Amir Khan and Hrithik Roshan from the current generation, and Nana Patekar and Kamalahasan from the older generation. But I cannot stand Shah Rukh Khan. Is it true that he and Karan Johar are bisexual? Oh, I simply love to gossip about Bollywood stars. It helps me deal with my depression. I like Milind Soman. I believe it was he who released your (R. Raj Rao) novel, *The Boyfriend*, in Bombay in 2003. Does that mean that he is also...? I have the CD of his movie *Rules: Pyar Ka Superhit Formula*.

You know, I think sex is a private thing between two consenting partners (homo, hetero or transgender). Why do we talk so much about it in public? I don't like group sex, nor do I fancy sex in public places likes parks and loos. It's not my fetish.

4

kamamaureemootoo

Editors: Please introduce yourself to us.

Kama Maureemootoo: Well, I am Kama. I am twenty-two, a student of literature at Ferguson College, basically from Mauritius. I am a young man, fascinated by life and the strange world we live in, and having a deep passion for poetry, dance, philosophy and travelling. Hmmm... yeah, I guess that's it.

Editors: There are various sexual identities that are prevalent today. For example, gay, straight, bisexual, transgender, *koti*, etc. What would you say is your sexual identity?

Maureemootoo: Gay.

Editors: Why?

Maureemootoo: I don't see myself as having a girlfriend, or getting married. I like to dress well. I see gay/straight as either–or categories in the Western sense. I've been to France and UK with my parents when I was seven years old. I have white Western friends in France, UK, etc., and several Mauritians are in the West too. So, maybe all these people unconsciously influenced me.

Besides, back home in Mauritius, we as gays see the issue in pretty much the same way as in the West. There are lots of Western families in Mauritius. There is a certain amount of sex tourism in Mauritius, like in Sri Lanka. There was an article in a local newspaper about a homosexual guy from France looking for partners, but the press wasn't hostile to him.

Editors: Is Kama your real name or pseudonym? Are you aware that it means 'pleasure' in Sanskrit?

Maureemootoo: It's my real name. Dad chose it. He read somewhere about *Kama Deva*, the god of love. Well, yeah, it also means pleasure, and there's the *Kama Sutra* and the like. I got to hear a lot about all that since I am in India. In any case, it is my real name. My mom is a Hindu and my father is a Christian.

Editors: Coming back to the question of identity, what do you feel about the politicising of sexuality?

Maureemootoo: I am not sure I got the meaning of the question. I just checked in the dictionary for the exact meanings of politicise. If I got the meaning right (to cause an issue—in this case sexuality—to become political), well, I think it's all pretty stupid. The fact is that one's sexuality is part of the private sphere of one's life, so we should just be and let be, live and let live.

So, as long as what one is doing, does not hurt anybody and/or create a nuisance for society as a whole, there is no question of politicising sexuality.

But then I am not sure if I am getting the meaning of the question right, and in case I didn't, please just explain it to me, and I'll reply back. [*After the editors elaborate on the subject of politicising sexuality*...] Having said that, now that you've explained the meaning of 'politicising' to me—I think that to live and let live, you do have to politicise the issue to an extent. Or, the mainstream will not let you live.

However, I do not like drawing too much attention to myself. I have to be cautious, considering my age and the fact that I'm financially dependent on my parents. Maybe ten years later, my views will be different.

Editors: If you were to prioritise your various identities, in terms of race, class, sexual orientation, etc., where would sexuality be on the scale?

Maureemootoo: Let's see...

Kama,
Human being,
Young man,
Student,
Mauritian,
Dancer and poet (I am so pretentious!),
Gay.

Editors: Why would you put sexuality at the bottom of the scale?

Maureemootoo: I don't have to say I'm gay, just as a heterosexual doesn't have to say he's straight. I don't see my sexuality as something that's 'different'—though society does so. It's like having black or blond hair, or curly hair, or my eyes. I know I'm not being realistic. If I can change just ten or twelve people around me, that's enough. There's nothing special about my sexuality. So I don't need to emphasise it.

Editors: How did you get to know about the support group Samapathik in Pune?

Maureemootoo: A few weeks after landing in India, I decided (now that I was settled) that it was high time I found out what the gay scene was like out here, and above all, look for support groups or other gay people. And like anyone of my age, I just logged on to the net. It was a bit hard to find it though. Had to do a lot of research, but bless the Internet! My research paid off!

Editors: Has being a member of Samapathik made a difference to your sexual life—well, not so much in terms of sexual activity or friendships with like-minded people, but in terms of acceptance of your own sexuality? In other words, has Samapathik helped you come to terms with yourself?

Maureemootoo: Well, I think I'll say no… no, because I think I had already come to terms with my sexuality long before. So on that front, there was anyway no help to be offered!

But I must mention that Samapathik really helped me to understand the scene out here and all those things that seemed so weird to me, like guys holding hands, or eunuchs, etc. And also, it really helped that I knew that there was someone out there to whom I could turn if anything went wrong, and though nothing actually went wrong, it felt good and reassuring to know there's someone I could count on. But, like I said, coming to terms with my sexuality was done a long time ago…

Editors: What is the same-sex scene like in Mauritius from where you come? Is there a law against homosexuality as we have here?

Maureemootoo: The scene back home is pretty contradictory! On the one hand, we have the same law that you have out here. (Mauritius was a British colony before it got its independence.)

But in practical terms, as far as I know, nobody is concerned with that law because it has never been used against anybody, and so nobody cares anyway about the law.

In practical everyday life, being gay is not such a big deal back home; even being a transgender or things like that don't matter. People don't care at all. But here comes the contradiction: people don't care at all as long as it's others who are all these things. The mentality's a bit like this: people are free to do what they want with their sexuality and I really don't care and am not bothered *but* only as long as it's not my son!!! Or my brother, for that matter!

But ultimately, on the whole, it's quite accepted. It's not that bad at all. The general population may think it's weird or funny or against nature, but nobody will deny that homosexuality exists. Everybody knows it exists and it's part of life. And what I feel is that personally people may feel it's strange or against nature, but they won't ostracise anybody or stuff like that. So I think that's pretty cool.

Editors: Is there a gay movement in Mauritius?

Maureemootoo: As far as I know, there's no gay movement or gay support groups in Mauritius. People meet on the net. There was just one gay bar in the country, which has now closed down. People meet each other by coincidence, in the streets or in shopping complexes. They identify each other by their clothes, way of walking, etc. Eye contact can work wonders. There may be cruising areas, but I'm not sure—my generation prefers to meet people on the net. The social aspects of gayness, like having friends, gatherings to know the other person first, building up relationships, are more in Mauritius than here. Here it seems to me, people are only interested in getting into bed. Some friends and I thought of starting one, but we didn't succeed. Mauritius is so small with such few people.

Editors: When you first came to India as a student, what expectations did you have about queer-related issues?

Maureemootoo: I didn't have any expectations at all. I didn't even think about it. Now when I look back at it, I realise that it was quite unwise!

The thing is, my coming to India was really sudden. I just got a call from the Ministry of Education one day telling me that I'm being offered a full scholarship to go study in India for three years, and if I was planning to accept it, I had to be there within two weeks. So I was just too excited by the whole thing, and I was so thrilled about coming to India that I didn't even think about the gay scene out here. The only expectation, or should I say hope, I had in my mind was that Indian guys were cute. But I had no expectations at all when it came to the gay scene, which now, when I think back, is scary.

Editors: Why?

Maureemootoo: India is Jim Corbett, backward, etc., and I hoped Indian guys are cute. In short, I thought of it as a snake-and-tiger land.

Editors: As a dispassionate outsider, what is your view about the same-sex scene in India? Have you been to support groups in cities other than Pune—Bombay for instance, or Delhi or Bangalore?

Maureemootoo: Well, honestly, I do not really think much of the same-sex scene out here. It's just so weird that all people are looking for is sex, sex and sex. I mean there's so much more to homosexuality than a man having sex with a man, or a woman having sex with a woman.

You ask what more? By more I mean, a relationship, people getting to know each other before hopping into bed.

I think the whole thing is just too sex-oriented.

And then, what I think is really sad is the whole marriage scene. I mean, it really breaks my heart to see young guys in their thirties married with kids and cheating on their wives every weekend with a different man. The thing is that again, their homosexuality is being equated to the sex act, and not to asserting oneself, not to decide to stand by one's feelings and one's preference. I think that's sad.

Editors: Have you ever been in a relationship? If so, would you mind describing the experience for us? If not, why not?

Maureemootoo: Well, I've been in quite a few of them. Not that it was anything great, or that it lasted too long. So, really, there's nothing much to say about my relationships. Most of them were real cool; one of them was excellent—I was really happy for once. But then shit happens—so things do not always work out well, but that's ok! It's part of life.

Editors: Please cite at least one example.

Maureemootoo: Most of them were with confused guys who do not know if they're gays or bisexuals. This one that was 'excellent'—for once I felt good—was not just about the sex, but about having someone to hold on to before going to bed, though we didn't live together. He was a foreign student in my class (from Sri Lanka). To start with, we were just friends, but after we came back from our respective vacations (home) we realised how much we cared for each other. But then, overnight, silly that I didn't see it coming, he came and told me it was all over between us—he had found a girlfriend.

I was shattered. I think I have a talent for attracting confused guys. Back home, too, I've had confused friends of this kind.

Editors: The queer world is divided on the issue of same-sex marriage. There are those who are all for it, for personal as well as social reasons. Equally there are those who are opposed to it on grounds that it amounts to replicating what heterosexuals do, and in any case, marriage has not worked wonders for them either. What are your views on the subject?

Maureemootoo: Ha Ha! I like that question!

Well, whether it's hetero or homo, I'm anyways against marriage. I think marriage is pretty ridiculous for various reasons.

But not to deviate from the question, I'd say I really don't care who's getting married to whom—be it a man to a man, a man to a woman, or a woman to a woman. It's all a question of personal choice. If people want to get married, they should be free to do so, whether hetero or homo.

But personally I'm against marriage!

Editors: But what are the reasons you think marriage is pretty ridiculous?

Maureemootoo: I've always seen marriage as an institution. I'm against people who get married to prove their love (in Mauritius). In fact, I asked my parents if they would be happier if they lived together without marriage. There are arranged marriages in Mauritius, but they are the exception not the rule. (But maybe my point of view is changing.)

I don't like the idea of that stupid sheet of paper that proclaims people are wedded together.

However, I fully endorse the monogamy principle on which marriage is founded. Maybe it's my strict Christian upbringing. I don't think I hate marriage only because I am gay—I would have had the same views even if I were heterosexual.

Editors: Is marriage socially compulsory in Mauritius as it is here? Do you plan to get married in spite of what you say against marriage? If not, would you face resistance from your family, from society at large?

Maureemootoo: Well, marriage is quite important back home, but the major difference between home and India is that nobody is forced into marriage back home. If it happens, it's in real rare cases, because ultimately, back home, if one does not want to get married, nobody will force him/her to do so. Marriage is more important for girls than for boys, though.

And I am *not* planning to get married! And my parents know that already! They know my views on marriage already!

Editors: Do your parents/members of your family know about your sexual preference? If not, do you plan to come out to them? If yes, please tell us how they reacted?

Maureemootoo: As my friends generally put it, that's the *Kam-irony*! The thing is that I am out to everybody, all of my friends, or even most of the acquaintances in college, etc., but I'm not out to my family/parents yet. I dunno why. I suppose I will when the right time comes, but as of now, I just intend to keep things the way they are. Let's see later....

I'm thinking of telling them when I go home this time. I have an older brother, and I am sure he knows. I don't know if he's gay himself.

Editors: What are your views on the issue of coming out (of the closet)?

Maureemootoo: I think it's really important. It's important for one's self, it's important so one can be at ease with others and I think it also helps to come to terms with one's sexuality. In any case, I think we should all just be what we are, and assert ourselves for what we are.

Editors: In your approach to gayness, are you utopian or status-quoist? We mean to say, are you happy with things the way they are, or do you wish they would improve in the future?

Maureemootoo: I think things should improve. I hope things improve. On the whole in most countries things are pretty ok, but I think it's high time that the world wakes up to the fact that there is no such thing as 'normal'. There may be heteros, and blonds, and tall people, etc., but I think it's time for people to realise that there is no such thing as normal or abnormal. All that is just convention... that's where I think things should improve.

Editors: As a university student, would you like to see sexuality studies acquire the status of an academic discipline, as it has in universities abroad?

Maureemootoo: Hmmm, no, I don't think so. I mean yes, it's part of our studies, particularly if one is in the humanities, and you can't really escape it. But I don't think too much should be made about the whole thing. The thing is that I see homosexuality as just a normal thing. It's got nothing special about it. It's society that makes a fuss about the whole thing.

So I think if sexuality studies gets too much prominence, it would be rendering it as something 'special', something that is distinct, and I don't think there's a need for that, for according to me there's nothing so distinct about sexuality.

So, I think the small part that sexuality studies has right now in the universities is just fine.

Editors: What would your lifestyle be like, once you finish your studies and return to your country?

Maureemootoo: I don't have a clue. I really don't know. What I know is I want to travel round the world, and assert myself the way I am. I'm learning *Kathak* in Pune with Pandit Nandakishore Kapote and would like to pursue it.

Editors: Is there a connection between your being gay and liking dancing, especially *Kathak*.

Maureemootoo: No, not that I'm conscious of it. I've not seen it that way. But maybe a straight guy will be shy of taking up *Kathak*, unlike me, a gay.

Editors: Have you ever thought of emigrating to the West, because it's sort of gay-friendlier?

Maureemootoo: Yeah, I must have thought so pretty often when I was around thirteen to fifteen years old. But not any more.

Editors: Did you come to India as an escape? Will you change your mind about emigrating to the West to settle down there?

Maureemootoo: No I didn't come here as an escape. I wanted to leave home to experience living alone, doing all my cooking, washing, etc., but not necessarily for sexual reasons. But, now I'm scared to go back home because I've got used to having my own space (in the broadest sense), but there I'd have to live with my parents. I can't see myself as having sex in my parents' house, even in my own room. I would do it in public places like the beach, or at a friend's place. Even on the streets —where after 9 p.m. no one's to be found. Or in cars. I don't know if I'll change my mind about settling down in the West in the future.

5

christopherbenninger and ramnaidu

Editors: How long have you been together?

Ram Naidu: We recently finished fifteen years. On 10 April 2008, we celebrated our wedding anniversary.

It was at Kuala Lumpur, where my brother lives. Christopher took all of us, including my brother and his wife, to a fancy restaurant. You see, we moved in together on 10 April 1993, and consider that as our wedding day. We actually went to the Chaturshrungi temple in Pune and got a priest to marry us! Chris moved out of his house the previous day with one briefcase, in his Maruti Gypsy. We were quite nervous. Neither of us slept well that first night, so Chris thought maybe we should solemnise our relationship in this way. After that, we sat on a bench outside the temple and looked at the sunrise. We said to each other, 'Yes, this is a new life.'

Editors: Where and how did you meet? We believe your first meeting was sort of dramatic.

Naidu: I was a student of the Armed Forces Medical College (AFMC) in Pune, in charge of the creative club. Work often took me to Manney's bookshop in downtown Pune. This was where I set eyes on Chris for the first time. He was browsing through a coffee-table book on Rajasthan, pondering the picture of a young man. I went up to him and asked him if he found the guy in the picture good looking. He answered in the affirmative, and I sensed at once that he was gay. I asked him to a coffee. He gave me a false name—Richard—and said he was a Canadian. He lied to me because he was plain scared, and thought it unwise to disclose his identity. Besides, he was married and closeted. As for me, I knew I was gay at the age of sixteen. But I was studious and did not really have much sex. I grew up in Vijayawada, a small town in Andhra Pradesh. I studied hard to get into medical college, and my efforts paid off when I got admission in AFMC. In Pune, I had all the freedom I desired, and realised without a shadow of doubt that I preferred men. So during my first two years in college, I just chilled out, slept with 100 different men if you like, till I met Chris. It seemed all of Pune wanted to sleep with me, and this flattered me to no end. When I met Chris, there was instant chemistry. I realised that he was the kind of guy I was looking for sexually. Chris emanates a sense of assurance, passion, etc. It was there, all over his face.

Editors: Why do you consider it necessary to see your relationship as a marriage?

Christopher Benninger: Actually, I'm against the word marriage. Let's say we're lovers—real lovers, not casual lovers. Marriage is an institution created by heterosexuals. It's a Christian–European idea brought to India by foreigners. In the West, marriage is a part of civilised society, but Eastern religions view it differently.

Naidu: In my opinion, it is a marriage, and this is one of the strongest things about our relationship. My role models here are my own parents, who have had a very successful marriage. It's a construct they have established and I felt I should replicate it. I don't see my mother and father ever leaving each other. Similarly, the day we were blessed by that priest in the Chaturshrungi temple, I felt I would be Christopher's for life. I have to be with him as long as he is alive. Yes, I love him too, but it's a commitment deeper than love. It's a commitment never to leave him as long as he is alive.

Editors: Does marriage, then, mean stability? The gay world is notorious for short-term relationships, for lovers walking out on each other because nothing binds them legally. Nor do they have to worry about cumbersome processes like divorce.

Naidu: Stability yes, but also security. I would be insecure if I were in a relationship that wasn't sanctified by anything religious, legal. For that reason, marriage is sacred.

For us in India, marriage is for life. Divorce is not something that most married couples in India would consider as an option. It's still regarded as a dirty word, though that may be slowly changing, especially in the metros. Call me old-fashioned if you like, but when it comes to relationships, I'm an arch conservative.

Editors: Christopher, is it true that your business partnership with Ram is a front, an alibi that will legitimately make it possible for him to inherit your property in the event of your passing away? I mean, since same-sex marriage is not recognised in India, is this the sort of loophole you've discovered?

Benninger: Yes, because we're business partners, it effectually makes it like a legal marriage. But it's not as if I made him my partner merely to get over the problem of both of us being male. He's an unlikely business partner, given his educational background and his interests. Now that he's in the business, though, no one can fault the dedication and involvement with which he works for the company. He attends to all boring administrative and financial matters, leaving me to look after the creative side. So much so, I would be lost without him. The main thing, however, is that I consider him family. Not just him, but his father, mother and brothers as well. The basis of this is obviously trust. Do you know almost all architecture partnerships in India have failed because the partners cheated each other at some point? With us, it's almost certain that that will never happen. If you really study our business, you'll find that it's Ram who started the company, while I was the mere proprietor. Today ours is a private limited company, which is a notch higher than a simple partnership. Ram is as responsible as me for all the successes we have attained in the business, all the awards and the laurels. Then, there's also the question of language. As an Indian who knows the local languages, he's almost indispensable.

Editors: You will appreciate that we ask this question because an almost 30-year age difference separates you. Ram, what do you have to say about having a life partner twice your age? Does it make Christopher both lover and daddy at the same time? In the heterosexual world, such a vast age difference would, almost certainly, seem exploitative to many.

Naidu: Well, maybe I was looking for an older, more mature man because I was way too mature for my age. Yet I did not see him as an old man. I have met more handsome men than Christopher, but that is not what I was looking for. It wouldn't be difficult for me to find a guy of my own age. I have already told you that when I came to Pune it seemed as if the whole city wanted to sleep with me! Nor did I fall for Chris because he's a white foreigner, exotic to me. No, it wasn't like that at all. In reality,

I was looking for an anchor, not a shift. I reiterate I wasn't looking for a white man, no. I was looking for someone intelligent and intellectual who could change my outlook on life. I was looking for quality, for someone I could talk to.

Benninger: You know, we make a big thing about age in India, as compared to anywhere else in the world. In Europe or America, it's normal for any man to say that he has a lover of eighteen, twenty or twenty-five years of age, without that immediately being related to his own age. Somehow, you're made to feel guilty here if you have a partner much younger than yourself, as if you've committed a crime. I mean, if a younger man is attracted to an older, or vice versa, what's the harm if they get together? It's no one's business but theirs. In any relationship, it's for the two people involved in it to negotiate it in a way that makes the relationship succeed. This concerns a whole lot of things, of which age is only one aspect. There are other equally important—or more important—things such as values, academic interests, monetary background, spiritual beliefs, personal temperament, the ability to adjust to one another and so on.

Editors: You may consider yourselves wedded to each other, in a manner of speaking. But that's a bit like Sancho Panza riding a donkey and imagining he's on a stallion. In truth, you don't enjoy any of the benefits pertaining to taxes, loans, life insurance, family pension, etc., that married heterosexual couples do. What do you say?

Benninger: Sancho Panza indeed! Well, I've already said that as far as I'm concerned, I prefer to see us as lovers, and not a married couple. Having said that, I concede the point you make. In fact, the strongest argument in favour of gay marriages anywhere in the world is that it gives the partners the kind of benefits you refer to in your question, which cannot be sustained by mere love. In our case, I've explained how our business partnership is one way of getting round the problem, at least to some extent.

Editors: Tell us, is this a marriage of convenience? I mean Chris, as a foreign national, there are many restrictions on you here, such as the owning of property, which you can circumvent on account of your association with Ram. Also, why did you choose India in the first place?

Benninger: Foreigners can own property in India if certain criteria have been fulfilled. Even in 1976, in the middle of the socialist regime in India, foreigners could come to India and start a trust. Why did I come to India? Well, I saw a lecture on the country when I was in class six and that kindled my interest. I must have been eleven or twelve years old then. When I was in college, I came to India on a fellowship—the year was 1968—and I liked what I saw of the country. No, I don't see myself as a missionary or any such grandiloquent thing. I'm just a professional. The paradigm of colonialism does not have meaning any more. I was attracted to the colours of India from an aesthetic point of view. For example, I love the sight of men in turbans. When I first came to India, I met Balkrishna Doshi, a great architect. I regard him as my guru. In the 60s and 70s, I saw India as a frontier for new ideas. The face-to-face approach was still prevalent in India of that time. I met Mrs Indira Gandhi so many times in the 60s and 70s. I would have stayed on in India anyway. I consider myself a self-declared Indian. Would Corbusier be able to devise a new capital in Europe? India is a young country, modernistically speaking.

Editors: Chris, what about the fact that before you met Ram, you were married to this woman who now lives in the same city as you, and by whom you have a son in his early twenties. I believe even the divorce hasn't come through yet. Correct me if I'm wrong. But do you see this as a hurdle? I mean, in the event of a dispute, the law in every way will side with your former wife and son rather than with Ram. I also know that when your mother died in the US, your son wanted to see her will. Ram, does all this make you feel insecure sometimes?

Benninger: I had no property or wealth when I left the house. I was earning a meagre salary of Rs 12,000. Whatever wealth I had at that point

I gave to my wife. This included my car, a Bhupen Khakhar painting, some knives and spoons. All editors of architecture journals know that I'm gay and Ram is my partner. All our clients and employers in the office, too, know we're gay. My wife's not agreeing to a divorce out of a sense of power. She knew I'm gay practically from the time we were married. My relationship with her was idealistic. She was an intellectual partner. She may be gay too, for she had no interest in initiating sex with me. It was me who initiated it with her, and that's how we had a son. I certainly did not understand my sexuality when I was of Ram's age. A guy in the hostel once hugged and kissed me and I pushed him away. Later I wondered why I did it. Nor was I a devout Christian or any such thing. I never believed in god.

Naidu: You asked if Christopher's ex-wife makes me feel insecure. No, not at all. After all, what can she do? Christopher's mine and she'll never succeed in separating us, for he's never going to return to her, no matter what.

Editors: And now to some more personal questions about your relationship. Do you see yourselves as husband and husband, or husband and wife? If the latter, are you not perpetuating stereotypes? Because once again, it amounts to aping heterosexuals. They have issues such as childbirth to deal with, which we don't. Are your domestic lives strictly demarcated?

Naidu: I know why you ask this question. It's because I sometimes joke about being pregnant with Christopher's child and so on. In actual practice, we're neither husband and husband, nor husband and wife, as you put it. We're just a gay couple. I'm born a male and I don't always have to see or think of myself as a woman. See, I have this thick moustache which makes me look as macho as you can possibly imagine. Having said that though, I'd like to point out that all human beings incorporate both masculine and feminine characteristics in themselves. In my case, maybe my feminine characteristics outweigh my masculine ones. I'm proud rather than ashamed of this. If you see me attending to the domestic side of things at home, dealing with servants and things like that, it's hardly because I'm playing the role of the wife. It's got more to do with the fact that Christopher is busy with his work and I do not want him to be disturbed with mundane chores. To an outsider, it may seem like he's the breadwinner and I'm the homemaker, but that's a highly superficial way of looking at it. As we've already explained, I'm an integral part of the business too, in some ways attending to more important aspects of it than Chris. I've also taken on the management of domestic affairs because of the language problem. Christopher's assimilated to Indian ways a great deal, but he still finds it a bit difficult to speak in Hindi and Marathi. One more thing, if you're thinking of the roles we play in bed, I'd say that even that can be fluid rather than fixed.

Benninger: I think Ram has said it all. I just want to add that we'd be the last ones to perpetuate stereotypes. Even when I was married to a woman, I hardly assigned only wifely duties to her. She was a professional companion to me, as is Ram now.

Editors: Incidentally, have you both ever thought of adopting a child?

Benninger: If we'd wanted to adopt, we'd have done it by now, isn't it? No, I don't think that was really on our agenda. Once we got together, our main concern was to establish ourselves in the field of architecture, which, I think, we've succeeded in doing, given our impressive list of clients today.

Editors: From the way you've worked your relationship out, I assume both of you are strong advocates of monogamy. But Chris, Ram is much younger than you, and therefore sexually more agile. What if he indulges in sexual activity with men closer to his age? Will you permit that? Or will it destroy your relationship?

Benninger: You know, it wouldn't bother me at all if Ram had sex with someone nearer his age. But it would have to be restricted to sex alone.

If the person starts to make demands on his time, or thinks he has rights over him, more than me, that would be unacceptable to me. But no, if it were just the question of a fuck, it would be preposterous of me to make it an issue. I'd compare it to something like a Hindu vegetarian, say surreptitiously having a piece of meat. I think these things have got to do with how secure or insecure one is in a relationship. In the early years of our relationship, I'd be jealous if he even went alone to a sauna. But later I became more secure. Now, if there's a gay party or some such thing, I frequently tell him to attend it by himself, without dragging this old man along. I feel quite happy to see him enjoying himself and having a good time. I'm fully alive to the fact that he's much younger than me, and his bodily needs are different from mine. Ironically, I think it's Ram who would be more jealous if I had an affair with someone.

Naidu: That's true. I would feel jealous if Chris even touched someone. But may be that's my nature. I couldn't see him in bed with someone; it would destroy me. And yet at the end of the day I don't think I wouldn't be able to handle it.

Editors: Chris, you were with a woman earlier, and now you're with a man. Would you say you're confused about your sexual identity?

Benninger: I may have been confused earlier, when I was married. But I'm not confused anymore. I know that I'm gay, and was gay always. My marriage was one of those sad things that just happened, as it happens to most people, especially in India. But you mustn't read too much into it.

Naidu: I think sexuality is a fluid thing and we go through different phases. People are different at different times of their lives. So when Chris married this female, maybe he thought he was attracted to her. Later he discovered that he wasn't.

Editors: Ram, I know your parents and brothers have accepted your relationship, and think of Christopher as a sort of son-in-law. This seems miraculous, considering they're from a small town in Andhra Pradesh. How did it come about? Were they okay right from the start, or did you have to work on them?

Naidu: In the beginning, maybe it was difficult for them to accept. But I talked it over with them and made them see things from my point of view, and then it was okay. Certainly, they weren't judgemental. They are intelligent, loving, caring parents and the happiness of their kids is more important to them than anything else. There was no breast-beating at home, nor did they ask me to leave the house, or say they disowned me, and so on. None of the horror stories that we hear of in the media, or read about in the newspapers happened in my case. Maybe I'm blessed. My father, especially, realised that sexuality is not the only thing in life, and too much mustn't be made of it. There are other, more pressing concerns. And Christopher, he regards my family as his own. Whenever my parents and brothers—one of them is also unmarried—visit Pune, they stay with us. Both Chris and I try to make them as comfortable as we can. There are no conflicts at home. It's pretty hunky-dory, actually. I'm not suggesting it's like this in all cases, but maybe our family is the exception rather than the rule.

Editors: Chris, you say your clients and employees know you're gay, and know that Ram is your lover. Yet, you are not as open about your relationship, as say, the fashion designer Wendell Rodericks. Are their residues of conservatism still lurking somewhere?

Benninger: I don't think one has to wear one's sexual orientation on one's sleeve or shout about one's gayness from the rooftops. I told you that our family, friends, clients, employees and all those who matter to us in our personal and professional lives know about us and about the exact nature of our relationship. Beyond that, we don't have to rub it in. I think gay people are often responsible for alienating themselves from the rest of society by their bad behaviour, by this desire to make their presence felt at any cost. It probably comes from a sense of insecurity, something that neither Ram nor I share or can be a part of. You have yourself said somewhere that if you're gay, people look to you for clues as to how to deal with you. The signals that we send out to the world at large must enable us to earn their respect and admiration. It mustn't put them off. It should be our endeavour to make people—the mainstream if you like—see that we're no different from them. We have the same capacity for love, friendship, humanity and tolerance as they do.

Editors: Like issues concerning class, caste and gender, sexuality too has been politicised. Perhaps, this is the only way in which change can be brought about. What do you have to say about politicising gayness, and about gay activism? If you're against it, doesn't it make you status-quoist?

Benninger: I have nothing against the politicising of gayness, if that is what one wants to do. But it certainly cannot be prescribed as the only worth-while activity for anyone who's gay. Also, in the anxiety to be political, the more romantic aspects of gay love mustn't be thrown overboard. Unfortunately, it seems to me that this is what has been happening. The gay movement in India today, as we once discussed in a QSC meeting, has become almost synonymous with HIV and AIDS. Is there any one left who can celebrate gay love the way, say, Wilde, Whitman or Genet did? Today, everyone has become a killjoy. Mention the g-word, and everyone goes alarmist, assuming it guarantees AIDS. Gay politics is fine, provided it goes beyond this, even if it means foregoing wealthy NGO funding, and addresses larger social and legal issues, such as the notorious Section 377 and a whole host of other issues that concern the day-to-day lives of gay people.

Naidu: I've attended the meetings of several gay support groups, and I'm sorry to say I find them boring. The levels of ignorance and intolerance prevalent have to be seen to be believed. There is so much in-fighting between the various groups in India, while the need of the hour is to come together and strengthen our base. It seems to me that each one who starts a group ends up being on his own trip. The concerns of others don't seem to matter to them anymore. Then there are the lesbian groups that can never see eye-to-eye with the male gay groups. All this has put me off activism quite thoroughly. I still believe in it in principle, but the way it is practised in our county is quite revolting.

Editors: Many Western countries have legalised gay marriage. Do you wish that this would someday happen in India too?

Benninger: I think I have already answered that by saying marriage is a Western, and a Christian-European institution that we do not have to import into gay life here. Monogamy, yes, but marriage shouldn't be the only agency that can compel people to be monogamous. However, if legalising homosexuality and gay marriage gives people financial advantages, if may be worth considering purely from that point of view alone.

Naidu: My views, as you know, are different from Christopher's here. To me, nothing can match the sacredness of marriage, which heightens the way in which the partners view each other, as compared to when they were just lovers. For this reason, I'm pro gay marriage. Of course, to expect gay marriage to be legalised in India is just a pipe dream at this stage.

Editors: Your lifestyle. Would you say there's anything specifically gay about it, other than the fact that both of you are male? Or is it simply the lives of wealthy persons in India?

Benninger: In the first place, we're not wealthy. As for our lifestyle, I'm not sure I know what you mean by a specifically gay lifestyle. Yes, maybe we have more disposable incomes than people who've got to raise kids and so forth, who might have to save up for the future. Both of you know us for a number of years now, and you've seen that our lifestyle is no different from that of other upper or upper middle-class people in the city of Pune. I mean, we have got office by day, entertainment in the evening, almost everyday, and we travel quite a lot, mostly on business. I must be spending more than half the year flying. Ram accompanies me on some, but not all of these trips. His parents visit us once or twice a year and we look after them to the best of our ability. We read, see TV, exercise, go to the gym and enjoy good food. We have our regular dose of sex. What else? We celebrate religious festivals like the *Ganesh* festival and Christmas, and do *poojas* like the *Satyanarayan pooja*. Purely out of a sense of fun, not because we're religious.

Naidu: Yeah, we believe in the good life, but is there anything wrong in that? We're not Bohemian, and I don't know if gay people are supposed to lead Bohemian lives. The image we try to project is that of gentlemen of talent and business acumen. Not gay lovers. Our lifestyle is exactly like that of the more successful people in the field of architecture. We've been living in a rented apartment for quite some time, but at last we're building our own house that will be different. Each of us drives his own car. Okay, so we're wealthy, we're capitalist. Gayness doesn't always have to be seen from a leftist or socialist perspective.

Editors: Chris, as an architect, has your sexuality influenced your work in anyway. Can there be said to be some such thing as gay architecture, just as we have gay art, gay sculpture and gay literature?

Benninger: There are an abnormally large number of people who are considered to be gay architects. But none of them say they're doing gay architecture. Maybe that's only possible in literature and painting, not in arts like architecture and music. I don't know. Minarets, steeples, etc., are by no means examples of homoerotic architecture. The mural in the dining hall of the Mahindra World College, and in my own institute, Centre for Development Studies and Activities (CDSA), is that of a nude male with balls and dick.

Editors: So sexuality isn't, for you, your only or main identity. Obviously you have other identities as well.

Benninger: Sexuality isn't my primary identity, no. Being an architect is far more important to me—it's my dominant identity.

Naidu: Calling yourself gay is a very stupid way of describing yourself. Yet, we have been an inspiration to many young people on account of our relationship. I did a research project in the Anthropology department of Pune University on gayness. Does that make me a status-quoist (because of the anthropological perspective)? You rely on things like gayness and so on if you are not good at other things.

Furthermore, my identity is overshadowed by the larger identity of Christopher. If he's Indian, I'm Sri Lankan. Maybe if this were not the case, if his didn't overshadow my identity, it would be different.

6

satishranadive

Editors: Tell us something about your background.

Satish Ranadive: I was born in the Ahmednagar district of Maharashtra in 1976. I'm the youngest child in a family of four brothers and two sisters. My father left home and went to Bombay in search of work with two of my elder brothers. Mainly, my mother brought us up at home. I studied in my village till the seventh standard. Thereafter, I moved to my *mama's* (mother's brother's) village in Ahmednagar district itself, but stayed in a hostel. I managed to pass my tenth standard exam and then came to Ahmednagar city to do my twelfth, and later my graduation. During these years, I lived with a cousin of mine, who's in the police, in his quarters. After graduation, I left for Pune to do my M.A. I have a double M.A., one in Hindi and another in

Sociology. I've also done a diploma in Labour Relations and a Hindi translator's course from well-known institutions in Pune. I've done social work in and around Pune. In school, I once gave a speech on Independence Day, which my mother attended. I started my working life in Nagpur in 1996 as a teacher in the Central Board for Workers Education that comes under the Ministry of Labour. I taught several workers. I trained for four months here and then conducted my first training programme for women workers in my native village, Gunawadi. I enjoyed working in this field and did similar training programmes for workers in other villages, mainly in the Ahmednagar district. In 1999, wandering in search of employment, I came to the Maharashtra Centre for Entrepreneur Development in Pune and ironically enough started training programmes for the educated unemployed. To improve my training skills, I worked as a trainer in the Nehru Yuva Kendra too. Here, I met several corporators, politicians and businessmen. I tell you all this about myself to demonstrate that I'm highly educated and have a desire to do well in life, like any normal person. I'm no loafer type.

Editors: When did you first realise you were bisexual?

Ranadive: In my village school in Gunawadi, which was a co-ed school. A classmate and I thought we were in love with the same girl, so I bashed him up one day, especially as he was threatening to reveal all to my mother. This girl was well-off and she's a doctor now. A few months later, as we were walking to school one day, we saw a small girl, say about ten years old, relieving herself in the fields. I passed a dirty remark. The girl complained to her mother who came to our school and complained about me to my teacher. The teacher admonished me. From that day somehow, girls put me off. I stopped seeing them as sexual objects—in fact, I stooped looking at them at all. Boys replaced my fantasies. I enjoyed being with them much more than I liked the company of girls. There was one boy, Pramod (name changed) whom I was particularly fond of.

Editors: Did this proximity to boys in the hostel lead to sex?

Ranadive: Yes, invariably. I had my first full-fledged sexual experience not with a girl, but with a boy, when I was in the eighth standard. I still remember his name—Harshvardhan (name changed).

What a nice name! You see I was very attractive then and a bit effeminate too. So I was an easy target for older schoolboys. However, though I was effeminate, I had no interest in playing the female role. I saw myself as a man, and whether it was a boy or a girl I was with, I could only do what men are supposed to do. However, we rarely went the whole way in our escapades. Most often, it was what adolescents anywhere in the world indulge in as they begin to discover their sexuality—mutual masturbation and so forth. Contrary to popular belief, in villages we begin [our sexual lives] early. It is in cities that kids tend to be inhibited and lead sheltered lives with their parents. More so, if they belong to the educated middle classes. Villages rarely offer the same scope to lead sheltered lives. Those who did not stay in the hostel had to walk long distances everyday to and from the school. Anything could happen on the way and our parents or guardians wouldn't have a clue. Moreover, their minds don't work the way those of urban parents do.

Editors: What about later on? Were you able to think of women again?

Ranadive: The encounters I had with the boys in my school kindled my interest in men. I gradually grew addicted to homosexual activity, and to date must have been with scores of men. I became adept at non-verbal communication—I began to check men out on the streets and they knew from the look in my eyes, and that alone, what my intentions were. If it wasn't the streets, it was the usual public parks and loos, where men cruised each other. Once we established contact, we normally went to a lodge. I realised that sex with men was relatively hassle-free as compared to sex with women. We passed off as mere friends, and thereby did not arouse suspicion in the minds of people. Moreover, there was no fear of unwanted pregnancies. AIDS was an issue, yes, but with a condom (or two condoms) one was pretty safe. I must reiterate, though, that in all those encounters with men, my condition was that I played the active role. If anyone insisted to the contrary I just walked away. I was mortally afraid of anal receptive sex, not just the pain of it, but also the damage it could do to my psyche.

Editors: We detect an anxiety in you to be active, to play the man's role, as it were. Why?

Ranadive: It's true I have a thin, almost womanly voice. My style of walking may also resemble a woman's. But there's a reason for this. It's because from early childhood I played with girls more than boys. I hate it, however, when people assume that because of my voice and my walk, I'm gay. It's too much of a stereotype. Having said this, I must admit that on occasion I've used these very (effeminate) characteristics of my personality to hook men if I fancied them. I can both exaggerate my effeminate traits, and play them down, as I do at work. It's up to me. When I exaggerate my effeminate traits, I'm not conscious of my masculinity. But at other times I am. In any case, I'm bisexual. I've had flings with girls too. Besides, I'm conservative. I believe in strict gender roles. Nature made man to be the penetrator and that's how it should be. Without this, how can the life cycle continue? I may be homosexually inclined, but I'm still a man. I'll never agree that I'm a *koti*, even if you convince me that my body language is that of a *koti*.

Editors: What's the strangest encounter you've had with a gay man?

Ranadive: It was in Pune, during my M.A. days, when I lived in a hostel and had unrestricted freedom in terms of time and so on—did not have to get back by a certain time, as at home. Once, on my way to Bombay, I landed at the station 3 hours before the departure time of my train, which was 10 p.m. I loitered about in the area. A man came after me. Let's call him G.S. He said he was an engineer in a well-known company. I was irritated, but he pleaded with me to go to his house. He was a married man, whose wife and kids were presently away. I capitulated. His flat was well furnished; he seemed affluent. I read the newspaper, freshened up; we had dinner and mangoes as well (it was summer). We talked. He said something about taking part in plays in his college. Then, before I realised what was happening, he went inside and came out a while later dressed in a ladies night gown, with long hair, falsies, *kajal* (kohl), *bindi* (vermilion dot on a woman's forehead to signify that she's married), a nose-ring and ear-rings. His gait was that of a woman. I was taken aback. For a moment, I thought it was his wife who had entered. He also twisted his mouth like a woman—I liked that. So he was a—what do you call it—transvestite. I had never met a transvestite before. He was also gay. He said he kept his ladies clothes, including a sari, under lock and key and wore them only when his wife was away. She had no clue that he liked to dress in ladies' clothing. We went to the bedroom where there was a long mirror in which we saw ourselves. We looked quite strange together—like man and wife, you may say, though he was taller. This was his fetish—shorter man, taller woman. We spent the night together and made love. I forgot all about my train ticket and my trip to Bombay. The next morning at the time of leaving, he put Rs 350 in my pocket. I vehemently refused to accept the money. I was no male prostitute. But he insisted, and said it was a gift, given with love.

Many months later, I thought of G.S. and went to his flat. But this time it was his wife who came to the door and informed me that he was not at home.

Editors: Have you ever had sex for money?

Ranadive: No, I've never had sex for money, though G.S. gave me money. And I took it because I needed it. But there's this young guy, Sawant [name changed], whom I met at the Pune station. He would take people to a lodge, have sex with them and then ask for money. When he tried to do the same with me, I lectured him. Told him he should work honestly for a living. I was bent on reforming him, and even took him to Nagpur once when I went there on a training programme. But there too, Sawant hooked a Muslim guy in the washroom, befriended him and then stole his wallet. I got to know of this only later. I felt every bad and admonished Sawant. Told him I did not want to be his friend. But it was too late. The damage had already been done. Then I realised that Sawant was using me to procure victims because I was the more delicate-looking. I dumped him there and then. The point I'm trying to make is that once someone gets addicted to having sex for money, it's very difficult for him to drop the habit. He would, in all likelihood land up in jail. I don't know where Sawant is now—languishing in jail most probably. It's immoral and indecent for a man to sell his body. As for me, although my parents were not very well off, they sent me money regularly as long as I was a student. So I never had to consider selling my body as an option. Having said that, I must admit that money is a great temptation. If an older, wealthier guy offered it to me, I wouldn't be inclined to refuse it on grounds of principle alone. But I still wouldn't see myself as someone who has sex for money. That's not my identity.

Editors: Most Indian men get married, even if they are attracted to other men more than to women. What are your views on this?

Ranadive: Oh, I'll get married too. One hundred per cent. I've already seen over twenty girls. Some of these proposals came via the family, others I found out on my own. If I'm still unmarried, it's only because I haven't found the prefect match yet. The girls I've seen so far, if they're good looking they're not educated, and vice versa. So I've kept it on hold for now. No, I won't tell my wife about my gay life. But if I'm caught, I'll confess I'm interested in it since college days, and I like experiencing it occasionally. There's no point trying to deny it and lose my wife's trust as a result, as some men do. I don't think the woman I marry will leave me even if she finds out about my gay life. After all, we're Indians. We tend to have kids soon after marriage, and kids cement the relationship. Moreover, I'm not that sort of gay or bisexual person who's revolted by the idea of sleeping with women. Obviously, I'll be able to satisfy the sexual needs of my wife too, so there's no reason why she should want to leave me. You know something? This may sound strange, but if my wife says she would like to have sex with other women, I'll allow it. I might even welcome it. I'm even on the look out for a lesbian woman with whom I can have a marriage of convenience. But she should be interested in community work. She should be willing to work with me for the welfare of the gay community, and even help me to set up a gay support group. What do I think of same-sex marriage? I'm not horrified by the idea. It's just that the laws of the land do not permit it. But if I were in another country, where the laws permitted it, I would certainly consider it as an option. You see, at the end of the day, we are products of the culture. We are conditioned by our culture, and all our ideas are informed by it.

Editors: Will your family ostracise you if they find out about you?

Ranadive: No, I don't think they'll go that far. And if they do, I'll stand up to them and answer them, and ask them point blank if they know of the developments that are taking place in foreign countries.

Editors: You have many gay-bashing stories. Recount some of them for us.

Ranadive: In all, I have got into trouble four times in different parts of the state of Maharashtra—Bombay, Pune, Nagpur and Ahmednagar—because of my hunger for physical contact with another man. The first time was at the Churchgate station in Bombay. I cruised a Parsi guy, but before we could take off together, a gang of hoodlums seized me and indecently asked if I came there to get buggered. I protested, wanting to know why they picked on me and spared the others in that washroom. At this, one of them put his hand into my back pocket and threatened to beat me up if I didn't part with cash. And then, do you know what I did? I screamed, appealing to passers-by to help me get rid of the *goondas*. I claimed they were pickpockets. It worked. The rogues ran away, while a good Samaritan accompanied me all the way to the bus stop just outside the station, and did not leave till he put me in a bus that took me to Chembur, where my brother lives—and to safety.

The second time was in Nagpur. The pattern was similar. I found myself in Sitabardi, a neighbourhood known for same-sex cruising. A hoodlum came up to me and said, 'My brother, where are you going, didn't you recognise me?' I did not, but he insisted he knew me. His accomplices were near at hand, but I did not know that. Soon they approached me too, and like the first guy, claimed they knew me. Then something came over me, and I asked them to identify themselves, with name and address, failing which I would take them to the police station. I realised they were after my gold chain. Giving them the slip, I walked away as fast as I could, and hopped into a bus bound for Dharampeth, where I lived. In retrospect, I wonder why they did not give me chase, or at least follow me. Was it because I mentioned the police?

The third time was in Ahmednagar. I met a guy called S.D. at the bus terminus and went with him to a lodge, for which he paid. He was a confidence trickster. He made me part with my phone number and started calling me up at home. We met quite often. One day, I took him home to introduce him to my brother and *bhabi* (sister-in-law). The guy was handsome, though effeminate. He resembled—of all people—the singer Anuradha Podwal. His girlish way of speaking aroused my brother's suspicion. I tried to cover up for him by saying that he was from Jalgaon, and people of Jalgaon spoke that way. As if my brother was born yesterday to believe this! Nevertheless, the guy spent the night at my place. We slept in my room on the same bed. The next morning we went out into the fields to answer nature's call. I still remember the way we squatted close to each other. I cautioned the guy to act a bit 'manly' so that he wouldn't inadvertently out me. At this point, he started to refer to me as *dada* or elder brother. A few weeks later, he landed up at my place without telephoning. I was not at home—was in Pune to attend college. He even brought my *bhabi* a present—two saris. He spent the night at our place once again, but this time it wasn't incident-free. The rogue tried to decamp with some cash, to the tune of Rs 15,000, which my brother had carelessly left in a trunk to pay some bills. Luckily, my *bhabi* woke up with the sound and accosted him. He apologised. When we counted the cash we found that Rs 100 was still missing. We thrashed it out of the chap and threw him out of the house. After that, I never saw him again. I'd like to caution all gay men here—beware of confidence tricksters and sweet talkers, and never make the mistake of giving them your name, address and telephone number till you are 100 per cent sure of their antecedents.

Finally, Pune. I was at this notorious public loo near Main Street. I went inside for a leak and was witness to all the torrid same-sex activity going on in broad daylight. When I came out, a muscular guy followed me and chatted me up. Meanwhile, two others approached us. They appeared to be Muslims and their mouths reeked of country liquor. One of them was a mechanic dressed in navy blue apparels. As soon as they joined us, the muscular guy—who was obviously hand-in-glove with them—vanished from the scene. I was trapped. The bastards grabbed me by the shirt and threatened me. Once again, I resorted to my action plan. I managed to free myself, went to the Udipi restaurant opposite, and complained to manager. But the waiters took the side of the mechanic. They knew him, since they worked in the same neighbourhood. As I sat at a table, the two *goondas* followed me into the restaurant and joined me, sitting bullyingly close. I walked out of the restaurant, so did they, and at this point the filthy mechanic got hold of my shirt again and started beating me up. I hit him too. By this time a small crowed had gathered. Without knowing what the issue was, they tried to pacify both sides. They succeeded in putting an end to the ugly episode. The public has tremendous power. I scrammed to the nearest bus stop, hopped into the first bus that appeared and fled. At home, my *bhabi* saw my soiled, crumpled, torn shirt and interrogated me. I fibbed about falling out of a running bus. In retrospect, it seems to me that if I had money in my pocket, I could have flung it at the faces of the hoodlums and saved my self-respect. So here is another piece of advice to cruising gay men—make sure you always have a fair amount of cash in your pocket for emergencies.

Editors: Do you think support groups is the answer to these sordid incidents that all of us experience at some point or other?

Ranadive: Definitely. But a lot of gay men who become members of support groups do so only for sex. This is unfortunate. We need to devote ourselves to serious work for the welfare of the gay community. As I said, I have plans to start my own support group some day. I am inclined towards social work. Maybe, I'll approach some NGOs for financial help. We need a self-help group for gays, which I would like to start. If not NGOs, maybe banks could be approached for financial help, though this maybe difficult as long as homosexuality remains criminalised in India. Many gays are in creative trades like dress designing, catering, dancing, fashion photography, etc. We can solicit their help to start vocational guidance programmes for members of the community, in order to help them discover their talents. We should be encouraged to save for the future. A lot of gay men with disposable incomes tend to blow up their money on partying. What comes in the way of achieving these utopian goals is the business of sexual identity. The majority of gay and bisexual men in India are merely interested in sexual activity, but run for cover the moment we suggest that their orientation really is (or should be) a part of their sexual identity as well. I've interviewed several *kotis* on my own. 'We are not interested in identity politics', they irresponsibly say, 'we will never give our arse for free.'

7

manoharshitole

Editors: Please introduce yourself to readers.

Manohar Shitole: I'm a homosexually inclined man, 44 years of age. I knew I was homosexual since adolescence, since the age of thirteen or fourteen. By training, I'm an engineer. I'm also an amateur artist, pen-and-ink sketches being my speciality. I'm married and have a daughter. I described myself as homosexual, and yet that was never a part of my identity. Identity-wise, I did not know who I was sexually. Perhaps I know now, but it's too late for anything to significantly change in my life. All through my life, I have been repressing my feelings for men. It's only in the last couple of years that I have been having clandestine sex with men. This suppression of my sexual nature affected me deeply, both from within and without. I lack confidence; I cannot really approach people and talk to them. No, I'm not exactly shy; it's just that I lack resolve. In day-to-day life, my morale and self-esteem tend to be low. My bottled-up sexual feelings played havoc in my life. My body was pale and thin. My mind was jumbled, even though I'm not the nervous sort. There is nothing else I can say about myself by way of introduction.

Editors: How do you view your homosexuality? Do you view it as an abnormality?

Shitole: When I got married, I was very tense. I wasn't sure if I'd be able to perform with my wife. This anxiety can make any man a nervous wreck. In my case, it triggered off my visits to a series of sexologists. The first of these was a husband-and-wife duo, well known in my city. I told them about my innermost fears, my revulsion to sleep with my wife and satisfy her. I tried to speak to them as objectively as I could, reminding myself all the time that they were medical professionals for whom I was only a case study. And yet, I simply couldn't bring myself to tell them about my homosexuality. I simply lacked the guts. I tried very hard, I was on the verge of disclosing it to them a thousand times, but in the end it remained unsaid. Naturally, therefore, the sessions were a failure; the money was wasted. I received no succour. All that this doctor couple said to me as we parted was, 'Manohar, why do you stand on the bank of the river and debate if the water will be hot or cold, or whether you'll be able to swim or not? Just jump into the water, take the plunge.'

To this day, I don't know whether they spoke these words because they guessed what my problem was.

The second time I decided to seek professional help, I looked up the yellow pages of the telephone directory for a list of doctors and treatments. I found a 'penis specialist' and consulted him. After preliminary discussions pertaining to my age, profession and such like, I mustered up the courage this time to tell the doctor about my attraction for men. It caused confusion in me, I told him, and so I wanted his guidance. I think the 'penis specialist' got even more confused than me on hearing my revelation. He did a physical check-up on me, and told me nothing was wrong with me physically. He told me that the cure for my problem was not physical but mental treatment. He thus washed his hands off me by referring me to another medical practitioner.

This guy called himself a medico-psycho practitioner. I had three to four sittings with him. He told me to be as frank with him as possible, failing which he wouldn't be able to help me. So I told him everything. His reaction? He informed me that homosexuality was a common occurrence in men, and even the patient who saw him just before me was gay. He explained that all men were homosexually inclined to an extent, and what differed was the degree of same-sex attraction each of us felt. This put me somewhat at ease. I tried to see homosexuality as nature's gift. What this third doctor made me see was that even if one tried to get rid of one's homosexual feelings with therapy, it would never completely disappear. It would stay with me till the end of my life. The last time I went to see this doctor, you know what he said to me? He said, 'Bravo! Do not be afraid. Enjoy yourself.'

Editors: Are you aware that in America and several other countries, homosexuality is no longer viewed as a mental illness?

Shitole: I wasn't aware during the time I was seeing these sex doctors, but I am aware now.

Editors: Did you see marriage as a possible way to take your mind off homosexual desires?

Shitole: Yes. I wanted to wipe this thing out from my life. It was hassling me to no end. I wanted to clear my mind of the fog that engulfed it. I guess what compels us to change is this thing called society. There is the image of man in society. Every man, once he matures physically and is financially settled, is expected to get married and raise a family. Parents have these expectations of their children, and we are supposed to fulfil them. I imagined that I had to follow the same path; I had no other choice. The only course was for me to change my own nature. It was this that took me to the sex doctors. But in spite of all the sessions I had with them, and in spite of being married for ten years and producing a child, I still have this feeling, this desire within me. It's something I can't really express to anyone. Outwardly, I tried to be normal—I did my duty towards my wife, child and parents. I behaved—or pretended to behave—like a decent family man. But the urge to have gay sex did not go away. Each time I tried to suppress it, it returned with twice the force. I was an unhappy man.

Editors: What's your wife's position in all this?

Shitole: My wife is not orthodox, but neither is she very modern. If I go home late, she doesn't ask me why I'm late. She doesn't nag me, as some urban wives are apt to do. At the most, at the time of leaving, she might ask me what time I'll return. Many wives ask so many questions to their husbands, it becomes very difficult [to live together]. If you lie once, you have to lie a hundred times to cover up the first lie, and in this way the problem is compounded.

Needless to say, I have given my wife no clue about my gayness. Within the family I try to behave as normally as I can. Very few times in the last two years or so, have I spent a whole night with a friend (read lover). If I make this a regular practice, my wife might start to doubt me. I usually make out with a male friend only when she's away with our daughter at her parents' place. To deflect suspicion, I have sex with my wife whenever she demands it. There are really very few times when I want to have sex with her. I do it just to please her and keep her happy. Sometimes I try to avoid it by giving excuses. I tell her I'm tired, or that it is very late, or that the neighbours might suddenly drop in! But I cannot do this too frequently. Otherwise, she might begin to doubt me. As a family man, I know I have duties to perform. After all, like all devoted Indian wives, my wife works for the home, for our daughter, for me. I have an obligation to keep her happy at all times. Yet, whenever I have to sleep with her, I need time to prepare myself mentally. I never get emotionally involved in the act. It tends to be mechanical from my side.

Very rarely, very rarely indeed do I initiate sex with her. It's always she who does so. Moreover, my wife is the only woman I am willing to satisfy sexually. Even if I were straight, I wouldn't look at other women. I believe in being loyal to one's spouse. I don't care about Karishma and Kareena (Kapoor). But I have a tremendous sexual attraction towards men, and to my bafflement, it is as much within me today, in my forties, as it was when I was a young man.

Editors: Have you ever considered having a relationship with another man that would sort of parallel your married life? Or is this morally incorrect to your way of thinking?

Shitole: No, it's not morally incorrect. I need to be happy too. But having a relationship with another man, or even a steady male friend, is easier said than done. In the last few years, I have met many gay men and even slept with them. But for a relationship to happen, there must be compatibility. This usually isn't to be found, and the reason obviously is that homosexual activity for most Indian men is a part of their secret double lives, which they'd rather not admit even to themselves! For example, I like men who are gentle, to whom I can connect at a deeper level and share thoughts, habits and manners. But such men are a rare commodity. Only occasionally have I met men like Sandip (name changed), who lives in the Konkan, and with whom I have tried to have a more or less sustained relationship. From our very first meeting at a gay party in Mumbai, I liked him. He liked me too. I liked him though he is a *KoBra*. You know what that is? It's short for Konkanastha Brahmin! I mean, they have a reputation for being narrow-minded and miserly, but Sandip is different. We are both very clear about the fact that we cannot live together, like husband and wife. Besides, each one of us is free to have sex with anyone we fancy, even though we're committed to each other. That's the understanding we have, as two men. Can a man and a woman ever come to such an understanding within a marriage? Of course not. Sandip and I are lovers, but we are also friends. We do not have sex every time we meet—we cannot, even if we want to. It all depends on the circumstances, and the opportunities available. But we can be friends at all times. You know Sandip has even come and stayed at my house with my family. In fact, when his younger brother and sister-in-law shifted to our city, they took a lot of help from my family. Without having a clue as to what the exact nature of the relationship between Sandip and me is! To them, we're just good friends. His brother now considers my wife as his own sister. There is a deep relationship between all of us. I think this is how men like me circumvent the taboos that exist in certain kinds of relationships.

Editors: You spoke of compatibility. How exactly would you define it?

Shitole: I meant both physical and mental compatibility. To me, being on the same wavelength as a person is far more important than his merely being attractive to me sexually. That is why I prefer middle-aged men as lovers, though young people are a greater turn-on. But young people usually lack maturity. During sex, they tend to think only of themselves, conveniently forgetting that their partners are also in need of pleasure. In any kind of sexual activity—gay or straight—the partners need to be in tune with each other. Their approach to sex and their thinking must be similar. Otherwise, the experience isn't rewarding enough. For example, I might like deep kissing, but if my partner has a problem with this and refuses to yield, it will naturally put me off. It'll put him off as well. I think the real joy of sex is when the two persons involved respond to each other's body language. If not, it simply amounts to play-acting. Very artificial. When two people meet for the first time, things might look rosy, fantastic. But as the affair progresses and emotions come into the picture, it brings pain and frustration in its wake. Most gay men want to avoid that because of the social conditions prevalent in our country. As a result, the gay community has earned a bad name as people who only want sex, not love and its attendant responsibilities. But we cannot be blamed for this. It's mainstream society and its hostility to us that is responsible for shaping our attitudes. As a married man, I know this well enough.

Editors: How do your colleagues at the work place behave with you?

Shitole: I have more than a hundred workers in my charge at our unit. But somehow, my homosexuality has always made me feel that I am not fit enough to be their boss. I mean would they accept my authority if they knew who or what I really was? This is the question that keeps bothering me, and I am very conflicted. For the working class in India, especially, a homosexual man is not man enough and is no different from a eunuch. And, as you know, eunuch is a metaphor for a weak, not a strong person. It is this thought that hampers effective communication between me and those under me. I can't talk to them properly. My mind keeps telling me, you can't handle them. This is one of the things that drove me, in the first place, to these quack sexologists I spoke of earlier. I think gay and homosexual men are better off being self-employed.

Editors: We guess what you are talking about here is masculinity, and the forms it takes in day-to-day life in India. Any views on this?

Shitole: Yes. Masculinity is prevalent everywhere. The acid test of whether a man is gay/homosexual or not is his insistence on being a 'top only' guy. That's what most men insist on, and it leads me to the conclusion that very few people are genuinely gay/homosexual. To these men, being 'bottom' guys challenges their masculinity, leaving them with a sense that they are not manly enough. And this they simply can't accept about themselves. To a real gay or homosexual person, this top/bottom dichotomy shouldn't be so important. Should it not be more about the feelings, the emotions? Why should being active or passive assume an either/or framework in their scheme of things? What's the harm in being versatile and playing both roles in accordance with one's bodily responses? But what interferes here is the male ego and male identity. It ensures that things remain at the level of sexual activity and do not blossom into full-scale relationships. So apart from society and its hostility (that I spoke of earlier), it's masculinity that also comes in the way of gay love in India.

Editors: You referred in passing to a gay party that you attended in Mumbai. Can you describe for readers what it was like?

Shitole: It was in a bungalow at a beach in the western suburbs. There was an entry fee that included a beer and some food. But for extra drinks and extra food, the guests had to pay out of their pocket. There were about a hundred people who were present. Most of them were young—say in their twenties or early thirties—and all of them were gay. The majority of them seemed effeminate in their speech and mannerisms. Of course, there were some who were different. They did not look gay at all, though they were gay. Sandip was one such. We quickly made eye contact and started speaking to each other. But we weren't really very audible to each other as the music was extremely loud—much beyond the permissible decibel level. I don't know how the neighbours didn't object and contact the police. Or perhaps, there are no full-time residents there, other than the poor locals, mostly *koli* fishermen, I suppose. There were only the bungalows of Mumbai's super-rich who come here on weekends. Then there was dancing. How can you have a party like that without dancing? People danced, literally with gay abandon. Some were graceful, others clumsy. Some had come with partners, others searched for partners in the crowd. Those who didn't have partners just danced in a group with all the others. Some were shy and refused to come to the dance floor, even though others tried to drag them on to it. Initially both Sandip and I were shy and did not dance. We came from middle-class Maharashtrian backgrounds after all. But after a while, and after a couple of beers (I hope my wife doesn't read this), we landed on the dance floor too. No one seemed to eat much. Everyone danced more than they ate and some threw up in the washroom. By midnight, the dance floor was packed with everyone jostling for space. That's when all the physical activity like fondling and kissing started to happen. Since it was an overnight affair, people retired to whatever corner they could when they were tired, to have a few hours of rest. Maybe some of them made out with each other in the dead of night, drunk as they were. I did not see anything. And even if I did, it's not something I can describe here.

All in all, both Sandip and I enjoyed ourselves, but we both felt that one party was enough. I don't think we really want to be a part of the party circuit of Mumbai and Pune. We prefer spending whatever time we get together intimately, by ourselves. This is not to suggest, however, that parties like the one we attended do not have their usefulness. They are one of the few networking places that can bring like-bodied and like-minded men together, other than conventional spaces like parks and public toilets, and now the Internet. After all, Sandip and I found each other at this party.

Editors: What are the hazards of being gay in India?

Shitole: One of the main hazards is that 90 per cent of the men who go cruising are fake. They are there only to cheat and loot innocent people who are merely seeking an outlet for sexual release, because they're human like everyone else. A few years ago, a day before New Year's eve, I was a victim of such malicious men. A man followed me as I went for a leak into a public loo on a quiet residential street, pretended to be gay and invited me to his flat. I had no clue that he belonged to a gang of hoodlums who approached us and blocked our path as soon as I started my scooter, with the rogue on the pillion seat. As soon as this gang of four made their presence, I discovered that the bastard who spoke to me in the loo was actually one of them, and his propositioning me was only a ploy. Though I tried to put up a fight with them, they were five while I was one. So one of them grabbed my spectacles, another took hold of my scooter. Two others clutched my hand and dragged me to a nearby bench. There they started raining blows all over my face, head, hands and stomach. Even my feet, for god's sake. They said, 'We know why you are here. Now we will show you who we are. We have connections in the police.' Next, they snatched my wallet. Unfortunately, it was one of those days when I was carrying money in my pocket—I normally don't. They audaciously stole the cash in my wallet, about Rs 500 or Rs 600, returned it and then resumed beating me all over again. As it was late, close to midnight, there were no passers-by to come to my rescue. The rogues took advantage of that. Besides, it was very cold and their blows hurt. Eventually, they let me go. I was extremely nervous, shaken. One blessing was that they hadn't inflicted any physical wounds on my body. I did not bleed. The papers in my wallet were also intact. However, I had a swelling on my face and a hairline fracture in my ribs. I couldn't sleep the whole night. I kept thinking of the excuse (for my condition) to give to my wife when she returned from her parents' the next morning. When the time came, I told her I had a scooter accident, as well as a toothache, hence the swelling on the face.

There are other hazards too—like contracting HIV/AIDS. I am very scared of this nowadays. I'm not sure one is safe even if one uses a condom. A third hazard for closeted homosexual men like me is that we can easily be blackmailed and outed to our families, employers and neighbours. The shame of this would be too much to bear. Even death is preferable to being held to ransom on account of one's sexual inclinations.

Editors: Your drawings. We get the impression that you attempt to sublimate your sexual fantasies in them. Would you agree?

Shitole: Yes. That's more or less true. Whenever I see a cute guy, I fantasise. There is an artistic quality to these fantasies. They're not just about sex alone. They're romantic rather than sexual, and the settings are very important to me. I imagine myself on the eighteenth or nineteenth floor of a high rise building, making love to the guy of my dreams. Or by the sea, or in a thick forest. Sometimes I imagine the chap in question to be my boss in the office, wearing a suit and tie, and standing very close to me as he explains something. On the way back home, he gives me a ride on his bike and I clutch him tightly. The thing about fantasy is that there are no limits to it. One can imagine anything, and no one other than oneself will know. So it's an excellent way to vicariously satisfy one's longings and desires. Art is an excellent alibi, like literature. Some of my drawings are explicit, others erotic. Some may verge on pornography. But the nice thing about art is that it is invested with respectability. If one did the same thing in real life, one would be dismissed as a man without morals, a man without character. But when something is represented in the form of a drawing, its implications are different. Its intentions are noble, and the person in question is viewed in a positive light as a man of talent, even genius and not in a negative light as an immoral man. Art belongs to the realm of representation that is on a higher plane than reality. I can draw penises and partially naked men as an artist, but I cannot openly give vent to these fantasies in day-to-day life. Of course, I'm aware that these days, the moral police in our country do not even spare artists. M.F. Hussain is a case on point. This is very unfortunate.

Editors: So, Manohar Shitole, where do we go from here?

Shitole: It is easy to talk about the past. But when I start thinking about the future, there are unbearable worries, tensions and anxieties. So I will not get into that. I am no philosopher.

8

thomaswaugh

Editors: Tell us about yourself.

Thomas Waugh: I was born in Ontario, Canada, the year after India's independence, and have taught film studies since 1976 at Concordia University, as well as sexuality and queer studies and curriculum about AIDS for many of those years. Concordia is an English-medium institution in Canada's French-speaking metropolis, Montreal. I have been a visitor to India since 1970, when I taught English in Punjab for two years as part of a volunteer organisation, and have felt lucky to have met so many queer Indian brothers and sisters over the years, including many who don't use the same labels as I. Over the last two decades, I have extended my research in film studies to include Indian cinema, including stirrings of what might be called queer Indian cinema. I feel most privileged to have been able to integrate theories and cultures of my own queer sexual identity into my academic work.

Editors: When did you come out to the world about your gayness?

Waugh: I have always been out to myself, even as a child, but without self-conscious labels, and at puberty, and thereafter gradually grew into an awareness of myself as a homosexual. I did not act on that identity, at least in terms of genital contact with another man, until I was twenty. I didn't start coming out to people in my life, other than my very slowly proliferating network of partners of course, until a few years later, and I didn't come out to my parents until I got a permanent job around 1976. I didn't come out professionally until I published a first-person article on queer cinema in 1977, I believe.

Editors: What, especially, was the reaction of your family towards your sexual orientation, considering that your father was a priest and your mother a teacher?

Waugh: My mother went berserk and said she never wanted to see me again, so most of my liberal Protestant father's energy went into calming her down and making me feel still loved, rather than whipping up negativity. I think this was a test for his progressive Protestant liberalism and he passed with flying colours. I still have the incredibly beautiful letter he wrote me. My three siblings were less supportive (which was unusual for my peer group) and engaged in emotional blackmail regarding how my parents would react. My mother soon came through. Our religious denomination (to which I no longer adhere) is the most liberal church in Canada and through the 1980s struggled with the issue of Lesbian Gay Bi-sexual Transgender (LGBT) members and clergy. I was proud of my fiercely protective mother in those years and the way she rose to the occasion in the struggle around homosexuality in her church—even to the extent of leaving my late father's conservative congregation and joining another parish. She now has Alzheimer's disease and asks me how my wife is.

Editors: Can you briefly trace Canada's journey towards gay liberation?

Waugh: Canada, under Liberal Prime Minister Pierre Elliott Trudeau, followed Britain's lead and decriminalised same-sex relations between two adults in private a few weeks before Stonewall in 1969. So our emerging movement in the 1970s was focused most on anti-discrimination cases and human rights charters, unlike the American focus on decriminalisation. We had little success in that decade, except in my province of Quebec, which forbade discrimination based on sexual orientation in 1976. The next milestone, after much judicial and police harassment, was our new constitution of 1982, whose Charter of Rights and Freedoms contained general equality provisions without mentioning sexual orientation. Few of us at the time, and probably not Trudeau, realised this charter would be applied to LGBT people. But the Charter soon began to be interpreted by one court decision after another in our favour, and by the end of the century, all provinces and territories adopted or were forced to adopt non-discrimination human rights charters. Same-sex marriage came next, legalised everywhere by 2003–2005. In short, you could say there's a top–down governmental or judicial dynamic to what you call 'our journey', but of course I have not mentioned the dynamic growth from the 1960s onwards of grass-roots communities, media, markets and other aspects of the public sphere, especially in the large cities where the majority of Canadians live. Within the legal framework, there's still a lot of work left to do: the current Conservative regime is trying to criminalise youth sexuality by raising the age of consent from fourteen to sixteen, and is resisting the push for gender identity as grounds for non-discrimination and resisting the widespread consensus in favour of repealing our inherited colonial laws about prostitution and pornography. General social attitudes about sexual diversity have also evolved radically since 1970.

Editors: Your views about same-sex marriage, now that it's legal in Canada?

Waugh: I know some of my progressive friends think same-sex marriage is no big deal, and some think it's even a backward step, providing an institutional foundation for us to be assimilated through aping hetero-sexual structures, rather than maintaining our inherent subversive queer role in society. I think this can be a utopian thinking and know too many deliriously happy couples for whom legal marriage has been a very meaningful breakthrough in their lives. Although I will probably never get married, except for some mundane pragmatic reason, on the level of everyday life, the legal recognition is important: my common law partner has access, for example, to free tuition and medical coverage as a result of our relationship. If Lesbian Gay Bi-sexual Transgender Queer (LGBTQ) ideologues ally themselves with conservative oppo-nents of same-sex marriage, they do so at considerable social risk—not only to the legalities of couplehood, but also to essential things like inheritance law and parenting rights. At the same time, I empathise with the arguments that the Canadian 'journey' has been overwhelmingly legalistic, with progress focused on winnable legal issues, rather than more fundamental concerns of sexual minorities that sometimes would not fare so well as respectable monogamous couples in the courts, such as intergenerational sexuality, sex-work and pornography.

Editors: As a film studies professor at Concordia University, is your sexual orientation an issue among your colleagues and students, as it tends to be here in India? Or is it completely inconsequential?

Waugh: There has been only a little bad blood, for example, the faculty union refusing to support benefits for same-sex couples in the late eighties, or our first gay studies film and literature course in 1988 be-ing denounced in the university newspaper by a colleague in another department, etc. Otherwise in a large liberal downtown institution, there's a strong culture of diversity and tolerance. Moreover, since I have established queer studies as perhaps the most important field of my intellectual contribution, recognition of my scholarly work implies polite acceptance of sexual diversity, even where individuals might have private doubts. So it is neither a major issue nor inconsequential. There are lots of queer faculty, including a couple of transsexual professors. With the latter also, an academic focus on gender politics (a strong women's studies programme, for example) seems interconnected to an institutional culture of diversity.

Editors: Have you experienced hostility or prejudice from the orthodox conservative element in academia as a result of your research in queer pornography?

Waugh: Not really. But I'm always looking over my shoulder. Because, in all modesty, I think I pioneered some new areas of research, I think recognition followed which might not have happened had my work been mediocre. One secretary once refused to type one of my pieces on gay male eroticism, but I didn't press the issue. Some of my colleagues in the US heartland have run into problems, however, in teaching and researching pornography.

Editors: Is there a queer mainstream in Canada and other Western countries, which tends to be white, to the exclusion of queer persons of colour? Does it introduce a sort of racist dimension to the issue?

Waugh: I shouldn't sound complacent, for there's much work left to do, but I think the LGBT public sphere has become increasingly diverse in recent decades: in Toronto and Vancouver perhaps even more so than in Montreal. This was my impression when I wrote my book on queer cinemas in Canada. My classes on queer cinema at Concordia are quite diverse: I just read a wonderful paper on the queer subtext in *Sholay* by a woman student of Sikh descent.

Otherwise, I'm not sure what the notion of a 'queer mainstream' would mean, but it is true that sometimes I wake up at public events and notice the crowd is pretty white, or at least not reflecting the demographic mosaic of the Canadian population. Is this about racism or about other more benign cultural dynamics about the integration of newcomers in any society? Probably both. It is also true that the middle-class white gay male market is the most powerful in terms of spending power in Europe, North America and Australia, and therefore most visible in the public sphere which is so significantly shaped by markets. Of course, the market has no conscience, racial or otherwise. Finally, we should focus on class as well as on race and culture, for the poor are also invisible and excluded.

Editors: Gays and lesbians in Canada: unity or disparate agendas?

Waugh: In terms of political lobby groups, community organisations such as film festivals or pride parades, and academia, strategic alliances between men and women are the tradition of the last couple of decades, never without tensions of course. The dark days of a quarter-century ago when there seemed to be an anti-sex consensus on the part of lesbian-feminist voices and groups, and when male-identified groups tended to be so clueless about sexism and reproductive rights, etc., seem to be a thing of the past. One legacy of the 'dark days' is that lesbian feminist hysteria about pornography eventually impacted on our criminal code in a 1992 decision, and now queer erotic culture is still paying a heavy price in terms of censorship and self-censorship. Otherwise it's been a lot of work, but women and men seem to have learned to collaborate when we share interests, all the while recognising important differences. Most recently, I relived some of the old 'disparate agenda' stress when a couple of female reviewers felt that I hadn't given women equal balance in my book on queer Canadian cinemas (as a historian, how could I invent a 50/50 balance in a sixty-five-year trajectory in which the first lesbian-authored film did not show up until the late 1970s?). I relived a parallel kind of disparate agenda crisis again at a recent workshop on queer film festivals I had organised. Tension flared up between younger transgendered folks and my generation of lesbian and gay veterans over the 'withdrawal' of a film by the San Francisco LGBT festival, *Frameline*, that had been objected to by voices within the trans community there, and words like 'offensive' and 'censorship' became very inflammatory. In other words, different agendas are healthy and normal and we live and learn by them, all the while needing to better our skills at working together in full respect of difference.

Editors: There is a sizeable transgender population in your country? What issues concern them?

Waugh: There have been sizeable and visible transgender communities, especially conspicuous in the largest Canadian cities, for decades. Transmen (female to male) are increasingly visible these days in university communities such as Concordia. The constituency is diverse of course, but concerns include the provision of unisex washrooms in public spaces, access to surgery and other healthcare services under provincial medicare plans, legal recognition (ranging from the acceptance of gender identity as a protected category in rights charters to the overcoming of bureaucratic hurdles to official gender change, including recognition of name changes by institutions), and for many the decriminalisation of sex-work as well.

Editors: Is there a lot of homophobia in Canada as in the US?

Waugh: Homophobia in Canada is better hidden and less institutionalised, but no less present than in the US. Our distinct legal framework, including constitutional protection for the last quarter-century and partial decriminalisation over the last forty years, gives us a false sense of security. Those of us living in the large and diverse metropoles forget what it can be like in the hinterland and the rural regions, both in terms of homophobic violence and in terms of relatively benign forms such as heteronormativity and queer invisibility in the public sphere.

Editors: After visiting India for almost forty years, have you perceived any changes in the gay scene here, a more visible Right wing now than earlier?

Waugh: When I first came to India as a young guy in 1970, I perceived a lot of same-sex eroticism (as well as a certain amount of gender diversity in the form of *hijra* culture, of course), but this was never spoken. I saw no gay scene as such but I didn't know how to look for it (unless you can call my couple of furtive encounters with horny like-minded men a 'scene'). My most traumatic memory of discovering queer India back at the start of the 70s was seeing three boys, ranging in age perhaps from eleven to thirteen, hauled up before the school assembly and publicly humiliated for having been caught diddling with each other. The 'instigator' was expelled I believe, and much was made of the fact that he was a 'scholarship boy' to boot. I, the closety foreign teacher in the audience was shamefully silent and powerless.

Now I perceive a huge universe of same-sex eroticism between men and between women, and a growing and diverse openly queer culture, in the arts and media, in the public sphere, in academia, in my own personal networks, especially in the metropolitan areas. I've been reading Arvind Narrain's and Gautam Bhan's superb anthology *Because I Have a Voice: Queer Politics in India*, and I'm amazed by the richness and diversity of the experiences and debates represented in the almost thirty selections. At our 2007 India–Canada queer culture conference in Pune, I was bedazzled by the brilliance and power of the leaders of queer India which we had assembled.

Of course, the political Right might seem to be better organised and more visible now as a political movement than earlier. But don't forget the Emergency that happened in the mid-1970s, a very traumatic period of retrenchment. Was the effective 'consent' to dictatorship at that time not a kind of Right wing resignation? I can't forget, also, how the culture I first immersed myself in, around the rural Punjab public school with its military aura was also profoundly conservative almost by definition. In some way it might be better to have the haters come out of the woodwork as they did in the 1990s rather than have them quietly profiting from the silences.

Editors: What is your take on the following: most Indian men want to have their cake and eat it too, that is, be secretly gay and also wanting to be a part of the heteronormative families, as a result of which they marry women?

Waugh: It's not my place to criticise individuals and the choices they make in the absence of options based on economic, cultural and social power. With regard to being judgemental about hypocritical closet cases, I'm of two minds: of course, I'm outraged at the rich, powerful and cowardly, for example, Bollywood directors known to be gay, who will not publicly put themselves on the line. Nevertheless, so many of my Indian friends, partners and lovers over the last thirty-eight years have not identified themselves as gay and have valued their familial environments, and my great affection and respect for them will not allow me to judge them. Of course, queer identity is not incompatible with familial networks, and that is something we are rediscovering in the West, I would say. Finally, part of me tends to be self-righteous about people who lie to their spouses or even worse, endanger them through infection with STDs, but on the other hand who among us can throw the first stone?

Editors: Has AIDS hijacked the gay movement in developing countries like India and South Africa?

Waugh: No. At least not to my knowledge. From the little I know about such countries, the two movements energise each other. And having two intersecting movements around related issues builds strength through alliances and basic power in numbers. With regard to the West, I have just finished reading Ann Cvetkovich's *An Archive of Feelings: Trauma, Sexuality, and Lesbian Public Cultures*, and I'm struck by her account of AIDS activism in New York in the late 1980s and the momentum it gathered through the unusual alliances it formed, for example, between politicised lesbians and hitherto unpoliticised HIV+ gay men, most of whom would never have ended up in the gay movement were it not for their infection. Who is the most famous gay person in South Africa?—Zackie Achmat, the HIV+ ex-sexworker AIDS activist who through his Treatment Access Campaign has probably contributed as much to the gay movement in the narrow sense as anyone else. How did South Africa end up with equal rights for queers in its constitution?— through the example of gay anti-Apartheid activists like Simon Ngode, who never even dreamt that racial politics was hijacking the freedom cause for sexual minorities. AIDS reminds us how important coalition politics is. In India, I gather, this was one of the lessons of the *Fire* [a movie written and directed by Deepa Mehta] eruption; the importance of alliances between the women's movement and queer politics. Let a hundred flowers bloom.

Editors: Mention some of the gay men and women in India who come across to you as exemplary.

Waugh: Other than my thirty-eight years worth of Indian friends, partners, lovers and tricks, and the two editors of this volume, R. Raj Rao and Dibya Sarma, and other writers and artists, from Mahesh Dattani and Hoshang Merchant to Shohini Ghosh who have really gustily fulfilled their vocation as the legislators of humankind? I have great admiration for historians Saleem Kidwai and Ruth Vanita, and for the scrappy pioneer Ashok Row Kavi, who served for so long as the most visible and most accessible whipping boy and media spokesperson in India. Finally, when it comes to everyday courage, vision and persistence that have had important local effects, I would point to folks like Pawan Dhall in Kolkata and Manohar in Bangalore, both of whom insist on linking queer politics to the cause of all oppressed people.

Editors: Is the Indian government shortsighted to continue with the anti-sodomy law?

Waugh: Not only shortsighted, but hypocritical and in violation of both the Indian constitution and the International Charter of Human Rights, of which it is a signatory.

Editors: From the point of view of your work in film studies, what is your response to the emerging queer cinema in India?

Waugh: I'm very excited by the emerging pockets of lust, subversion and social vision that I have encountered, too numerous to mention in this space. With mini digital video, the momentum is increasing and distributors like 'Under Construction' (Magic Lantern Foundation) have a whole suitcase full of short documentaries and fiction that form the groundswell. Let me just mention the pioneering work of the late Riyad Wadia, whose *Bomgay* was really ahead of its time in 1996, for all its quirks (fried eggs on Rahul Bose's nude belly in the Bombay Fort Library). And, also, the important intersection between Indian queer cinema and diasporic queer cinema, evident in such works as *Bombay Boys*, and breakthroughs in regional cinemas, such as the Marathi short fiction *The Bath* by Sachin Kundalkar, a haunting and ambiguous story about a young Pune hustler and his John, who is more into care-giving than sexual exploitation.

Editors: Can queerness ever reach the levels of acceptance in India that it enjoys in Canada? Should that be our aim?

Waugh: I would say no! That should not be our aim. Indian activists, artists and community leaders should determine your utopias, and Indian cultures, economies, and democratic secular institutions and public spheres will determine the speed, shape and dimensions of your trajectory towards whatever those utopias must be. Globalisation notwithstanding, I don't think India should follow the West. In the West, the paradigm shift of the 60s and 70s did not happen on its own through spontaneous combustion. Rather, there was a convergence of factors, from the women's movement and the youth counterculture to the generalised shift in the role and makeup of the family, economically determined, not to mention the encroachment of the ever-proliferating marketplace into previously uncolonised areas of private life and desire. The Indian family remains such an economically important institution, although I'm not familiar with what social scientists are saying about possible fault zones therein. Whether or not India will produce a convergence of effects similar or analogous to what shaped the LGBTQ revolution in the West is an open question.

Editors: Will you write a book one day exclusively on queer India cinema?

Waugh: As soon as I make more progress on my Hindi, I think it might be fun to write a collection of essays on angles of queerness in Indian cinema: both Bollywood and the regional cinemas, documentary and fiction and experimental forms, diasporic and *desi* (local), covert and overt. The subject of queer/India/cinema is too sprawling and contradictory to be a single comprehensive and linear monograph.

Editors: The queer South Asian diaspora in Canada—an identity crisis, race and sexual orientation in conflict with each other?

Waugh: I can only judge on the basis of the many films and videos by queer LGBTQ South Asians in Canada, by artists like Atif Siddiqi, Nila Gupta, Kevin D'Souza, Safiya Randera, Ian Rashid and Michelle Mohabeer, all the while wanting to avoid too many generalisations. Obviously, these artists are working through some of the individual and collective dimensions of belonging to multiple minority identities. But I would say notions like 'crisis' and 'conflict' are too reductive in the face of the very complex sensibilities expressed in their work. Of these artists, I would say Michelle, whose ancestors were indentured labourers in Guyana, is the most programmatic in dissecting the dynamics of racism in Western society. Her work often explores common ground among lesbians belonging to various visible minorities.

9

narendrabinner

Editors: Please introduce yourself to us.

Narendra Binner: I'm Narendra Binner. Kindly make sure you use a false name and not my real name in your book. The name you give me shouldn't bear any resemblance to my own name—it should be as different from it as possible. This is necessary, considering that I'm HIV positive and few people know of my HIV positive status. There's nothing extraordinary about me. I'm about 40 years old; I was born and partly brought up in rural Maharashtra, but later moved to the city with my parents, brothers and sisters. Early in life, I lost my parents and that too tragically. This thrust many responsibilities on my head, although I'm not the oldest sibling; there are two brothers and two sisters who are elder to me. For one thing, it meant discontinuing my studies after the tenth standard and taking up a job to look after myself and my two brothers younger to me.

But it also meant having to get married at a very young age. I'm embarrassed to say that I got married at the age of twenty-two to a distant relative of the family who was of the same age. If I had my way, if I had so much education as to be able to think for myself and not be governed by society's rules, maybe I would never have got married at all. That is because, although you can call me bisexual, I'm much more sexually attracted to men than to women. But as you know, in middle-class Indian society, marriage is compulsory, more so for people like me without parents. Wives are needed to cook food, keep the house, etc. There isn't much romance in the marriage. That's one of the main reasons I married early. But, as I said, the loss of my parents also prevented me from completing my higher secondary (twelfth standard). This has severely affected my job prospects. Although I'm in a government job, I'm in class four cadre, and cannot make it to class three because I haven't passed my twelfth. So I have an ill-paying job and find it difficult to make ends meet. Of course, my family is small—I have just two kids—a son and a daughter—and they are very understanding and accommodating. That, then, is all there is to my biography.

Editors: When were you diagnosed as being HIV positive?

Binner: About five years ago, in September 2003 to be precise. It was a traumatic moment for all of us when the blood reports arrived. My wife was hysterical, and her relatives had to be summoned from another town to calm her down. Both she and I were also counselled by a doctor couple who run a clinic. I myself thought it was the end of my life and I was just thirty-five years of age then. But five years have passed and I'm still alive. All by the grace of god.

Editors: Do you have any idea as to how you were infected—who is the culprit?

Binner: My wife frequently asks me this question. But I can't tell her anything because I have been leading my gay life in secret and she doesn't have a clue about it. To you, of course, I can speak frankly. And the truth is, I don't know how I contracted the virus. In those years (early 2000s), I was quite promiscuous as a gay man, and had unprotected anal receptive sex often. I discovered a group of army men in a cruising area who came to look for men every night, and I was hooked. They looked so sexy in their uniforms and with their soldier haircuts and muscular bodies that I was swept off my feet. I made friends with some of them and visited them in their quarters regularly. We had unprotected sex, and I played both the active and passive roles. Some of these men were married but were away from their wives on postings, so they desperately sought out other men like me. They too were turned on by me and said many nice things about my sex appeal. What none of them told me was that he was HIV positive. Maybe they did not know it themselves or if they did, they deliberately kept the fact hidden from me. People don't go around telling those they want to have sex with that they have HIV or AIDS, for it will obviously drive their partners away. Moreover, even if they had told me, I might still have not been put off, because I had a pressing need for same sex activity and in my view there was no one hotter than those military guys. I would give anything to sleep with them. Of course, I knew about the risk of HIV, but I am an optimist and think of diseases and such like as things that happen to other people, not to oneself. Why did I not use a condom? Oh, condoms reduce the thrill of sex. As I once read in a magazine, using a condom was like having a chocolate with the wrapper on!

Editors: How did you first get to know that you were HIV positive?

Binner: I wouldn't have known I was carrying the virus within my body, had it not been for a bad attack of herpes that I had in September 2003. This, as you may know, causes a belt of highly painful blisters to form all around the waist. The blisters were so painful, I had to crawl like an animal on all fours to go to the bathroom and so on. I was in agony, groaning and moaning all the time. I thought it was the end of my life. The lay public refers to this disease as *nagin* (snake venom) and believes it is a curse for one's evil ways that can only result in the death of the victim. I was aware of this superstitious belief and it scared me all the more. Finally, when I could bear the torture no more, my family got me admitted to a private hospital close to my house. There was no question of my riding my own motorcycle to get to the hospital, so a kind neighbour took me there on his motorbike. As soon as I was admitted, the treatment began and within a day, the pain subsided. There's nothing to beat modern, allopathic medicine in its effectiveness. Soon I was feeling much better, what with all the powerful and expensive drugs administered to me, and I thought I was ready to be discharged from the hospital. But the doctors in the hospital dropped a bombshell at that moment. They said I would require an HIV test. This is because herpes—I didn't know it then—is one of the opportunistic infections connected to HIV, like TB or pneumonia. I underwent the test and the results came back positive. I was shattered. As I said, my wife grew hysterical on hearing the news, because she thought it was the end of our lives together. Luckily, her relatives were around to console and comfort her. Just to be sure, I got the same test done at another private clinic, and this confirmed that I was indeed positive. I had a tough time hiding the news from my office colleagues who came to see me in the hospital, together with my boss. If they got to know I was HIV positive, it could cost me my job, my only source of livelihood! To this day, the people in my office do not know that I'm infected. But here I'd like to say a word about the highly discriminatory and insensitive ways of doctors and especially nurses in private hospitals when it comes to handling patients with HIV. In my case, they emptied the entire ward as soon as my reports arrived in order to isolate me. As if the other patients in the ward would get HIV just by being in the same room as me! When my wife questioned them, the head matron, a Keralite, told her that my life was now over [since I was infected], but they had to think of the welfare and well being of other patients. It was almost as if she was saying that my disease was a punishment I had got for my evil ways, so there was no need for the hospital to be kind and considerate. Because AIDS is a sex-related disease, there is a great stigma attached to it. This can be devastating for patients, who are made to feel exactly as leprosy patients felt in the past. Hospital staff themselves need to be counselled before they are assigned to AIDS patients. In the other private clinic that I went to, the atmosphere was much better, with the doctor couple who run the clinic speaking to my wife and me in the most gentle possible manner, counselling us and not making us feel like we were the biggest sinners in the world.

Editors: What measures did you take on being declared positive?

Binner: It took me a while to come to terms with the fact that I was infected. You may say that for a long time I was in denial. I refused to accept that I was ill. Outwardly, my health bore me out. I did not look or feel like a sick person. But AIDS is such a thing that you can't escape from discussions on it on TV, in the newspapers, etc. It is this that gradually made me realise that I was carrying the dreaded virus in my body, and had to take precautions if I wanted to live. So I concentrated on my diet, making it a point to eat healthy food to the extent that I could afford, and exercise regularly. I closely followed all the health tips given to HIV and AIDS patients in a supplement called 'Family Doctor', issued with the Marathi newspaper, *Sakal*, which I read. I started drinking only boiled water. I quit smoking and drinking alcohol, and so on. All this seems to have paid off because, as I said earlier, it's five years now since I was diagnosed and, *inshallah* (god willing), my CD4 count (red blood corpuscle count in the human body) is still above the danger mark. That's one thing I did not want to do as often as my doctor recommended it—get a CD4 test. I take it about once a year or once in one-and-a-half years, but the doctor feels I should get it done every six months. This is a bother, not only because of the expense, or the fact that the clinic is far away from my place, but also because I'm scared of the results. Yes, I'm aware that a CD4 test can now be done free at government-run health centres. I'm also aware of organisations like National AIDS Control Organisation (NACO). But I prefer going to the private clinic because it's hassle free and I don't have to wait for long to have the test done. Also, the rates for the blood test have come down even in private clinics. There is a sort of rapport that has developed between my doctor and me, which I find reassuring and comforting.

Editors: Did being HIV positive mean changing your gay lifestyle in any way?

Binner: I had grown fairly promiscuous at the time I was infected. The promiscuity has no doubt come down. But it's not as if I've put my gay lifestyle behind me. Sex is a basic need that has to be fulfilled even if it is contrary to reason. I have a steady partner whom I see off and on. He's young and unmarried, and I haven't told him about my positive status. This is wrong, I know, but then I'm scared of losing him if I tell him. In any case, we don't usually have penetrative sex, and even if we do, I make sure I wear a condom. Is the guy himself positive? I don't think so, though he hasn't got himself tested yet. With this guy, it's more of an emotional thing than physical sex. After I was infected, I needed a sense of feeling wanted, because though my family continues to be supportive, it's still not the same as before. I'm a human being and like all human beings I need love. I can't cope with rejection. I feel much better when I'm with this friend of mine than when I'm with my family. That's why I never stay at home on Sundays and holidays. Under the pretext of overtime at the office, I snatch time that I spend with my sweetheart. We sit in a park, or, when I've just received my salary, maybe even in a beer bar. Sometimes, we go to his house if his folks are out, and on occasion I've brought him to my place as well, when my wife goes to her parents' house with the children.

Editors: So what is the exact state of your health today?

Binner: I've already told you. My CD4 count is still high enough. The time for me to start Antiretroviral Therapy (ART) hasn't come as yet. I feel quite strong and fit and go about my day-to-day activities like any normal person, exactly the way it was before I was diagnosed. Apart from that initial attack of herpes, I've had no serious opportunistic infections either. Just an occasional fever or a bout of diarrhoea that I get treated with the usual medicines, and then I'm fine again. My doctor says I'm a 'slow progressor'. That is to say, the virus isn't multiplying in my blood at an alarming rate. May it always be just like that.

Editors: It's been nearly five years since you were diagnosed. How come your neighbours, your colleagues at the office, your employers, etc., do not have any clue that you are HIV positive? How have you managed to keep it such a well-guarded secret from them?

Binner: No one knows. They did not know when I was first diagnosed in 2003, and they do not know today. Why should they? One does not go about broadcasting these things, especially when the illness is AIDS. In any case, my family and I are reticent by nature and not given to loose talk. But the main reason, I guess, why no one knows or suspects is because my health is fine and, touch wood, I never have taken seriously ill after being diagnosed. Even my relatives, though they know, behave with me as if I'm just fine, and the topic never comes up when we meet during social occasions like *poojas* (religious ceremonies) and weddings. They also continue to visit us at home, as before. This is a progressive way of dealing with the disease. All those stories one hears in the media of AIDS patients being thrown out of their homes and persecuted by society seem highly—or at least somewhat—exaggerated to me. I don't think, breathe and live AIDS every singly moment of my life.

Editors: What about your children? Do they know about it? Do their friends, their friends' parents and the school authorities suspect anything? These things can be very tricky, as reports that we receive from time to time from different parts of India show.

Binner: My kids are still small. They have not reached adolescence yet. My wife and I haven't told them about my disease, and at this stage they don't know. Maybe we'll tell them when they're older. Since they don't have any inkling about me being HIV positive, there is no question of theirs friends or friends' parents or school authorities knowing. Their friends continue to visit our home and eat with us. I think it's fairly easy to be tight-lipped about anything that one wants to keep secret and prevent the world from getting to know. So I fail to see what all the fuss that you refer to is about. I guess it's the patients themselves who are responsible for it, because many people find it difficult to keep secrets and have a tendency to talk, and tell the person to whom they talk not to tell anyone else, and so on, but this is never strictly practised, and this is how news spreads. Of course, as I said, in my case, the main thing is that there are no visible signs of illness. If there were, it would be different, because then I would have to explain away the illness to all and sundry. But because I've never been seriously ill after being diagnosed, it's easy for me to keep rumours at bay, and I hope and pray that it always stays that way. For all practical purposes, I'm a normal healthy middle-aged male in the eyes of the world. They do not see anything amiss.

Editors: Has your wife undergone an HIV test? What is the status of her health today?

Binner: I must confess that my wife hasn't had an HIV test. I know this is foolish and contrary to all reason, but in a way she's more in denial than I am, and is plain scared to get the test done. She's not a college-educated woman, and though she reads up on health issues in the newspapers, and is aware of the dangers of HIV and AIDS, she's unwilling to go for a check-up. I too do not insist that she should get the test done. It's been five years now since I was diagnosed, and she's never taken ill in all these five years, no opportunistic illnesses connected to HIV or any such thing. So I guess she must be okay. Since the birth of our children, our sexual activity reduced considerably, as a result of which my hunch tells me that she's not infected. I was increasingly drawn to men during those years and it suited me fine that my wife and I were not leading an active sexual life. As it turns out, this was a blessing in disguise.

Editors: What sort of relationship have you had with your wife since you were diagnosed?

Binner: My wife was so angry and upset after I was diagnosed that she made it very clear to me that she did not wish to have 'wifely' relations with me ever again in her life, and that's how it has more or less been since then. We live together with our kids as two friends might, or even a brother and a sister may! This of course sounds strange, but that's how it is. I'm not perturbed by the arrangement, and on the contrary, I find it convenient, because I'm relieved of the duty to perform, which is the 'husbandly' duty of all married men. HIV is the pretext that saves me from having to sleep with my wife, in whom, naturally, I'm not sexually interested because I'm much more of a homosexual than a heterosexual person. Of course, as stated before, my wife doesn't know this. She has no clue about my homosexual life. When I was first infected, she found it hard to imagine how it happened because she knows me to be a faithful husband. But she, like most women, was thinking of faithfulness in terms of extramarital affairs with other women and those, of course, I've never had. It was beyond her imagination and her awareness to figure out that I contracted the virus by sleeping around, not with other women, but with men. I'm not sure she knows this even now, because we've never openly discussed it at home and it has never come up in our conversations. We live our lives as two adults tied down to each other with neither of us having the option to alter the status quo. Divorce is not an option in the section of middle-class society to which we belong, and neither of us wants to jeopardise the lives of our children.

Editors: There are AIDS support groups for gay men in the country today. Are you aware of them? Do you think they make a difference in the lives of HIV and AIDS patients?

Binner: No, I'm not aware of these groups. I know of organisations like the Humsafar Trust in Bombay, run by Mr Ashok Row Kavi, and I also know that a lot of their work now is related to AIDS. But I'm not aware of any support groups specifically for HIV and AIDS patients only. Please tell me about them. I'm sure they would make a difference in the lives of unfortunate people stricken by the disease, especially those who are discriminated against by their families and by society. Having AIDS doesn't mean that we cease to be human beings with sexual impulses. But we are often made to feel that being diagnosed amounts to the termination of our sexual lives. Perhaps groups like the ones you refer to are a boon then, in our lives. AIDS patients can at least continue to have sex with each other, can't they? More than that, they may begin to care for each other to a degree that the outside world, including one's immediate family, is incapable of. Hats off to the NGOs or whoever who have started these groups.

Editors: Then there's the contrary view that AIDS is really an invention of powerful drug cartels that want to foist their medicines on the world. What would you say to that?

Binner: I don't know. I'm not university educated and I don't have independent opinions on these matters. People, all over the world, have been dying of AIDS for the last twenty-five years and more, and so the disease, and virus that causes it, cannot be imaginary, it must be real. Having said that, I'd like to point out two things. First, AIDS is a strange disease because it has no symptoms of its own. People don't die of AIDS per se, they die of diseases like TB or pneumonia or even a simple thing like diarrhoea, which doctors call 'opportunistic' infections and connect them to AIDS. But how can we be so sure that they actually have a connection? I mean, AIDS is nothing but low immunity, the immunity system breaking down, but there are people without HIV, and without low immunity, who also contract diseases like TB, pneumonia and diarrhoea. Are we sure then, that it's the HIV virus that is responsible? Which brings me to my second point, concerning myself. I tested positive in September 2003, and got my CD4 done a second time a few months later to confirm the diagnosis. But now it has been five years since that time, and I'm fine, without medication. How come my CD4 has stayed constant all these years, so that the time for me to start my ART hasn't arrived? If there is the HIV virus in my body, and if it's multiplying, there should be a drop in my CD4, isn't it? These are questions that sometimes bother me, and make me wonder whether the whole thing may not be a hoax, a cruel joke being played on me, and if, in the last analysis, I'm not sick, but a normal, healthy person.

Editors: What steps do you take, diet-wise and exercise-wise, to ensure that your CD4 count stays high enough to delay commencement of ART?

Binner: Exercise-wise, I don't do much. I keep talking of going to the gym, but it never actually happens. Nor am I into things like yoga, which is excellent for a healthy life. Why, I don't even take regular walks because I'm addicted to my motorbike and take it with me wherever I have to go. Of course, I live in a neighbourhood far from the main road, surrounded by farmland, where the air is fresh and pure and unpolluted. This I guess plays its own role. Those who live in polluted localities easily catch throat and lung infections and so on. As for diet, I eat a lot of fresh vegetables, dry fruits—to the extent that I can afford them—and fruits like bananas. I make sure I have my meals on time. Our diet at home is mostly vegetarian, with *chappattis*, vegetables, *dal* and rice comprising the meal. Once a week or so, we might have chicken or fish. I do make it a point to eat an egg too, once every two days, and I frequently drink a glass of milk, or eat a bowl of curd. So this then is how my diet looks. My doctor tells me that once ART starts, I'll have to be even more careful about my diet.

Editors: Once you begin with ART, how do you plan to meet the expenses?

Binner: I don't know. I haven't thought of it yet, and will cross that bridge when I come to it. ART can be had for free at places like NACO, but I'm not sure of the modalities; we receive conflicting reports in the newspapers. I mean, are the drugs eternally in short supply, so that one has to wait in a queue every month for one's quota of medicines? Furthermore, is the therapy given for free only to those whole annual income falls below a certain level? These are questions I have not looked into seriously, because they don't concern me yet. But I guess someday I'll have to confront them head on. Of course, I'm sure to qualify for free ART even if it's linked to one's annual income, because my salary isn't very high at all. But I don't know if I want to be seen with all those poor and sick people every month, waiting in a pathetic queue for their quota of medicine. I'd rather go to a private clinic and pay for the treatment, provided it is within my budget, because that certainly is more dignified. I'm also not sure whether ART has any side effects. Some people say that the strong drugs that are administered do not go down well with all, and patients have been known to die from the side effects, especially poor patients who cannot afford the healthy diet that is daily needed to complement the ART. I don't know. These are scary questions, which worry me and give me tension if I start thinking about them. It's much better to lead one's life on a day-to-day basis and not think of the future. I'm a reasonably happy man today, but I'm not sure how long this will last. ART is the thing I dread most, and I hope that the day never comes at all when I have to start my treatment. My wife has a small job and she has been saving up some money, but it breaks my heart to think that we will have to use her meagre savings just to foot my medicine bills. I'll have to look for extra part-time work to make the ends meet, once I begin with ART.

Editors: Do slight setbacks in your health cause you to panic, or are you not the worrying kind?

Binner: No, I am not the worrying kind. As I said earlier, I am optimistic by nature. I do get sick once in a while with a fever or diarrhoea, but I do not tend to connect this with HIV. I tell myself that these are normal viral infections that all people get regardless of whether they're HIV positive or negative. And I go to a local doctor and get myself treated without revealing anything about my HIV positive status. Luckily for me, I've been having even these illnesses only occasionally, and ordinary medication promptly cures me. All this may change in the future when my CD4 count drops to a level when I have to begin with ART, and my immunity becomes low, exposing me to all kinds of infections. But right now, by the grace of god, my immunity is quite all right.

Editors: Does death scare you?

Binner: Actually, no. I don't think of death much, and I have the will to live. At the same time, I'm ready to die any time, even today, if death comes knocking at my door. I'm not worried about my wife and children, because I know that in the event of my death, my wife's parents, her brothers and their families, will step in and look after them. They're a very close-knit family, because of whom, I'm sure I'll be able to die in peace.

Editors: But have you planned for your family in case, god forbid, you succumb to the disease?

Binner: Not much. My income isn't large enough for me to have savings, insurance policies or investments at this point, when I'm just about to turn forty. Most of my money goes in running the home. Leading a reasonably comfortable life has always been my priority, as a result of which I own my small flat and my motorbike, and have everything at home like a colour TV, a fridge, DVD player, a PC, etc. My family at least has a roof over its head for I finished clearing my housing loan a couple of years ago, and now the flat is in my name. Real estate prices being ever on the rise, the flat will fetch much more now, than when we bought it. So in case of dire emergency, maybe my wife can sell the flat and move in with her parents, taking the children along with her. Or may be she'll manage to get more part-time work that'll enable her to continue to stay in the flat and keep body and soul together. The most important thing is that I'm in a pensionable government job, so my contributory provident fund and pension will come to the aid of my family in the event of my passing away.

Editors: AIDS today is not seen as the fatal disease it was about twenty-five years ago. There are positive people all over the world who have been living with the virus for life. Does this instil hope in you?

Binner: Yes, indeed. For me, it's other people who die of AIDS—not me. The fact that my CD4 count has stayed above the danger mark all these years has made me confident, even if initially I was overcome by despair when I was first diagnosed. I'm sure that even when I start my ART, I'll be fine, and will be able to live to more or less the same age that I would have, even if I were HIV negative. I've heard and met people from Western countries who say that HIV now is perceived as any other non-terminal and non-fatal disease, say, like diabetes, that one can continue to live with, provided one strictly follows the doctor's orders, takes ones medicines on time and takes all the required precautions. I believe that that's slowly what's happening in India as well, though we still have a long way to go. I also fervently hope and pray that with all the research going on worldwide, the day is not far off when a permanent cure for AIDS will be found, that will bring hope and joy to all the unfortunate patients and their families, affected by the disease.

10

armanpasha

Editors: Tell us about yourself by way of introduction.

Arman Pasha: I come from a middle-class family in Bangalore where all my family members are highly qualified professionals in their respective fields. I too am highly qualified. My hobbies include listening to soft Hindi film music and net browsing—where I keep chatting with guys from all over the world and try to know about places and people over there. The qualities I look for in a friend are that he should be frank, friendly, understanding and jovial. I always smile, whatever problems I may have. I try to understand my friends' problems too, and keep advising them. I enjoy advising friends and trying to get solutions to their problems.

Editors: When did you realise you were gay?

Pasha: My first encounter with gay sex happened with a guy called Suraj. He was a childhood friend. We used to go to school together and return home together. It was a routine from our days in primary school. That year I had appeared for my graduation exam. It was a difficult time. The college days were over. All my college friends were busy with their lives. As it happened, I also broke from my girlfriend. It was because our friends began to spread rumours about me, and my girlfriend could not take it. I was really lonely and miserable.

One day, Suraj appeared with a video cassette. It was a porno movie and he wanted to watch it with me. He maintained that it was a real hot movie and I had never seen anything like that. I was alone in my house and was easily persuaded. The movie was really good. It was summer. I was wearing only a Bermuda and a T-shirt. In summer I never wore underwear when at home. As you know, Bangalore can be really hot in summer.

After some time, I noticed that Suraj was staring at my crotch rather than concentrating on the TV screen. On the screen, the girl was giving a blowjob to a guy with a big black cock. I was aroused. Suraj could clearly see my erection protruding through my Bermuda. We were sitting on the carpet. Suddenly, Suraj moved towards me and grabbed my cock. I was too shocked to ask him what he was doing. He soon stripped me of the Bermuda and began to masturbate me. I did not know what to say or what to do. Then Suraj began fellating me. I was embarrassed. At the same time, I was enjoying the damn thing. I ejaculated very quickly. I was groaning, but he was deeply engrossed in what he was doing. I was feeling shy and embarrassed. Soon Suraj abruptly left. I couldn't watch the rest of the movie.

When Suraj returned the next day, I could not face him. He left without meeting me. For many days afterwards, I remained uneasy. I used to dream about the incident every time I closed my eyes. I could not concentrate on anything. The following week, Suraj tried very hard to meet me. But every time I would devise ways to avoid him. I was troubled emotionally. I thought whatever we did was unnatural and sinful. Though my family is modern, religion played an important part in our lives. I thought my family would never approve of this kind of behaviour. I was experiencing a strong sense of guilt.

One day, my mother asked me to wait for the electricity–meter-reading man who was to come home to read the meter. Someone knocked on the door and I thought it was him. I opened the door and saw Suraj standing there. This time I could not run away from him. He entered and began to apologise for his behaviour. He said that he was sorry for what had happened. He was even ready to fall on my feet. He had charm and I liked his company. I said OK, and told him to be careful next time. He promised that he would never do this kind of thing again.

We were in my room chatting. I was feeling sleepy. I told Suraj that I would like to sleep now. He said that he would also like to take a nap. It was very common for Suraj to crash in my room. We were lying together and chatting. Soon I realised that Suraj was trying to reach my crotch. He had a way of seducing people. He was what Michael Jackson sang about a smooth criminal. I had to cooperate with him.

Then it became a daily routine. In the beginning, we used to do it every day, later every alternate day. It continued for six months. Then I completed my graduation and Suraj began to drift away, mingling with low-class people, fagging, boozing and stealing. I saw him stealing myself. But I was afraid of him; what if he went and told my folks about what I was doing in bed with him.

One day, he came to my room quite drunk and ordered me to remove my clothes. I was very upset with his behaviour. I scolded him severely and asked him to leave my house at once. He left meekly and never returned. That was the last time I saw him. It was the time when internet chatting flourished. I was hooked to the internet; I went to cyber cafés regularly and made a lot of friends.

It was after meeting Suraj, however, that I became aware of my gay side. After the first encounter, I was confused. But with the second encounter with Suraj, I came to realise that I was attracted to guys too.

Editors: You mentioned that you were in love with a girl before the Suraj incident happened. Do you remember having any feelings for men before Suraj?

Pasha: Before Suraj happened, I was aware of the existence of a gay life. But I never thought I was a part of it. I knew these five students, who were from Bangalore, studying there and living together in a flat. I was very close to them, since they were good friends and never did anything wrong. But a friend of mine who also knew these guys used to tell me that their intent was not good. Indeed, after some time two of these guys confessed to me that they were gays. I did not have any problem with them being gay. They were good friends.

Editors: After Suraj, what? Did you find any other man, or another girlfriend?

Pasha: After Suraj, I was hooked to browsing on the internet and kept meeting friends. I met this guy who was from Delhi. Just by chatting on the internet, I fell in love with him. But it did not work out. He confessed to me that there were a total of three guys who were in love with him. One was from Mumbai, another from Nagpur and the third one was me. I asked him to stop three timing and choose any one among us. Then he stopped chatting with me. Even when he was online, he would refuse to respond to my messages. I got the message.

Editors: What do you identify yourself as?

Pasha: I think I am bisexual. Before knowing that I was attracted to men, I had sex with five or six women. I am comfortable having sex with women.

Editors: What do you look for in a male partner?

Pasha: To be frank, I never go by the face value of a man. For me, the guy should be good-natured, friendly and understanding. I usually prefer a bottom/passive kind of guy.

Editors: Are you thinking of getting married? If yes, do you think you will continue with your homosexual activities after marriage or will they stop? Do you think your wife might find out about you?

Pasha: As a member of Indian society, I can't think of living alone. Therefore, I have to get married. I think after marriage too, my homosexual activities will continue, as I have many friends who are married and continue to be gay. I think I will join their gang.

Editors: Are you aware of the existence of gay support groups in India?

Pasha: When I realised I was gay, I had no support system. I wasn't aware of the existence of any gay support groups.

Editors: Now in some parts of the Western world, marriage between same-sex couples has been legalised. Do you see yourself living with a male partner as husband and husband?

Pasha: If I were in the US or anywhere else in the West, I may have thought of marrying a guy, but I don't think I can even dream about it in India.

Editors: Any recent encounter with a gay man that you would like to share with us?

Pasha: Let me tell you this incident. I got the address of this guy on the pen pal section of a newspaper. He had placed an ad for a male friend. I responded. Soon, we became friends. We talked to each other over the phone and got very close to each other. Yet, for me, the relationship was going nowhere as he did not know about my sexual orientation.

I decided to tell him about myself. I wrote a long letter and explained the fact that I am gay. After posting the mail I thought I have lost a friend. One week later, I received his mail. First he thanked me for trusting him and telling him about my sexuality. He wrote that my sexuality did not bother him in any way whatsoever and, he will be my friend for life. He wrote, 'I'll be your friend till my blood is red.' He said that he was not gay. However, he requested me not to stop mailing or calling him. Later, I met him too. He was a pharmacy guy who knew about being gay. Sometimes, he made fun of me for loving men, but I couldn't protest as he was a good friend of mine. He kept insisting that I should get married to a girl and settle down.

Editors: What is it like being gay in India?

Pasha: In the closet, nobody has a problem. It is the public display of homosexuality that makes people uncomfortable. People think that gays are 'cheapies', they are whores. That is why I hardly eye guys in public. I only respond if someone else initiates it. I would never stare at any one in public. The public is very orthodox.

This incident occurred recently. I went to meet a friend of mine and from there I travelled by bus. At one place I had to change the bus. I walked to the bus stop where I noticed a big crowd. At the centre of it, a bus conductor was hitting a young man of about twenty-eight to thirty. Someone in the crowd informed me that this guy was sleeping in the bus when the bus reached the last stop. There too, he wouldn't wake up till the conductor forced him to get down from the bus. Once awake, the guy was angry that he missed his destination and slapped the conductor. Now it was the conductor's turn to beat the guy up.

Soon, I came to hear another version of the story that the conductor was telling his friends. According to this version, this young man was found trying to molest another guy in the bus. Therefore, everyone was hitting him. The young man said nothing, but tried to cover his face with his palms. The conductor was suggesting that they should take the boy to their office and strip him.

It was 10.30 in the night. I was waiting for my bus. After fifteen minutes, the guy who was beaten up arrived at the bus stop. The conductor had finally left him alone. He stood there and soon began to eye another man who was sitting at the bus stop. Now, I knew which version of the story was true. It is a shame that gay men in India have to live in such conditions. We do not have any freedom like other civilised countries. We do not have any choice to live and lead our own lives the way we want.

Editors: What do you think is the major hurdle for gay men in India—the law, society or something else?

Pasha: I think the issue lies within you. If you are not comfortable about yourself, about who you are, nobody can help you. I know who I am and what I want and, therefore, I can handle the folks around me. Let me give an example.

Recently, I met this guy called Santosh in an internet chat room. He was from Mangalore. We exchanged our phone numbers, and talked on a few occasions. He told me that he was coming to Bangalore and wondered if he could see me at my house. I said why not. He came over to my place and we talked for a long time. He arrived around 9 p.m. and by the time we were through it was 10.45 p.m.

I went to drop him at the bus stop. The bus did not turn up till 11.15 p.m. I suggested that I should drop Santosh home on my bike. On the bike, he informed me that he was in love with a boy and he was very possessive about his lover. When I asked him who he was, Santosh informed me that he broke up with his lover. I was sad to hear that. I asked him how. Then he told me that he broke up with his lover because of me.

I was shocked to hear this. I had no idea what I was doing in their love story. I demanded an explanation. Santosh then told me that this lover of his had met me six months ago. I did not remember who he was. Anyway, he went and told Santosh that he had slept with me. Santosh was upset at this and they broke up. I was feeling 'fuck all'. Because of me, Santosh split with his lover and now, Santosh and I were best of buddies. But till now, Santosh would not tell me who his lover was, whom I knew long ago.

I still think about this event and wonder what went wrong. I have seen this on many occasions. Many relationships break only because they don't trust their partners or they are too possessive. I can only say that give a chance to the partner to say what he wants to say. Don't jump to conclusions. Don't give up a relationship too soon. Have faith in your partner. Till date, I wonder where I went wrong.

Editors: Have you ever been the victim of homophobia or gay bashing?

Pasha: To be frank, I have never fallen into any awkward situation. It may be because my friends' experiences taught me to be alert. I am alert. I also ask my friends to be alert.

Now, let me tell you about a friend of mine who had gone through a very bad time. His name is Francis. He works for a five-star hotel. He is a simple, friendly, understanding guy, who always keeps smiling even when he's in trouble. It happened two years ago.

There was another guy called Shiv, who worked along with Francis. They were close to each other, and Francis was terribly attracted to Shiv. But Shiv was straight and there was not much hope for Francis. But Francis could no longer bear to be without Shiv. So, one day he wrote a poem confessing his love and gave it to Shiv. Now, Shiv very un-poetically asked Francis what that poem meant, and poor Francis told him everything in detail; how he was helplessly in love with Shiv and so on. Shiv was not only straight, he also despised queens. He informed everyone that Francis was a pervert. He also began to abuse Francis in public. His other co-workers were cool about Francis and they did not give it much thought. But Shiv stopped talking to Francis. His hatred to Francis was apparent whenever they used to see each other in the course of their job.

Francis was very troubled by the entire affair. He could not afford to leave the job as he had three younger brothers to look after. It was at this point that I met him. He was always thinking of leaving the job, and was always facing Shiv's hostility. I offered him a shoulder to cry and told him that there was no point in feeling wretched. He should stand up to the issue. I believed in the 'give respect get respect' theory. I said as much to Francis. Soon, whenever Shiv tried to bully Francis, the latter would fight back and bitch about Shiv. Shiv was taken aback and gradually he stopped making fun of Francis.

Editors: So you are saying that being gay is a constant fight with your surroundings?

Pasha: No. What I am saying is identifying your priorities, identifying what you want and what you expect from others. Take hold of your life and don't let others dictate what you should do.

There is another friend of mine whose name is Bhaskar, who is a classical dancer. He performs in five-star hotels, in stage shows. He also runs a dancing school for children. He is very innocent and caring, but also very secretive.

He was in love with a guy called Chander for more than a year. I was his friend, but I hardly knew anything about his love life. Whenever he talked about Chander, he got very emotional, on the verge of tears. He told me that he was very happy having Chander as his partner. With him, he said, he forgot every other worry of life.

Bhaskar's mother was old and she lived in the village with his sister. She had a kidney ailment, and soon she was shifted to Bangalore for better treatment. This made Bhaskar very unhappy, for his house was now occupied by his mother and sister and he could not give much time to Chander. He was torn between two loyalties. Now, he spent more time outside with Chander. Gradually, Bhaskar's sister came to understand Bhaskar's attitude and decided to shift their mother back to the village. Bhaskar was happy with this decision. Once they were gone, Bhaskar got busy with his daily routine with Chander. He did not give his mother much thought. After two days news came that his mother was no more. Bhaskar was upset at this and he rushed back to the village to see his mother for one last time.

After completing the funeral, when Bhaskar returned back to Bangalore, things were not the same. Chander avoided meeting him. After a few days, he came to know that Chander was seeing someone else—a rich guy who could spend a lot of money on him, even though Bhaskar spent a lot on Chander. Chander had high expectations; he was like a chameleon that kept changing colours.

Bhaskar was devastated. It was at this time that I met him. He was crying and saying that it was because of Chander that he lost his mother. I told him that he should have taken care of his mother's health and then worried about Chander. But, now, what was the point in crying over spilt milk. It was foolish. I am sorry to say, the ending is not a happy one. After he lost his mother and his love, within a year, his siblings forced him to get married. Though he was averse to marriage, this time he did not want to make his family unhappy.

Now, he tells me that he is very happy with his wife, but I know for sure, he has neither forgotten Chander nor his gay instincts.

Editors: What's the gay scene in Bangalore like? Have you heard of the famous gay support group, Sangama?

Pasha: I can't really tell you what the Bangalore gay scene is like, because I do not party as such and I do not move among 'that' kind company. I have a set of straight friends who do not even know that I am gay. I work in the BPO sector where I cannot talk about my sexual orientation. That's not a problem because I have a group of gay friends who are constantly in touch and meet each other whenever possible. We support each other. We are all good friends.

Editors: But being gay is not about having sex, it's about a lifestyle...

Pasha: What do you expect me to be, a laughing stock? How I seek release is nobody's business but mine. Just as how I live my life is nobody's business but mine.

Editors: You are a Muslim. Does your religion hinder your being gay?

Pasha: You mean, the scriptures advocating punishment for homosexuals and its being a sin and all that? No. If it were a sin, god would not have made me the way I am. This is a simple justification and I strongly believe in it.

Editors: Would you like to say anything else by way of conclusion?

Pasha: At the end, I would like to say that you should not fall for a guy who does not bother about you. You should be with a guy who respects you, understands you and loves you. I have seen many guys in my friends' circle who keep begging others to accept them, even while they get no response. First see a person's heart, then his face and other things [sic]. Also don't trust a guy until you know him well, as I have seen many guys who see a street-smart guy and they will be ready to do anything for him and that guy would take advantage of that in many ways—physical, mental and financial. As I say, money is not everything in life, first see a person's heart and then other things.

11

aslamshaikh

Editors: Please introduce yourself to us.

Aslam Shaikh: I am Aslam Shaikh. I am about twenty-five years old. I am an auto-rickshaw driver. I live in a slum in Pune with my aged parents, wife and two small daughters. What more do you want me to say about myself? Yes, I'm a circumcised Muslim. I go to *namaz* (prayer) on Fridays and celebrate all the *Ids* (Eid). But other than that we are like any other Maharashtrians of the area. I speak Marathi quite fluently with my passengers, neighbours and other auto-rickshaw drivers. At home, however, we prefer Hindi. I prefer saying *Bismillah* (god's name uttered for good luck by the Muslims) rather than *Bhavani* (god's name uttered for good luck by the Hindus) on receiving my day's first earnings. Education? I've studied up to the eighth standard in a school run buy the civic corporation.

Editors: Is driving the only thing you do for a living?

Shaikh: Yes. All right, no. I need not hide anything from you since you are going to change my name in your book anyway. And none of my friends and relatives is going to read your book because it is in English. So there's no harm in letting you know that I worked for a fellow who was in the flesh trade. I helped him procure girls and find customers. In other words, I was a broker, a pimp, who traded in girls. Did I ever exploit any of the girls myself? No, never. It was a business, like any other, and I was serious about it. But I enjoyed my work because it was fun, and I love fun. This was before I started driving an auto-rickshaw for a living. I was probably not eighteen years of age yet and couldn't get a driver's license. Later, I started driving someone else's auto for a daily wage, but continued with this other job. A vehicle makes it so much easier. It gave me mobility. I still remember the registration number of that auto-rickshaw—606. It was my lucky number. Now I don't drive that auto any more. I've purchased my own auto with a bank loan. We've even rebuilt our shanty and rented out a part of the space below, first to a *canteenwallah* (one who runs a canteen), who made tea and *batata wadas* (potato balls) and even Chinese food in the evenings, and now to a hardware store.

Editors: How did you enter the flesh trade?

Shaikh: The man for whom I worked is actually my own maternal uncle. He came home one day and said to me, 'Aslam, you have dropped out of school and are sitting at home idle, so why don't you come and help me with my work.' He said this to me in front of my mother, who is his cousin sister. But, obviously, he didn't specify the nature of the work. This he told me later, no, not even in his house in front of his wife and kids, but he took me out to a beer bar and disclosed it to me over there. I was initially shocked, but soon took it in my stride. Shocked, not because of the kind of thing he wanted me to do, but because he was my own uncle, my own relative. But afterwards, I got over it. My uncle warned me not to mention what he had said to anyone at my home or his home. If I did, he threatened me with dire consequences. I was not mad to tell anyone. Once the work started, I was sometimes overcome with pangs of guilt, but such occasions were rare. I felt very good at the end of the day when I got my daily wage. The harder I worked, the greater was my remuneration. I was usually rewarded with a 100 rupee note everyday. How much does that come to in a month? Rs 3,000. See. Is that a small amount for an eighteen-year-old who's not even a tenth-pass? Even today, boys of eighteen don't earn that much. There's so much unemployment. Besides, the poor have limited options. They cannot always find respectable jobs like the well-to-do.

Editors: You traded in women, and here you are, giving us an interview for a book on alternative sexuality.

Shaikh: So what do you expect me to do—trade in men? Are you out of your mind? As if it happens that way? Women are commodities, not men. I don't know what you mean by male prostitution. You educated people are full of strange things in your head. Okay, so I have had sex with men, but that's different. That wasn't my job. I did it just for the heck of it. If women are not easily available, any man turns to other men. It's common, and there's nothing unusual about it. But we don't talk about it the way we talk about our encounters with women, or even boast about them. If we did, the person opposite will think we're mad and should get our heads checked.

Editors: How were you initiated into same-sex activity?

Shaikh: We were mere kids then, in our teens. We used to sleep outside in the open, in the parking lot of a near by building, as our shanties are small, especially in summer. That's how it started. In any case, no one suspects anything when young boys sleep together. Only if it's a boy and a girl, do they object. But you are making much of something that is of no importance.

Editors: What about your later experiences with men, when you were older?

Shaikh: I was not doing any of this out of choice. Basically, I don't like having sex with men. I'm a heterosexual. So if I was indulging in it all the same, there had to be an advantage for me. Those who are bigger than me, both in age as well as social position, pay me for sexual favours either in cash or kind. The minimum they give me is Rs 100. Some of them give me presents like *attar* bottles or cigarette lighters. Once I even got a pair of brand new jeans. However, when I go out with these men, I ensure that my manhood isn't challenged by insisting on the active role. You see, I am not a *hijra*.

Editors: What's the role that your main job—auto-rickshaw driving—plays in all this?

Shaikh: My job plays a big role. Unlike people who sit in one place, say, in offices or shops, I'm mobile. Constantly on the move. Naturally, I meet more people. Once a passenger hires my auto, it's just him and me. There's quite a lot of privacy [laughs]. Well, not the sort of privacy you have in a car, with all the tinted glasses rolled up, but private enough. The auto-rickshaw may be open on all sides, but no one can hear our talk, except maybe at traffic lights. So it becomes easy to transgress.

Editors: So, to put it picturesquely, what you are saying, in effect, is that it isn't just your vehicle that is for hire, but also you?

Shaikh: Yeah, in a way you could say that. But only passengers with mischief on their mind would see it that way. The majority of passengers wouldn't. Who are the people who usually hire an auto, instead of travelling by bus? Well-off people. Most of them, men and women, would think it beneath their dignity to befriend an auto-rickshaw driver. They think we're unclean, lowly. The words 'for hire' written on our meters apply strictly to our vehicles, not to us. Besides, I'm not a woman. That kind of connection comes naturally to men when there's a woman in-volved. But certainly not if it's a man. Perhaps, that is why there are no women auto-drivers or taxi-drivers in India, though I'm told they are there in foreign countries.

Editors: You know, in spite of all that you say, we think that the seeds of sex work were sown in your mind during the time you traded in girls. You're just in denial.

Shaikh: Every man secretly envies women for being able to cash in on their bodies, while we ourselves cannot. I am no exception to this rule. On the contrary, the envy may be greater in my case because, as you say, I was in the flesh trade. But are there red-light areas with male brothels which ladies can regularly visit, as men visit red-light areas looking for prosti-tutes? Obviously, no. I mean, I know of high-society married ladies who have adulterous sex when their husbands are away with college boys or young men from the working-class, and even pay them or give them gifts. But that is not the same as female prostitution, complete with red-light areas and brothels. Besides, the number of ladies looking for adulterous sex in India is very small because unlike men, women on the whole are decent, and are concerned about the honour of the family. It's a ques-tion of their self-respect, and they don't want to be caught and branded whores. They are concerned about what the neighbours say much more than we men. So where does that leave a man who wants to sell his body? He has to turn to homosexual men. But this is a compromise. It also challenges his masculinity because it temporarily makes him a woman. A man can't be with another man as a man. One of them has to think of himself as a woman. And it would usually be the guy who's being paid.

Editors: Do you pay attention to your dress, physique and general appear-ance?

Shaikh: Yes. I like to look smart. At least sometimes, if not all the time. I try to experiment with my hairstyle. At times, I grow my hair long; at other times, I shave it all off—have a *ganja* (bald) cut as it's called. I'm tall enough, but I like to wear leather boots that make me look even taller. However, when it comes to clothes, I'm severely constrained by my lack of money. Dressing good is an expensive business. I'm poor. I cannot afford all the fancy shirts, T-shirts, jeans and trousers that rich collegians wear. Though, Fashion Street is one place where you get inexpensive imitations of branded clothes and I visit it often. Fashion Street *zindabad* (long live Fashion Street). Still, you must realise that I'm the main earning member of my family. The Hindu auto-rickshaw drivers send their wives to work as maidservants and so on, in homes. But we Muslims do not. We're conservative. There are men folk in the households and our wives may not be safe. So, the upshot is that I have to make do with just a couple of shirts and pants. Once, a woman who hired my auto told me point blank: 'I don't like your appearance.' I felt bad, but took it in my stride. I wanted to tell her, 'Mind your own business madam', but kept quiet. Simply smiled.

Editors: How exactly do gay customers proposition an auto driver?

Shaikh: Oh, there are different methods they employ. Some might deliberately touch one on the back, shoulders or thighs and make it appear accidental—as if the movements of the vehicle made it happen. Others start by talking dirty, usually about women, but make their intentions known soon enough. Still others assume a great familiarity the moment they step into the vehicle—as if they've known you for years. As the ride progresses they begin to get fresh. Some come to the point straight away and ask if one is available. These are usually guys who have their own place. There, there would be no dangers of a police raid and so on.

Editors: So how do you stave off these advances?

Shaikh: I simply ignore them and convey through my body language that I'm not interested. Or I might stop my vehicle and ask the passenger in question to get off there and then. As I did once to a balding old man in his fifties, who wanted to know the reason. 'Am I not paying you the fare', he had the audacity to ask. But I told him I didn't want to ferry him, that's all. *Meri marzi* (my will). '*Naraz kyon hote ho* (why are you cross),' he asked as he got down, humiliated.

Editors: You mentioned police raids. Tell us about them.

Shaikh: It happens in the lodges. I know quite a lot about the lodge scene in my city. It goes back to the time I used to do this shady business with my maternal uncle. Lodges are visited by regulars who obviously are not doing this for the first time in their lives. They've done this before so they know where exactly to go. So do I, the auto-rickshaw driver. And so do the cops. There is no dearth of cheap lodges in any city that rent out rooms especially for the purpose. The lodge owners know what's going on, even if it's two men who have rented the room, but they keep quiet, because it's a question of their livelihood. If they didn't let out their rooms for this type of risky business, they would soon have to close down their establishments and return to their native places. The police cash in on their vulnerability and swoop down for their *hafta* (bribe). Things are usually sorted out at this level and rarely make it to the courts or the press.

Editors: You say you are married now. Do you regret being in the flesh trade earlier? Has marriage enabled you to view women differently?

Shaikh: The man who introduced me to this business is himself old now, and has stopped it. I was in it mainly because of him. Now that he has stopped, I have stopped too. Yes, I have begun to respect women more after marriage. I've reduced my same-sex activity too. I visited a doctor who told me it's bad for my married life. We want to have many children. We are Muslims, remember.

Editors: Does your wife have a clue as to what you do outside?

Shaikh: Are you out of your mind? Do men go and say such things to their wives. How should she suspect? What I do outside is my business, not hers. I'm a man, not a woman. It is my male privilege to do as I please. Moreover, she will never be able to find out anything about me, especially as my conduct with her at home is above board.

Editors: Are you scared of AIDS. Do you always use a condom?

Shaikh: Yes. I'm very scared of HIV and AIDS. At first, I didn't know much about these things because I was ignorant. But now I do. That's one of the reasons why I've become, sort of, monogamous. No sex outside marriage. I recently saw an AIDS sign painted on a wall somewhere. 'Save Your Life. Go to Bed only with Wife,' it said. Surprised? You think I don't follow English? I've studied up to high school, sir. I'm not illiterate. The doctor I referred to earlier, too warned me about AIDS, and explained everything about the disease to me. Condoms? I use them, but I don't like them.

Editors: You saw a doctor. Why?

Shaikh: Sometimes I am not able perform well. It's not like it used to be during the early months of our marriage. At such times, I feel frustrated. So I decided to go and see a doctor. He asked me a hundred questions about my sexual history and said he wouldn't be able to treat me unless I answered them honestly. So I had to reveal everything. This doctor gave me to understand that it was because of what I did in the past that I was suffering now. I don't know.

Editors: Have you vowed to give up outside sexual activity altogether?

Shaikh: I have already told you that it's a source of income for me. First, I had only one daughter, and now Allah has given me a second. I have to save for their dowry from now onwards. I don't know when I'll be blessed with a son. Auto-rickshaw driving is not a profitable occupation any more. Seen the queue of auto-rickshaws at any stand? We wait end-lessly, all day in the sun for passengers. It was not like that before. But now everyone has his or her own two-wheeler or four-wheeler. So, why should they take a three-wheeler [Laughs]? It's the banks that are at fault. They give loans to everyone to buy their own vehicle. But if a poor auto driver like me approaches them for a loan, they refuse. I do not have enough assets, they say. Sometimes, I seriously think of giving up auto driving. But then what else can I do for a living?

Editors: Are you very religious?

Shaikh: Not very religious, but I am religious enough. I do *namaz* on Fri-days. In Islam, all sex outside marriage is a sin. The Quran says that such people should be stoned to death. It's my helplessness that makes me stray. After I die, I'll have to answer several questions in the court of Allah. I hope he'll forgive me. What do you mean by saying that in Arab countries men keep boys? I have never heard of it. If that's the case, please help me get a passport and visa, so that I can emigrate [Laughs]! I am told there is a great demand for car drivers there. I know car driv-ing, though I don't have a licence yet. You have a friend, who recruits Muslims to send them to Dubai, isn't it? Please put in a word for me. It'll change my life.

Editors: Do you face discrimination from your neighbours or from other auto-rickshaw drivers, either because of your same-sex activity, or be-cause of your religion?

Shaikh: Because of my religion, yes. Not because of my same-sex activity. How should they know about it? I don't walk or talk like a woman. For all I know, the other auto drivers too are doing the same thing. I know of at least one Hindu auto driver in the neighbourhood who sells his body for money. I'm sure there must be many more. But religion, yes. I have had to change my auto-rickshaw stand several times because of the taunts and bad vibes. Like they say, half seriously, half as a joke, that you are circumcised. If they eat *wada pav* (potato patty in a bun) or drink tea while waiting in the queue for passengers, they don't share it with me because I'm a Mohammedan. Conversely, they don't accept anything to eat from me. Except, maybe, on *Id*. But we don't have too many people coming over to our house for *Id*, except our own relatives. Like I said earlier, I've tried my level best to assimilate. I speak fluent Marathi with passengers and with my auto driver colleagues. But the stigma of being a Mohammedan does not easily disappear. I wish I could leave my area and settle down in another part of the town, where there are many Muslim people.

12

anagarcia-arroyo

Editors: Please introduce yourself to us.

Ana Garcia-Arroyo: My name is Ana. Ana Garcia-Arroyo. Garcia-Arroyo is my surname. And I like it with a hyphen. Both parts joined. The first corresponds to my father's name. The second to my mother's. The Anglo-Saxon tradition and the Christian tradition keep on leaving the second half out. My mother's inheritance seems to be invisible to them. And I get angry then.

Imagine getting up in the morning with just one eye, half the face, five fingers, and then you realise that you are lame; one leg has mysteriously been taken away. So please, Garcia-Arroyo. For you, just Ana, if you consider yourself a friend.

Garcia-Arroyo. Ana Garcia-Arroyo.

No. I am not Garcia Marquez or Garcia Lorca... not like them. I am still an unknown writer. And a woman as well.

A woman who falls in love with women. And loves some special friends deeply. I live in Barcelona. I have lived here since the Olympic Games of 1992. I came here to take part in the marathon, but I still have not reached the finishing line. Life has many obstacles. You already know that. There are barriers that get tougher when you use your talent and your political sense. Well, I am still running; taking part in this restless game called life. They have tried to eliminate me many times. But I am still here...

When people ask me the 'great question': where are you from? The earth beneath my feet starts to tumble. My identity is at stake. I was born in San Sebastian, I say. That makes me of the Basque Country, in the north of Spain. But I live in Barcelona, and speak Catalan as well. My mother tongue is Spanish. English is my second language and Catalan the third. I do not speak Hindi. But I would not mind learning it. Sorry, I also forget to mention the most important thing: body language. I speak body language. Smiles, sweet eyes, a pleasant melody from the heart. The intellectual disarmament to encounter the other.

So then, I am Ana. I am Ana Garcia-Arroyo. I am from San Sebastian. I am from Barcelona. I am a woman. I am alternative: sexually alternative, ideologically alternative. I am a writer. I am a Doctor of Philosophy. I am a specialist in Indian Literature in English. Forget all that.

Editors: Many lesbian and gay people say it took them a long time to discover their sexual orientation. How was it in your case? Did you know pretty early that you were attracted to people of your own sex? Or did it take you a while to find out?

Garcia-Arroyo: I was 25 when it happened. And it happened because I fell in love. At school, I had always developed a special attachment to some female students and friends. But at that time I did not wonder what it meant because it was a segregated school, just for girls. In my adolescence, I discovered that I did not feel like the other people at school and I did not share their likes and dislikes. It was the age of going to discos and meeting boys there, but I hated all that. I preferred being at home, reading. But I did not have books to read at home. My parents were not educated, so for them books were not important. I remember spending the weekends playing the flute. I was good at that. However, my parents did not give me extra music classes. What for? Music was useless at that time. Or so they thought. Their expectations for me were to finish school and get a job; earn a living as soon as possible. Then some day, I would get married... So, I felt completely isolated. Alienated. There was no one to identify with. There were no role models. I suffered a lot in that small city where there were no opportunities in any field, expect the traditional ones. I sort of ran away to London to learn English. My mother let me go; my father did not like the idea. There in London, a colourful world started to appear in front of my eyes. It was very hard to live there as an immigrant. I was badly treated by a Lord's family where I worked as an au pair. But I remember that at that stage of my life, I was still looking for real love. I had some male friends. But they did not mean anything to me. My soul was still looking for someone to love, somebody to identify with. At the age of twenty-five, that person appeared. And it was a woman, not a man. It took me some time to accept it. But in the end, I did. I had to deconstruct all those prejudices that my own culture, the Church, my parents, etc., had shaped within me. It is not easy to do that. And it takes time. You need strength and courage. But love, real love, always triumphs in the end.

Editors: There are many different terms now that generally refer to same-sex love. Sometimes they vary according to different contexts and times. Which one would you prefer in order to define yourself?

Garcia-Arroyo: Having studied the terminology used to express same-sex love in Western and Indian cultures, as well as the theories of sexuality at different moments of history, I very much like the terms 'queer', 'queerness' or 'alternative sexualities'. 'Queer' and 'queerness' refer to all aspects of life and not merely the sexual. 'Queer' describes a plurality of perspectives and idiosyncrasies that distance themselves from the mainstream or from conventional norms. Queer has been inscribed with very pejorative meanings like 'strange', 'deviant' or 'atypical', but of course, this is very reductive and parochial. At the same time, 'queer' embodies a 'verb', a constant action, rather than a noun, a fixed identity.

The term 'alternative sexuality' more or less expresses this idea of not having a fixed sexual identity. What I mean is that we cannot classify human beings within the conventional categories (heterosexual, homosexual, gay, lesbian, bisexual) because apart from these, there are many other ways of expressing one's sexuality. So, nowadays, the term that best expresses this idea is 'queer', which at the same time can be used in other fields that combat the mainstream and the imposition of a series of categories and hierarchies.

In Spanish, the term queer does not exist, so when I express it in that language, I like using expressions like 'alternative sexualities', 'alternative energies', 'alternative arts and literatures', 'alternative medicines', you know what I mean? The world has to be alternative. All of us must have a voice and be represented equally and with justice.

Editors: State the importance of marriage in Spain. Is it regarded as more or less compulsory, as it is in India, especially for women? In which case, how did you resist it and convince your family that you wished to stay 'single'?

Garcia-Arroyo: In Spain marriage is no longer compulsory for either men or women. It used to be compulsory at the time of Franco's dictatorship, when there was just one regime, the military and the Church, and both of them were the same power. But after Franco's death, with the arrival of democracy and the Constitution in 1977, things started to change. The feminist movement in Spain has contributed enormously to changing people's minds. If I compare my generation with that of my mother's, we realise that there has been a great transformation, and social rights, in general, have improved a lot. My mother was born in a rural area, when the Spanish Civil War ended in 1939. She did not have a good education. She just went to the village elementary school to learn how to read and write. She was the youngest of five brothers and then her role, the one that was culturally imposed on her at the time, was to look after my grandparents until she got married at the age of twenty-three. At that time, marriage was a compulsion, especially for women. If you did not marry, you were left alone on the shelf. So either you married or you became a nun. In my mother's time, women were invisible in the public sphere. But all that, gradually, started to change with democracy, with education and with different activist groups arriving on the scene. Few of them were the women's groups.

Nowadays, women can take their own decisions regarding everything. You can ask for advice but in the end it is you who decide. Certainly, we still have a long way ahead... The masculine power (gender) represented by both male and female bodies (sex/biology) still governs all of us. This masculine power in the new form of globalisation (about 200 multinationals), and some institutions supporting globalisation, still dominates all of us. But in the microcosm, at a national level, in Spanish society, in our own homes, we can say that social rights, human rights, have gained a lot of prominence in a very short time. That is why I have given you the example of my own mother and me. Let me put it in this way: I am the daughter of a very low working-class family (my mother and father), whose parents, grandparents, were humble peasants.

However, I would also like to point out that the social and political changes in a country are brought about by both the politicians in Parliament (the ones we vote for) and the people of the country. People cannot leave everything in the hands of the politicians. People cannot consider themselves civil citizens just by exercising their right to vote. We have to fight everyday for a more equitable society. And equality here means a society, a world that is more fair and just.

So, going back to your question let me say again that nowadays, being a single woman in Spain is even considered prestigious. You have your own profession, your own flat, your own friends, you can travel around, you get on well with your family, you visit them from time to time or they visit you. And all this is natural and well accepted for both men and women. But let me tell you something funny that happened to me last summer when I was travelling around Orissa, visiting India with a female friend and researching for a book that I am writing now. (The book is an essay and deals with the main temples and some major tribes of Orissa.) I was in the capital Bhubaneshwar, visiting the Khandagiri and Udayagiri caves, when I met a young man who started to talk to me. My friend cannot speak English so I was doing all the talking. He was very friendly so we continued chatting. From the beginning, I realised that this young man wanted to know about me—what a foreigner, a woman at that, was like and what she did in the country. So he asked me about my life, my age, my profession, my social status, etc. At this stage, when I said I was forty-three and single, he was puzzled. Then, without thinking about it twice he just said, 'but what about your sexual life?' He felt a bit embarrassed afterwards, so he quickly added, 'I mean, a married woman has sexual gratification, but if you are not married, what happens?' I tried to explain to him that marriage is just an option in life, and that there are many other alternatives for both men and women. I told him that in Spain both men and women could have lovers if they just want to satisfy the sexual impulse. We no longer need marriage to have sex and we no longer need to procreate. This is a cultural imposition to control the race and create prejudices. But this idea has already been deconstructed and has no foundation at all, unless you want to strengthen hierarchies... Well, the young man of Bhubaneshwar was really astonished. I insisted that Spanish people accepted it naturally, and as I was almost imagining his thoughts, and probably his next question, I took the initiative and said, 'but this does not mean that we go to bed with anyone.' For many, many of us, love is really what matters.

Editors: Would you say that in Spain it is easier for two gay men to move in together than for two gay women? If so, why is this?

Garcia-Arroyo: In the past, it was easier for two women who loved each other to have a relationship and live together. As I said earlier, a woman could live alone in her own flat; and if two women lived together, socially, they were taken as 'friends in need'. For men it was different. A man living alone was manly, but when two men live alone, people tended to suspect that they were gay. This certainly has to do with the private sphere, but what about the public one? How did people react when two men or two women showed some kind of affection in public? Here we have to consider many different factors. In cosmopolitan places such as Catalunya with its capital, Barcelona, and a language and culture of its own, differences of whatever kind have always been more accepted than in the rest of Spain. Barcelona has always been a cosmopolitan place, the avant-garde of art. As a result, those who find themselves on the periphery are much easier understood and integrated here. This has to do with politics. The most important regions of the interior of Spain have always defended right-wing parties and the Christian Church. They have always carried out a kind of politics that did not differ much from fundamentalism. To give you an example, during the presidency of Mr Aznar, from 1996 to 2003 if my memory does not fail, the great majority of the conservative members of his government were descendants of the ministers of Franco's dictatorship. Their ideas and discourses became sophisticated as far as form was concerned. But about content, the content was the same: there was just one Spain, one country, one language, one history and one unique way of thinking. This kind of domination, this sort of omnipotence subtly spread around and controlled all fields, all institutions. It controlled the media and easily manipulated the masses. So, as you can imagine with such people in power, same-sex love was forbidden; for some of them it has always been a thing that goes 'against nature'. This is what the Church says even today. There are others, also belonging to the conservative party, who take a liberal homophobic point of view. They say we have to tolerate homosexuals and understand homosexuality but at the same time they maintain that they cannot go around kissing and loving each other openly, they have to do it at home. Theoretically, we scholars call this liberal homophobia.

Editors: What is the legal status of homosexuality in Spain now?

Garcia-Arroyo: This is connected to the previous question. Since June 2005, same-sex couples in Spain can get married. After so much fighting, same-sex marriage is legalised at last. Just imagine what this represents in a country that has traditionally been Catholic! Little by little, Spanish people have become aware of the cultural constraints imposed by the Roman Church. Women, homosexuals and all those in the margins were the most affected. But so were men. Men were also conditioned by the stiff roles imposed. They had to be macho. You see this term 'macho' is originally Spanish and we have exported it to other countries. Women in Spain should be ashamed of that. But some men started to get tired of it too. So what has happened is that the concept of masculinity and femininity and the different roles connected to them have changed, and are now more flexible for everybody. If you also consider the activist and artistic work done by different groups and also by intellectuals and writers, then the result is that when the elements converge there is social improvement. And these elements are the political consciousness of the majority of the people of the country on the one hand; and on the other hand, the social politics that the Socialist Party introduced as soon as it won the elections in March 2003. The president of the Socialist Party, Jose Luise Rodriguez Zapatero, and all the members of his government have always stood up for its social reforms. One of the new laws introduced pertained to same-sex marriage.

Editors: What about your family? Have you ever told them about your sexuality?

Garcia-Arroyo: I know that for many people telling their parents about their sexuality is one of the first things they think they have to do. And this is very logical because what you want is support and understanding from those close to you. In my case, I did not tell my parents because, from the beginning, I knew they would not be able to understand. I just did not want to create unnecessary problems. Everyone knows his/her parents and can tell what kind of reaction one might encounter. Let me just put it in a simple way. When people speak different languages it is impossible to understand each other. You might be able to communicate by using body language, but if you know that one party does not want to make an effort, then you can do nothing. Why waste your energies then? It is like giving a baby a dish of very spicy *dal*, or a beefsteak; even if you insist that it is good and has proteins and vitamins and so on, his/her body is not prepared for that yet. You cannot reform your parents in a day, a month, not even in years. Many of them do not change throughout their lives. However, and thanks to the changes that have taken place in Spain and the visibility of same-sex love, I very much believe that, by now, they know. They also know what kind of themes I usually deal with in my scholarly work, so the idea might have crossed their minds. Of course, you feel isolated, alienated and like an outcast. But not just for loving someone of the same-sex, for many other things as well. I do not deny that at the beginning, the first ten years, it was very difficult. But the more I studied and became politicised, the easier it was to use knowledge and art to counter homophobia in the different spheres of life; it was really worth doing that.

Another important thing that helped was that my parents and me do not live in the same town. They live in a small city in the interior of Spain, a very traditional and right-wing place. At twenty-one, when I came back from London, I just could not live in my parents' place, so I quickly moved to Barcelona. But let me also say that from my point of view, parents should not interfere in their children's lives. We are adults and we have to live our own lives whether parents like it or not. If we want to tell them about our sexuality or about our friends or about our plans for buying a house or whatever, it is up to us. We must have our secrets if we want to.

The important thing is that we should be clear about what we want to do. Alternative sexuality is *not* a problem. The problem is homophobia. The crime is homophobia. The criminal is the homophobe. The deranged, unnatural, insane mind is that of the homophobe.

Editors: Have you faced discrimination at any of the work places you have been to on account of your sexuality?

Garcia-Arroyo: Yes. I worked for about ten years in a religious school, teaching English to Higher Education students. I knew what kind of school it was, and everybody knows that the Church condemns homosexuality. Jobs, as you can imagine, are very difficult to find. Unemployment is one of the great problems in Spain. So I decided to 'play the game': do my job, get the money and live my own life. I decided not to give explanations about my private life. Some other non-gay people also do that. The first years were more or less fine. But then things started to change. The director of the school also changed and life there became unbearable. As a teacher, I have seen many violations of human rights, of all kinds, committed against students, teachers... And nobody said anything. The teachers also witnessed many atrocities and they kept quiet. They were afraid of losing their jobs.

I was teaching English there, but in my classes, my students and I also debated texts dealing with racism, gender, sexuality, cultures, women, etc. I wanted my students to learn not only English, but to think; to consider the different sides of a prism, to be in the position of 'the other'. In the end, the school sacked me—for this and for the publication of a book. It was the translation into Spanish of Suniti Namjoshi's *Feminist Fables*. The school found out. And they sacked me. As you know, Suniti Namjoshi is an Indian writer who defines herself as a lesbian feminist. I did the translation and wrote the prologue. In a religious school, topics like feminism and lesbianism are still forbidden. The school would rather get rid of people like me who dedicated her time to writing 'subversive' things.

Do you know what I did then? I took them to court. I was not going to keep quiet. The dismissal was very unjust, so I sued them. After a lot of fighting, I won the case. They had to compensate me financially. Curiously enough, neither they nor me could use the publication of a book as a valid argument. Who is going to believe that they dismiss people for the publication of a book? Especially here, in the West, where things are always 'politically correct'? (Excuse me! I mean, politically corrupt....)

Editors: You have made quite a few trips to India. What is it about India that fascinates you?

Garcia-Arroyo: Well, this is a difficult question. It is as if you ask me, or anyone, why you fall in love with somebody, how can you explain it? How can you explain falling in love? Yes, you can give the typical answers: you can say that the person has beautiful eyes, is intelligent, is attractive, etc. You can say that India is an ancient and very rich civilisation with many cultures living together; you can say it has beautiful landscapes and admirable human geographies. You can say things like that, but it is much more than that. I first went to India in 1989. It was a month-long trip to the north of the country. At that time, India was still a very remote country for us Spaniards. I knew nothing of India. I can say that I did not even have any kind of stereotypes regarding the country. I cannot even tell why I decided to go there, why it attracted me. Perhaps the reason was that it is a faraway country and I wanted to go far. Or probably, and this idea convinces me more, my soul, for some reason, was leading me there. I just had to be there. I had to start my studies, and there had to be a beginning. So I went to India and I fell in love with the country. It was like being the lover and longing to find out more and more about the beloved. I wanted to know... So I started to read, to study, to try to understand such a complex culture, its stories, its secrets, its idiosyncrasies, its shortcomings. This is what happens when you fall in love; this is what happens in a relationship; you love the other, you start to integrate the person within your soul, your mind... Sometimes you do not understand many things, but communication helps, and there has always been an excellent communication between the Indians that I have met and myself. And this is fascinating. There is a book in Spanish entitled *From the Ganges to the Mediterranean*. Well, for me it works like this. There is always a bridge that connects you to the other, if you wish.

Editors: Ana, you have studied the gay scene in India and have even written a doctoral dissertation on it, which is now published as a book in both English and Spanish. How would you compare the attitude towards same-sex love in India and Spain?

Garcia-Arroyo: Honestly, what most fascinated me was the richness of the Indian homoerotic past in many different traditions—Hindu, Muslim and Buddhist. Our culture has been constructed on Judeo-Christian foundations; we have been gifted with a vision that sees the world in terms of binary opposites. What is correct and incorrect, natural and unnatural, etc. Same-sex love has always been condemned by the Church. St Paul in a letter to the Romans says that explicitly. People have been prosecuted and killed for being homosexuals.

However, if you refer to the present moment, there are differences between India and Spain. As I said earlier, in Spain gay people can get married and there is more flexibility concerning roles. In India there is still Section 377 of the IPC that criminalises homosexuality. Marriage is still a very strong institution in India. In general, the roles (masculine and feminine) attributed to men and women are still very well marked, very stable. Certainly, this is the consequence of colonialism and nationalism. There is a long list of bibliographical sources in my book, both by Indian and non-Indian scholars, the work of artists and activists; there has been a wave of alternative sexualities emerging and claiming their place. The terminology and concepts used to define same-sex love may vary from country to country, but what is relevant is that alternative sexualities in India are now much more visible; many works have been published, discussions are held, and very soon, I believe, the first obstacle, Section 377, will be abolished. India is after all a democracy, and politicians will eventually have to understand that they cannot enslave their own people with laws that once colonised them.

Editors: Did your doctoral research out you in any way? Were people in the university hostile to you for working on such a project?

Garcia-Arroyo: Yes, although they would never admit it because, of course, this is not correct for a university, which is supposed to forge liberties and freedom… From the beginning, I had problems with the head of the department, a woman. There were some other professors as well who also supported her. When I started working on Suniti Namjoshi's work, she did not like my theme: India-feminism-lesbianism. I remember discussing theories and terminology related, for example, to heterosexuality, lesbianism, etc., and she accused me of propaganda. So Namjoshi's poems were propaganda, her stories were propaganda and my discussion of them and application and allusion to critical theory was propaganda. I had many problems with this awful woman. But I did not want to give up. She humiliated me a lot; she also humiliated the supervisor of my work, another professor. But I was there, alone, with nobody's support because she, the head of department, this dreadful woman, was respected by everybody. She thought she was a goddess; a queen and her words were gospel. However, I knew I would not give up. There was more at stake than just a doctoral dissertation; there was justice, ethics and human rights. So I continued fighting. It took me six years to research and write the doctoral dissertation. The irony is that in the last two years, I even worked in that very department as an associate professor. At that time, I still believed that everything could be sorted out and that this woman would eventually change her stance. I was totally mistaken. In fact, she was just preparing her last act: to get rid of me, nicely. Always putting the blame on me: I was incomplete, inefficient, a bad teacher, etc., etc. It was clearly a case of bullying. And as you know, in such cases, the victim always appears as inefficient and incompetent. This is the aggressor's job: to make the victim look like that….

So they kicked me out. They shattered all my dreams. I went into depression that lasted for about a year. I did not go to the doctor; I did not want pills. Writing helped me get over my pain. I started to write short stories and to read a lot. And little by little I could more or less start thinking clearly again. Earning a living is hard, especially if you are a woman of a certain age. I am overqualified for some; I am too old for others (here, if you are over thirty-five, you are old). To tell you the truth, all that still hurts. Certain wounds take a long time to heal....

Editors: Are you a devout Christian? Orthodox Christianity does not approve of homosexuality. How do you reconcile religion with your own sexual orientation?

Garcia-Arroyo: I am a religious and spiritual person, but it has nothing to do with being a Christian. I do not identify myself with Christianity, or with the institutional religion of the Pope, bishops, priests, etc. The church has lost a lot of power in Spain and will eventually fall. Their laws, discourses and vision of the world are very narrow and inflexible. So, for me, it does not mean anything. On the contrary their discourses make me laugh. They are so unsustainable, if you to take a look at history. But I am religious and spiritual from the point of view that I have a soul, which is connected to the cosmic soul. Yes, in that way my sense of perceiving and understanding religion have more to do with Indian philosophy than with Western parameters. I also believe in karma, dharma and rebirth.

Editors: What's the nature of the gay movement in Spain? Is there much activism, or is it restricted to bars and discos, as in many western European countries?

Garcia-Arroyo: Before the socialist government approved of the law concerning same-sex marriage, there were many different strains within LGBT activism. There was no consensus with respect to agendas. So it was more difficult to fight. Now the law allows homosexual couples to marry, but there are still many parochial people who discriminate against you for being gay or for writing about it. I gave you my own example earlier. The first step has been taken and that is legal. But we cannot stop here. There are still homophobes around and we cannot give up. But let me also point out that what has really helped ordinary people by generating awareness is TV. In about a decade, there have been series, films and documentaries, etc., which have treated the theme in a fair way. So this is also important: to educate people on TV, so that the gay person becomes part of the mainstream. The programmes and films have to be well made, of course. You cannot adopt a simplistic approach. You need a team of professionals to do the stuff tastefully. Many artistic works can challenge conventions, as you know.

Editors: Ana, as you said, you admire the work of the Indian lesbian-feminist writer Suniti Namjoshi, and have also translated some of it. What is it that drew you to Suniti's work?

Garcia-Arroyo: I came across her work unexpectedly. I was reading a review and her name was mentioned there very briefly. What drew my attention was that the reviewer said that she was a lesbian feminist from India. I had not heard anything of the sort before and by then I had already read quite a lot about India. So, I started reading her work. First, *Because of India* and *Feminist Fables*. I liked them very much. In *Because of India*, Namjoshi gives the reader some biographical facts. It was as if personal pain could only be overcome by the beauty of poetry. You see Namjoshi's work, even if we consider the fables, is very poetic. So I decided to do my M.A. on her *Feminist Fables*, and then I translated them into Spanish. I have to thank Suniti for politicising me. I have learned a lot from her, and grown a lot.

Editors: For Suniti, feminism seems to be the logical outcome of lesbianism. Do you see it in the same way? Are you a feminist?

Garcia-Arroyo: Yes, I am. Many women still have to face double discrimination, for being women and lesbians. For me, feminism is a question of justice and human rights. It is as simple as that. Feminism has made a lot of mistakes throughout history. And there are still women who affirm that if there are more women in power, things will be easier for all of us. We all know that there have been women like Mrs Thatcher or Indira Gandhi or the head of department at my university, who have done terrible things. It is not a question of sex, but of gender. It is not about biology being destiny, as the feminists claimed in the old days. It is more a question of gender, for example, Judith Butler's theory of gender. Many women in power are very masculine; they have adopted this masculine persona to get to the top and they behave aggressively like men. If we men and women continue adopting the traditional models imposed by patriarchy and consisting of power-hungry institutions, fierce competition, treason, violence, etc., the ones suffering the consequences are always the ones in the margins. And these can sometimes be women, sometimes men, sometimes homosexuals and sometimes the poor. Feminism is a question of justice and human rights. That is the way I see it.

Editors: How is a lesbian couple living together different from a straight couple living together?

Garcia-Arroyo: I think this question is wrong. We cannot work or think with such reductive binary systems of 'a straight-couple', 'a homo-couple', etc. This is a great mistake. I could direct you to Eve K. Sedgwick and her *Epistemology of the Closet*, where she elucidates clearly that there are just too many kinds of so-called straight couples (to give you a funny example, she talks of those who smoke after sex, those who do not, those who take five minutes, those who need time, those who are romantic, those who go for it, those who do it only after marriage, those who play a porno film, etc.).

The same thing applies to couples that happen to be of the same sex. Therefore, we cannot categorise people. There are just as many ways of living and loving as there are people. We must shun stereotypes.

Editors: You live in a beautiful apartment in Barcelona city which I [R. Raj Rao] have visited twice. There is a stereotypical feminine touch to way you have done up and decorated your flat, normally attributed to straight women. How would you defend yourself against this essentialist charge?

Garcia-Arroyo: Well, it might look stereotypically feminine to you, but you have not seen other flats. I do not entirely agree with you. It has, for example, oriental decoration, pictures, musical instruments, etc., that I have brought from the places where I have been. I can assure you that my neighbours find my flat very strange and queer. The furniture might be classical. But that was a question of money. Most of the furniture was given to me or bought second hand. When I came to live in my flat, I did not have money; I had bought the flat and I had spent it all. So, I had to do with things given or bought cheaply. You see, I finally managed to paint the walls last year. Now they look more modern because I like bright colours and they are like that—in apple green, orange, yellow. And I did the job myself. Painting, I mean. Otherwise it would have been impossible. Paying a designer or painter is astonishingly expensive here. So, that also has to do with money.

Editors: What is a day in the life of Ana like?

Garcia-Arroyo: It is difficult to answer this question at this moment in time because I am in a kind of transitory phase. Or at least this is what I believe. As I said earlier, in the past I used to teach English in religious schools. Then I took up doctoral studies, my specialisation being Indian literature written in English... My life started to change at that moment. When I discovered other literatures, other cultures, other worlds, my own being started to think differently, feel differently. I have also travelled a lot, and that always reaffirms a flexible mind. Position determines point of view, you know that. My position has changed a lot. I could not and I cannot think like a typical Westerner, because at least one half of me was not/is not a Westerner. I cannot think like somebody in the mainstream because society has relegated me to the periphery.

At the beginning of the new year (2007), I made up my mind to walk forwards, not backwards. To fight for what I believe in.

I think I have a political and ethical task, a compromise with India. I think that, within my human limitations, my compromise involves spreading Indian literature and culture in the world where I live. India has to be known, discovered; cultural prejudices have to be deconstructed. In that way, I think I can modestly contribute to expanding the richness of an ancient civilisation like India. Suniti Namjoshi says that the West does not need to be explained. Everybody knows about their goodness and humanity. And she is very right. So, going back to your question, at this moment, I have decided to give up teaching English (I do not see this as my vocation anymore; that was in my previous life, but I have been reborn again) and start a new life. Therefore, a typical day now is very uncomplicated: I spend the day working, shut up in my studio, reading and writing. I continue with my research on India. I have many projects in mind. As pointed out before, at the moment, I am finishing a book on Orissa, its major temples and tribes. It will be published in Spanish by a good publishing house here, so I hope it will get to many people. Then I want to start another book dealing with Indian women writers. You see, nothing at all has been published in Spanish about almost anything concerning India. All the publications are in English. But in Spain, very few people can manage with English, especially at a high level. So things have to be written and told in my mother tongue as well, and I can do that. So at the moment, I work for ten or twelve hours a day, seven days a week.

I get up everyday praying to the gods and goddesses to give me health to continue working and to help me. You see, I now live on my savings. And I believe they will last for about two years. However, my mind evokes Tagore's words that comfort me and give me strength: '...and where the old tracks are lost, new country is revealed with its wonders'.

The black side of the story, as I have told you, is that I have to continue paying bills. And living in this society of mine is so expensive that sometimes I feel like a Dalit: an intellectual Dalit. Occupying the margins of society (in many fields), where I have been relegated, owning to the circumstances that have pushed me there. However, I do not feel sad, because, at least, at this moment I have been able to choose, and this is always very important.

No, I do not watch TV or go to the cinema. I meet some special friends, talk to them on the phone or write to them if they live far away. I have very few real friends. I usually get on well with people, but only a few, the true ones, can understand my soul.

Editors: Ana, you have also done some creative work. I think you have written a novel…?

Garcia-Arroyo: Yes, I have written a novel in Spanish, my mother tongue. The title is *Colegios caros de curas,* literally something like 'Expensive religious schools'. I hope it will come out soon. I have had some problems with the publishing house, because it is a small place and problems keep on cropping up. The novel deals with education in such schools, the religious ones. It is based on my own experience there. Through the lives of the different characters, teachers and students, we see the real problems of these schools. There is the story, for example, of a gay student who does not hide his gayness. He is beaten up one day and the school tries to forget him.

There is the story of a teacher, who is also a lesbian and a feminist; she has to keep quiet to conceal her real identity, but she uses literary texts to teach her students certain topics that are forbidden in the school. There is the story of a female trade union teacher, who is constantly mobbed by the high religious hierarchy of the school for her socialist ideas; and there is an episode where the students demonstrate against the Iraq war in 2003, and the consequences they have to face. Many things like that happen in these schools today, in the Western world where I live, that is so proud of being democratic and tolerant.

Well, so that is my novel; a modest piece because it is my first exploratory experiment with creative writing. I know I am not Arundhati Roy, a writer I greatly admire for her masterpiece, *The God of Small Things.* But my novel also introduces some topics, connected to education, which I am sure many people would appreciate. I have always felt that one does not have to be afraid of telling stories.

Editors: What is the position, then, of contemporary gay-lesbian literature in Spain?

Garcia-Arroyo: Well, in the case of gay writers dealing with gay themes, we can say that they have always been more open. But about lesbian-women writers, it is a different story. Until very recently, women writers have encoded their lesbian themes, or they have written under pseudonyms. I think this is a universal phenomenon. I also have to say that nowadays, there are still very few publishing houses that want to publish gay literature, which is of course discriminated against in that the people of 'the same species' alone read it. This, perhaps, also makes us think about what kind of steps we should take to make this literature part of the mainstream. I am not saying that we have to shape and adapt our writing to mainstream tastes, but we should be capable of challenging the status quo. Let me give you an example. Nowadays, writers such as Sarah Waters openly deal with lesbian themes and are very successful among readers of all kinds. The main theme of the novel is usually lesbian, but the context is fabulous. Waters, for instance, contextualises her novels in the Victorian age and the enormous amount of information she provides makes it resemble a historical novel. The readers enjoy not only the lesbian story, but also other details pertaining to that particular age. This is just an example, but what I mean is that readers, whether gay-lesbian or not, want to go beyond the typical. We do not want to read the typical story of a man falling in love with a woman and going to bed. Nor do we want to merely change the gender, and say 'woman falls in love with woman....' In Spain, many novels published lately are like that, very boring in my opinion. But I am afraid some of them are very popular among younger gay readers. However, we can use the same argument for other novels that are gay-themed. Some of them entertain you for a day and then you forget them.

Editors: In terms of political bonding, does a lesbian feel closer to a straight woman or to a gay male? Personally, how do you feel about this?

Garcia-Arroyo: From a political perspective both women and gay people have always been relegated to a secondary position within the heteropatriarchal system. Women have been struggling for their rights all around the world; some things have improved, but there is still a lot to be done in all cultures and countries. Gay people, both male and female, are also fighting for their recognition and their space in society. What happens is that within this categorisation, a woman who also loves other women has to bear a double stigma: the first one corresponds to the cultural category of gender (woman); the second one is connected to the category of desire (lesbian). Then, the fight for political recognition and equal rights is multiplied by two. This is the general pattern. However, it varies and functions differently in different situations. I mentioned earlier that a woman in power could be terrible towards other men and women. And a powerful gay male can show no sympathy with anyone, and even maltreat everybody, just because he might be interested in other objectives, for example, getting more money and social prestige.

In the past, the first feminist movements of modern times put the emphasis on the identification of all women and the creation of a common feeling of 'sisterhood' that embraced them all. It was a quite logical reaction. If 'biology is destiny' as Simone de Beauvoir had expressed in *The Second Sex* (1949), that is to say that 'one is not born a woman, one becomes a woman' according to the cultural category of gender, then the most logical reaction (to fight against these patriarchal impositions) was to create a political bonding among all women that could oppose the supposed enemy, man. In 1980, Adrienne Rich expands this argument in her famous essay 'Compulsory Heterosexuality and Lesbian Existence'. Rich argues that there has always been a lesbian existence, although the terms have varied throughout history and across cultures. Rich introduces the concept 'lesbian continuum' to allude to a relation between women that goes beyond sexual intimacy and identifies and unites all women, including heterosexual ones. For Rich, all women share a special bond for having been oppressed by the patriarchal system. Patriarchy has defined women and lesbians, attributing them limited roles and spaces, and reducing their sexuality to the business of procreation. The bond of sisterhood that many feminists spoke of in the 1970s and 1980s, aims at counter-attacking men who are described as violent oppressors and destructive conquerors of women's bodies. In 1981, Monique Wittig complicates things a bit more with the publication of her famous essay 'One Is Not Born a Woman', in which she asserts that a lesbian is not a woman. What she means is that a lesbian is out of the cultural category of gender that arranges human beings into the binary system of men and women. Let me explain all this with a simple table that will help to clarify all that has been said.

Binary Systems

Sex/Biology	*Gender/Cultural Construction*	*Desire*
Male	Men/Masculine	Gay
Female	Women/Feminine	Lesbian

For Wittig, then, a lesbian is not subjected to the hetero-patriarchal system as a straight woman can be. A lesbian is beyond the categories of sex and gender, as she is not engaged in an interrelated system of servitude (domestic work, having and rearing children, marital duties). One of her conclusions is that there cannot be this common bond among all women as previous feminists believed. If we also add other categories such as race, class, etc., then the discrepancies increase. Based on Wittig's ideas, Judith Butler interrogates traditional feminism. Butler criticises traditional feminism that, on the one hand rejects the idea that biology is destiny and on the other, assumes that masculine and feminine gender roles are culturally constructed on 'male' and 'female' bodies. The hegemonic cultural discourse founded on binary structures (man/woman; male/female; natural/unnatural; heterosexual/homosexual, etc.) delimits gender. In Butler's *Gender Trouble: Feminism and the Subversion of Identity* (1990), she criticises those forms of feminism that define women as a universal homogeneous political group on account of the fact that every single person is a different individual. She introduces a concept of gender as performance, that is to say, how we behave at different times.

Gender cannot be said to follow from a particular kind of sex. If one is born female it does not imply that one has to become feminine and love men. As a result, a male can become both feminine, and masculine, and can love a woman or other men. And the same can happen for a person of the female sex. Gender is then a performance, the way we act, which has been 'naturalised' by the effect of repetition and hegemonic discourse. Consequently, we can deconstruct traditional gender roles by acting or performing differently. We can improve the way society views gender roles and break the binary understanding of masculinity and femininity. In a culture like India that has always rejected being trapped within binary systems, reductive and stable patterns of conceiving gender and desire are unsustainable.

As a result of all this, and going back to the beginning of the question, it does not make much sense to establish a comparative paradigm and say that a lesbian feels closer to a straight woman than to a gay man. It would also be nonsensical if we put it the other way round: a lesbian identifying more with a gay male than with a straight woman. From my point of view, it all depends on who this person is and what kind of spiritual, intellectual and corporal affinities intervene in the relation between two people. It is not then a question of being gay–straight, woman–man, masculine–feminine, traditionalist–radical or Spanish–Indian, for example. It is much more complicated than that. From my personal experiences of everyday life, I can say that one of my best female friends is straight; her husband is also straight and I get on extraordinarily well with both of them. And I am also referring to the political perspective, not just the affective one. I have also met other gay males and lesbians with whom I have never identified politically or emotionally. However, I also have two very good friends who are queer people with whom I identify politically and affectively. All in all, I could say that relations and identifications of whatever kind cannot be reduced to simple parameters. Human beings are much more complex than the categories we create, whereby some theoreticians and political tyrants have positioned us and still want to nail us. We do not have to let them have that kind of perverse satisfaction.

13

avinashgaitonde

I

Editors: Please introduce yourself to us.

Avinash Gaitonde: I'm Avinash Gaitonde. I was born in 1981. That makes me twenty-four years old, isn't it? I'm not college educated—have merely passed my tenth standard.

Editors: Avinash Gaitonde, it's hard to believe that you are really sexually attracted to men. I mean, you look so manly yourself. And the stereotypical image of the homosexual man is that he is effeminate.

Gaitonde: Believe me, I'm not kidding. I like women, but I like men more. I find it a bit disgusting to sleep with women. With men, it is different. It's a thing between boys. No hassles. That's what I love about gay love. In any case, I hardly understand women. You may say that I'm bisexual.

Editors: But you have been stalking us. What exactly do you want?

Gaitonde: I heard about you [R. Raj Rao] from a friend. Everyone knows about you. I came after you because I can give you what you want.

Editors: Will it be for free, or do you expect us to pay you?

Gaitonde: I'm not a whore. I don't have sex for money. It's true that I don't have a job at present. But this thing, I want to do only for love.

Editors: Why don't you have a job?

Gaitonde: I dropped out of college, that's why. I used to study in Fergusson College. But I had to discontinue my studies because my dad refused to support me. He thought I was wasting my time in college. He wanted me to start working and give him a helping hand with the household expenses. But this was not what I wanted. So my dad and I could not get on with each other. There were quarrels at home daily. Often, I would walk out of the house after a fight.

Editors: But you still live at home, don't you?

Gaitonde: Yes.

Editors: Well, you have got the wrong ideas about us. For us, gayness is a serous issue. It's a part of our politics. Gay people have been victims of prejudice all over the world, and it's about time they are empowered. There is a worldwide movement to liberate lesbians and gays and we're a part of it. We're known as activists.

Gaitonde: [Nods]

Editors: We're actually against people like you, who think that being gay only means having sex with multiple partners. It's very irresponsible and earns all of us a bad name in the eyes of the general public.

Gaitonde: But sex is important, isn't it? You have to make some time for it.

Editors: Okay, where do you want to have sex?

Gaitonde: You decide. But if you don't have a place, I can take you to a friend's flat. He and his family live in Bombay and the flat is kept locked.

Editors: And what will you say to your friend?

Gaitonde: I don't have to tell him anything. We have an understanding between us.

Editors: So, is this where you take your lovers?

Gaitonde: I don't have lovers. You are the first one.

Editors: You mean you have never had sex with anyone before?

Gaitonde: I have, with a guy from my colony. We were at school together. I stay over at his place sometimes.

Editors: Avinash Gaitonde, what does your father do?

Gaitonde: He's a police constable. Like Dawood Ibrahim's father.

Editors: Dawood Ibrahim!!! You don't want to be like him, do you?

Gaitonde: No, of course not. But what's wrong in making money? When I see all these rich guys in the neighbourhood, I feel envious. And angry.

Because they have hardly earned the money they flaunt, which obviously belongs to their fathers. It's just that they're *bade baap ka beta* (son of a big man), unlike me.

....

Editors: Hi, Avinash Gaitonde, haven't seen you for long. Where have you been?

Gaitonde: I've stopped hanging out in the *Chowk* (square). Did you know that the *chowk* is full of *goondas* (hoodlums). And I am not a *goonda*.

Editors: Shall we have a cup of tea?

Gaitonde: Forget the tea. You haven't told me when we can make out.

Editors: We don't have enough privacy at home. And we wouldn't like to go to your friend's flat.

Gaitonde: Then how about your car? We can park in a quiet spot and roll the windows up.

....

Editors: Hello, Avinash Gaitonde, you're looking very dapper today.

Gaitonde: And you're no less handsome.

Editors: Have you found a job?

Gaitonde: No, can you lend me 300 bucks?

Editors: Okay, but on one condition. You must tell us a little about your gay self.

Gaitonde: What do you want to know? As I may have told you earlier, it started in school. I was in an all-boys school run by the city corporation. I started screwing some of my juniors. Afterwards, I screwed girls also, but did not give up on boys. It's the act of screwing that I really enjoy. It does not matter if it's a boy or girl. But I must be the one who screws. After all, I'm a man. I would never let another man screw me. It would violate my manliness, if that ever happens.

Editors: Do your straight friends know about you?

Gaitonde: They do. They don't have a problem with it, though they sometimes advise me not to indulge in too much *samlaingik* activity. Why should they have a problem anyway? We're men, not women. Men can do whatever they please. It's only when it comes to women that society disapproves of certain actions. My friends do not see me as distinct from themselves. We're *yaars* (friends). Whatever happens, happens in *dosti-masti* (mischief among buddies), and it's fine with all of us.

Editors: Do you have a girlfriend? When do you plan to get married?

Gaitonde: Yes, I have a girlfriend. Her name is Vaishali [name changed]. I've slept with her many times. But her parents wouldn't accept me as her husband because I am from a lower caste. But just because I am from a lower caste, you mustn't think I am not influential. In fact, we're distant relatives of a local corporator.

Editors: So, will you have a love or arranged marriage?

Gaitonde: I don't know. I haven't thought of marriage yet. I have to first be able to stand on my own feet. Can you find me a job, sir?

Editors: We'll try. But tell us something. If, as you say, you're disgusted by girls, won't it be unfair to the girl you marry?

Gaitonde: Girls have to accept the husbands that fate gives them. Moreover, I didn't say I don't like having sex with girls. For me, a hole is a hole is a hole, whether it belongs to a boy or a girl.

Editors: By the way, we are having a New Year's Eve party at this friend's place to usher in the new millennium on 31 December 1999. She is female. Would you like to come?

Gaitonde: Yes, of course. Give me the address. But why is it at a girl's place? I thought you dislike girls.

....

[At the party]

Editors: Hi, Avinash Gaitonde, are you enjoying yourself?

Gaitonde: There's this guy who is after me. He wants me to make out with him in the parking. He's harassing me a lot. He is not my type really.

....

Editors: Avinash Gaitonde, the waiters in this bar seem to be terrified of you. Why?

Gaitonde: Didn't you know? I'm the don of this area. A no-nonsense guy who will break their bones if they do not serve me properly. They know that very well.

Editors: And now, you are trying to pick up a fight with another customer, like any common *tapori* (vagabond)?

Gaitonde: If the situation arises, I can even use a knife. I don't take anyone's shit.

Editors: Cool it. It's time to part. Anything else you wish to say?

Gaitonde: I can do whatever I want and get away with it. Sometimes I think I am above the law.

Editors: OK, what can we do for you?

Gaitonde: Get me a job in your educational institution and I'll be your slave. But for now, please pay the bill and lend me 500 bucks.

II

Editors: [On the phone] Hello, Avinash Gaitonde. Yes, of course we remember you. You still have our mobile number? That's amazing. When were you released from jail?

Gaitonde: How can I forget you, sir? I was at the *chowk* with Satish [name changed], this guy from the police lines who knows you. He said you frequently enquired about me. It's he who gave me your mobile number. Yes, I had it earlier, but lost it after all this *lafda* (scandal) happened.

Editors: We heard about the case and would like to discuss it with you. Do you mind talking to us about it?

Gaitonde: I have no problem. Let's meet at the same bar [where we met last time].

....

Editors: Avinash Gaitonde, we read all about this case in the newspapers. It is said that you and your friends gang-raped this poor girl and threw her out from the second floor of a building under construction. Is it true?

Gaitonde: It's completely false. The girl was of easy virtue. She wanted me to sleep with her. When some friends of mine appeared on the scene, she got panicky and jumped out of the window.

Editors: So you mean, you were wrongly implicated and sent to jail?

Gaitonde: Absolutely.

Editors: You know, we felt a little let down when we read your name in the newspapers. Because it appeared in connection with the rape of a woman. We saw you as a defector.

Gaitonde: The girl led me on. It's my bad luck that I managed to get seduced by her. I'm now convinced that it's much better to have boy-friends than girlfriends. Can you think of anything like this happening, if there were a boy in her place? Girls are so opportunistic. They tempt and trap men when it suits them, and accuse them of rape when they grow tired. Because of that bitch, I lost two good years of my youth in jail.

Editors: The girl's no more. She was driven to suicide by the taunts of her family. So it's not right on your part to speak of her that way.

Gaitonde: It's good that she's dead. At least other men will be spared of her vile charms.

Editors: What happened during the trial?

Gaitonde: I would have been released long ago. But the girl's parents are somewhat moneyed. So they kept the case going. But finally, nothing could be proved against me. Even the semen test failed. The judge acquitted me and the other guys who were arrested with me.

Editors: But we heard something else: that the parents of all you guys paid money to the girl's father to withdraw the case.

Gaitonde: This is utter rubbish. Tell me who told you this, and I won't leave him alive.

Editors: Okay. How was jail life from the point of view of homosexuality?

Gaitonde: *Samlaingik* sex is rampant in jail. It can be had by day and by night, in our cells and especially in the toilets. So many older men tried to *patao* (hook) me in jail. They wanted me to be their lover, but I was choosy. I fell in love with a boy younger than me. His name is Shriram [name changed]. He was just nineteen and went to jail for a petty theft. I loved him and still do. It wasn't just lust. We were in each other's hearts. Believe me, I love him like I've never loved any woman. Not even my girlfriend Vaishali, who ditched me and got married while I was in jail.

Editors: Did the jail authorities ever catch you together red-handed?

Gaitonde: Yes, once. It was the dead of night. We were in a compromising position. The guard on night duty happened to pass by at just that moment. He saw us and struck his *lathi* (baton) on the floor. 'Kya ho raha hai (what's going on)?' he shouted, but walked away after that.

Actually, the jail staff is so used to seeing this sort of thing all the time that they don't even see it as something wrong. They know that if men are kept away from women for that long, they will turn to other men to seek an outlet. Everyone needs a release. Some prisoners, of course, practice celibacy throughout their time in jail.

Editors: Do prisoners use condoms? Have you heard of Kiran Bedi? She did not allow them to use condoms when she was the Superintendent of Tihar Jail in New Delhi. Because, she said, that would mean acknowledging that same-sex activity went on in the prison. And this was illegal, because Section 377 of the IPC makes it a crime.

Gaitonde: I don't know what you are talking about. No one uses condoms in jail. Besides, who is going to bring us the condoms? Our parents or what? Only they are allowed to visit us in our cells. My friends could only meet me in the court, whenever my case came up for hearing.

Editors: Is this guy Shriram also released from jail? If so, are you two seeing each other right now?

Gaitonde: Yes, he was released a month before me. But right now he's in Kolhapur to learn wrestling. You see, he's very skinny and now wants to develop his body. Maybe he wants to join the police. Ha ha.

Editors: What about you? Why don't you join the police?

Gaitonde: You are supposed to be intelligent. How can someone like me who's been to jail get into the police? I'm debarred from any government job, even though I'm innocent. Moreover, I detest the police force. It's bad enough that my father and elder brother are both in the police. As for me, I would rather be on the other side of the law.

Editors: What do you mean? The Dawood Ibrahim syndrome again?

Gaitonde: In jail, I met so many underworld dons and their henchmen that it's very easy for me to join the underworld and become a sharp shooter or a *supari* killer (contract killer). In fact, I'm seriously considering doing so.

Editors: No, don't say that. Surely, there are other honest ways of living your life? Do you have any plans?

Gaitonde: Let's see. I may start a shop if I can get a bank loan. Can you help me get one? They need a guarantor or so I am told. Will you stand guarantee for me, sir? Or, another idea I have is to buy an auto-rickshaw and drive it. But even that costs money. Do you know how much a brand new Bajaj auto-rickshaw costs?

....

Editors: [On the phone] Hello, Avinash Gaitonde . We're driving and can't take your call now. What is it?

Gaitonde: I'm upset. I've been drinking. You haven't seen me for so long. I suspect you don't want to see me because I am a jailbird. You didn't mind befriending me earlier. But now, because of this dark cloud that came over me, I'm not good enough. Okay, we'll see. Every dog has his day. The other day you saw me on the street and ignored me. I saw you again today. I was with some friends from the area in a black Zen with the windows rolled up.

Editors: No, Avinash Gaitonde, it's not like that at all. Why should we not want to see you because you went to jail? It's just that we're extremely busy these days.

Gaitonde: You're not the only one. All my friends have been shunning me. This jail thing has been the curse of my life. I get the message. Goodbye sir, I'll never phone you again.

14

ankitgupta

Editors: Please give us some biographical details about yourself.

Ankit Gupta: My life has been pretty simple really. No major achievements and no major failures either yet. I am twenty-five years old and was born in a small town in Haryana. I have lived my life since then in various parts of the country, owing to the transferable nature of my father's occupation. I studied in all boys' schools for a major part of my childhood and then moved on to co-education in the senior years. I double graduated in visual arts and English literature from the University of Delhi and the University of London simultaneously.

Ever since the year 2000, I have been working. I have experimented with various things in my career—advertising, graphic design, copywriting, content development, editorials, etc.

Editors: When you first attained puberty, who were you sexually attracted to/aroused by—girls or boys?

Gupta: As far as I remember, the first thought of being attracted to someone happened when I was thirteen. The years of *Maine Pyar Kiya* I think; and yes, I was attracted, rather truly, madly, deeply in love with the image of Salman Khan at that point. It was the male form that I was fascinated with. The thought of women as a sexual object did not occur to my mind, as far as I can recall.

Editors: In your opinion, was there any particular episode in your life that started to attract you to men?

Gupta: I was always in an all boys' school. It was a convent and we had nuns and priests for teachers. There were several incidents, in fact, which I can talk about, but the earliest one I can think of was about this time, when all of us in school had the necessary medical examination. There was a medical examiner and his assistant in a small room in our school. All of us in the class were asked to strip so that all the vital statistics could be taken. The whole idea of being naked with so many other people in a room was nerve racking and at the same time exciting for me. I remember trying very hard to suppress the urge to just reach out and touch someone else. In fact, after the medical exam was over and we came back to our class, I remember hearing my classmates who used to sit behind me discussing it and finding it quite an experience. I could only hear them giggle and whisper about it, but the thought of it stayed with me for a very long time. That perhaps was the very first time that I can think of as an episode attracting me to other men.

Editors: Can you describe your first sexual experience with a man?

Gupta: The first time I had sex! I don't even remember!! The first time was hardly the stuff one hears about in books. It certainly wasn't magic or any of those things. It happened in a hurry, in the back seat of a car, due to non-availability of any other place. I was studying in a defence school, and at that point we used to have a lot of army cadets who used to teach us horse riding, golf, and so on. The first time I had sex was with my riding instructor. He was one of those typical handsome army men—all muscled and sexy. We used to talk a lot while he would teach me how to mount a horse and ride steady. The talk often centred on sexual experiences, which he had previously. He would let on subtle hints about the fact that he liked me and so on. And then one day he seduced me into staying late after class in the evening and visit his quarters. All of this was extremely exciting for me as a teenager—to be treated like someone important. In his quarters, he kissed me and then one thing led on to another and we had sex. It was my first experience and I remember having an orgasm just by his touch. Quite an anti-climax; he came soon after we explored each other. I remember rushing into it, wanting more and touching and experiencing. But still, when I look back at it, it wasn't anything special, with me just realising that this is how it is supposed to be done. This is what it means to have sex!

Editors: You mentioned falling in love with another man much after having numerous sexual experiences with men. How do you differentiate between love and sex?

Gupta: I don't think it is necessary to have sex if you are in love with someone. While at college in Delhi, I had the release, being far away and in a city where no one knew me. I could do whatever I wanted. Plus, it was the simple fact that it was more open; the gay scene in Delhi. Men were more open and I had easy access to sex. But while I was indulging in it, I was never attached to anyone of the countless one-night stands I had. There were times when I didn't even know the guy's name or what he did. I never met them again. Love, for me, was everything opposite of the sexual act. In my first relationship, sex was a bare minimum; it was more about knowing the other person, spending time, depending and building a world around us. I think, that is how I differentiate between sex and love. Sex is easy, it is just an organic need of the body, but love supercedes all of that; it is more demanding and needs you to invest in the whole emotion. You need to constantly give and not want in return.

Editors: You mentioned that the Delhi gay scene is open. How is it so?

Gupta: In terms of sexual escapades, yes. You can have sex with anyone here; probably you'll need to do some manoeuvring, probably you will need to spend some money, but you can have what you want. There are numerous parks serving as discreet cruising joints, there are parties if you have the right contacts, there are the newspaper advertisements. You can get anyone you fancy, if you have a fat purse, that is. Money speaks. But love is a different thing altogether, as I said earlier.

Editors: The institution of marriage saves heterosexuals from promiscuity. Since gay men cannot get married to each other, there is no check on promiscuity. Would you say that this is true in your case?

Gupta: I don't think it is true in my case or even generally true. Marriage may be sanctimonious, but it is never binding, at least not in my experience. I have seen friends who are married having affairs, and who have slept with several married men, have known parents of married friends who were having affairs with other people. I think it is more to do with having faith and trust in a relationship. Although today marriage in India may be an institution that does supposedly bind everyone in a certain kind of boundary, there still are enough heterosexuals on the prowl. Being gay, however, does in fact make it easier to fool around. The opportunities are more; sex is easy and freely available. In my case, I did have enough affairs, but each time I have been in a relationship, I have always held my ground and have been faithful. In fact, both the times that I was seriously involved, I walked away from the relationships because at some point my partners were unfaithful—for whatever reason.

Editors: So being faithful is important to have a relationship, gay or straight?

Gupta: Yes. What's a relationship after all? It's about two people deciding to trust each other voluntarily. Love is a matter of trust, isn't it? The point is you can't have the cake and eat it too. If you need a new partner everyday, that's fine, then don't hanker for a steady relationship. You have to make a choice.

As I said, I had numerous one-night stands, but when I fell in love, and began to live with him, I did not even dream of another man. But my partner did not think so. The most dangerous thing in a relationship is when you start to take your partner for granted. I loved him so much that I agreed to whatever he said. He began to take me for granted. He began to bring friends to our flat and enjoy with them in the bedroom while I sat there in the kitchen. How long could you endure? One day, my patience snapped.

Now, sometimes, he calls me up, when he's very drunk. He says he's sorry. I listen to him patiently and then I hang up the phone. Once the trust is broken, it can't be mended.

Editors: You mentioned you have no qualms about paying for sex. Does it mean that you endorse male prostitution? Can you describe the Delhi gay scene in terms of money?

Gupta: I really have no qualms about paying for sex. It is no different from buying something off the shelf in a supermarket. You want something, you pay for it. As simple as that. And if that translates into me supporting male prostitution, yes I do. For the simple fact that each of the times I have paid for sex and have received the services of an individual, it has always been a voluntary act. All of these men who sell themselves do it knowingly and are not forced into it. They need money and I have enough! So what's wrong if a consenting adult chooses to sell his body and another buys it at a price?

Editors: Do you see yourself getting married to a woman someday? If yes, does it worry you what your sexual life might be like after marriage? If you continue to have sex with men after marriage, will you tell your wife? If you don't wish to get married, how do you think you are going to convince your parents?

Gupta: I don't think I will ever get married to a woman. At least not in this life. As for my parents, I haven't yet decided whether I am going to tell them or not. They know that I am not the settling type and have always talked about how they don't see me getting married and starting a family. So it is actually easier. I am not sure how I will convince them eventually, and also know that it will not be an easy task, but still, once the time is right, I will let them know the truth—whether they like it or not. And at the end of the day, it is my life. I should be the only one who should decide what I want to do with it.

Editors: Do your parents have any inkling about your being gay?

Gupta: I am not sure. But I think my brother knows about it. We haven't talked about it though. He had met my previous boyfriend once; he had come to my flat in Delhi. He's aware of my somewhat queer lifestyle. But I don't think he has told anything to my parents.

Editors: You said you had two previous relationships; love as opposed to sex. But given the situation in India, with the law firmly in place and the general attitude towards homosexuality, do you think is it possible for two men to live together happily ever after.

Gupta: When it comes to a relationship, I don't think the law and the general attitude is a big hindrance. Especially in a big city like Delhi, or any other city in India, people really do not care what you do in your bedroom. I know many gay men and I know that people do not care with whom they live.

But the problem is with the gay men themselves. Most gay men—I am not talking about MSMs or those who have sex for money, but gay-identified men—associate their gayness with queer sexuality. That is, being gay means you like to have sex with men, and as many men as possible. In other respects, you are like any other heterosexual. It is this attitude that is hampering gay men in India from sustaining fruitful same-sex relationships.

Gay men are insecure. They want the best of both worlds and end up losing everything. That is what my two previous relationships taught me. And I am not planning any more relationships in the near future. If I want sex, I know where to get it.

Editors: Where?

Gupta: I know a person, who runs an agency for gay men. You give him a call and tell your type—big, small, fair, dark, anything. He will quote a price. If you agree, you fix a meeting time. You meet the person at a pre-decided spot, bring him home, or wherever you want to lay him, do the act, pay him the money and go about your business. You do not ask anything about the person—his name and so on.

There are times when I haven't talked to a person even after spending the whole night with him. You can get a person for one hour or for the whole night, depending on how much you pay. I prefer the hourly person. Once you are released, you do not want them to hang around in your house.

The latest trend in finding people is the classified column in the national newspapers. They advertise under the health and fitness columns. You will find some agency under the heading 'massage'. You call up the number given in the paper and state your preference. It's very discreet.

Editors: Can you profile men who have sex for money.

Gupta: I have seen people from very well-to-do families having sex for money. I know a well-known fashion designer who calls boys to his house to suck him off. For most of these boys, this is an easy way to earn money. Most of these are students. The money their parents send them is not enough. So if they can earn Rs 2,000–3,000 in one night, what's the big deal?

Editors: Do you identify yourself as *koti/panthi*, active/passive, gay/bi-sexual, etc.?

Gupta: I identify myself as a gay man.

Editors: What does being gay mean to you?

Gupta: It means that you are different. It means that you are special. That means there is more to your life than just to get married and procreate. You are no breeder. That means you are culturally more focused.

Editors: Have you ever been gay bashed or been a victim of homophobia?

Gupta: I think everyone who has an alternative sexuality has been a victim of gay bashing or homophobia at some point or the other, whether it is direct or indirect. I too have had similar experiences. Snide comments in school because I was more sensitive, or so everyone thought, because I wouldn't participate in bullying other children or teasing people, or some snickers when you rationalise about not opting for sports in place of books. But it has never been anything more than that. Maybe because I have always stood up for myself and have never been really affected by any comments on me, for I know that it isn't me the other person is talking about. It is someone else, and it's a figment of his or her own insecurity.

Editors: We've asked this question to others, but we would like to ask you as well. If your friends, relations, parents, family, employers, neighbours, etc., find out about your sexual life, do you think they will ostracise you?

Gupta: This is an interesting question! Most of my friends know about me. There was a time when I told all of my friends that I am gay. While I feared losing some of the valuable friendships, nothing of that sort ever happened. None changed their opinion about me. My friends include a lot of straight friends who may not be cool about homosexuality per se, but they all accepted me as I am. My parents don't know about me, but my sibling does.

At almost all of the places that I have been working, my employers knew about me. In fact, when I joined a multinational advertising agency, they propped the question of my sexuality in the interview and I was hired with their complete knowledge about my sexuality. They commented later about the interesting point of view and value that a member of the gay community added to the world of advertising and went on to even have a seminar on the subject! As for my parents, I can't really say what they would say. But I do know eventually, they will accept me.

Editors: What sort of support systems have helped you to come to terms with your sexuality?

Gupta: There wasn't any kind of a support system. I think all that I had was just my friends and the internet. The thousands of chat rooms and various websites allowed me to figure out that there were other people who are gay. Which made me realise that I was just as normal as men who had sex with women or the straight population.

Editors: But the queer identity thrives on being different, not being 'normal', but being different, isn't it?

Gupta: I am not the activist type who would shout about his sexuality from the rooftop. My sexuality is my own business. No one has the right to question it unless it bothers them. And I am sure I have not bothered anyone with my sexual orientation.

15

ganeshholay

Editors: Please introduce yourself to us.

Ganesh Holay: My name is Ganesh and I'm twenty-two years old. I live in rural Pune and have studied up to the tenth standard. My father is a farmer. We have our own farm near Pune, where we grow onions, potatoes, wheat, bajri and the zendu and lantana flowers. I've also done a bit of poultry farming. I help out on the farm, since I'm jobless now. The flowers are carried to Bombay for sale, but someone else goes to Bombay, not me. I'm afraid of that notorious city. I've strayed enough, and if I start frequenting a city like Bombay, god knows what will happen to me. My mother died when I was a child of six or seven. She was electrocuted at her place of work in the village on a rainy day. I have an elder brother and two elder sisters. I'm the youngest kid. One of my sisters got married at the age of fourteen or fifteen.

Editors: When you first attained puberty, whom were you sexually attracted to—girls or boys?

Holay: It was girls and boys both. I had an equal preference for both.

Editors: Was there any specific episode that started to draw you to people of your own sex, that triggered it off, so to speak?

Holay: It started in the usual way—schoolboys discovering and exploring their bodies. We were thirteen years old. That's when I first learned about masturbation. Village life offers ample scope to experiment. There are open fields all around and at night it's dark. One can indulge in forbidden activity without being caught. Besides, when boys hang out together, no one suspects what they might be up to. It's different if there are girls as well—then everyone sort of instinctively knows what's going on. Also, there's minimal parental control in villages, especially in the case of boys. We are free to do as we please. So you may say I received all my sex education from my classmates at school.

Editors: As you say, it's common for adolescents to experiment with their bodies. But in your case, it helped you discover something about yourself: that you were homosexually inclined.

Holay: Yes, I discovered that unlike the other boys, I was attracted to people of my own sex. In their case, it was always girls. I know it's abnormal (or at least thought so then) and never admitted it to my friends. My fantasies often were of men in the age group of, say, twenty to twenty-five, not very thin, not very fat, smart looking with moustaches. They were also effeminate.

Editors: Was your first sexual experience with a man consensual or forced?

Holay: I was still in school when it happened. We wore uniforms and had to tuck our shirts in. Once, on my way to school I entered a public toilet. It was one of those *Sulabh Souchalaya* toilets, with an attendant. The attendant at the counter was a man of about thirty. He was fair and looked as if he was from north India. He seduced me. He summoned one of his friends, and asked him to sit at the counter, while he motioned me to follow him to his room. Afterwards, I left for school, but throughout the day I thought of the guy. The mere thought of him disturbed me. That evening after school, I returned to the same place. The guy was there, but there was someone else with him as well. He merely smiled. I wished that the morning's experience would be repeated. At the hostel too, I kept thinking of what happened that morning. So I started seeing this man regularly. I enjoyed his company. This went on for five or six months, till he was transferred out. After his transfer, I continued to visit the toilet. I asked his successor where he was (his name was Munna), and he would retort, 'Why are you so interested?' Then, believe it or not, this other guy seduced me too. And he took me to the same room, where he attempted to sodomise me. I was dazed; my mood was off. But I did not stop seeing the guy—I went to meet him after a couple of days. Like Munna, I continued to see him till he was transferred out.

After that, I got hooked to same-sex activity. I indulged in it whenever and wherever I could—at the hostel, at ST bus stands, in movie theatres, in public toilets all over Pune, Ahmednagar, Nasik, etc. I knew the ropes, and sometimes it was I who made the first move, sometimes the other guy. It was consensual rather than forced sex. I don't want to blame the man who seduced me.

Editors: The institution of marriage saves heterosexuals from promiscuity. Since gay men cannot marry each other, there are no checks on promiscuity. Would you say this is true in your case?

Holay: I have never ever thought of or wished to get married to a man. It's ridiculous. I may have thought of having a steady male companion. But I have thought of marriage in the normal sense, which is to say, to a woman. This is for the sake of the family, but also because, like anyone else, I have the desire to settle down. I can't imagine settling down with another man. It doesn't happen in India. If you say it's possible in other parts of the world, like Europe and America, maybe you're right. You are learned men. But I do wish to have my own kids as well. Can I have kids by another man?

Editors: Do you think you will continue seeing men even after marriage?

Holay: I will be getting married very soon. In fact, I might be married before your book is out! My gay life will continue after marriage. I'm too addicted to it be able to give it up just like that. Yet, it scares me. I worry whether I'll be able to have a normal sexual life with my wife. I worry if I will be able to have kids, considering I've been so promiscuous. There is this view that if you shed too much semen, you lose your virility and cannot have kids. There is a couple in my village that has been married for eight years, but they do not have any kids. People think of the husband as impotent and the wife as infertile. They taunt them. I have taunted them too. They are ostracised by village society for not having kids. I worry that some day I may be similarly taunted. I once read in *Police Times* [a tabloid newspaper in Marathi] of an illegal gay club somewhere. The founder got married, went on a honeymoon, but ran away from his wife one night as she laid waiting on the bridal bed. He cut short the honeymoon and returned home. Every night, he would come home very late. Not only did he not sleep with his wife, but he would also torture her. When the wife couldn't take it any longer, she complained, first to her family and then to the police. The police summoned him and he confessed that he was gay. He told the police that he even sold his body to men. The woman divorced him, got married again, while the man employed two men as sex-slaves! Naturally, I'm also scared of being caught by my wife. But I'm optimistic. I'm sure I'll be able to carry on without letting her know. In villages and small towns, people don't give their wives the freedom that women have in cities. If they do, people call them henpecked husbands. I'll obviously marry a woman who's not very sophisticated, so it's highly unlikely that she'll find out about my gay life. Moreover, the woman I marry must also be less educated than me, though she won't be completely illiterate. I detest completely illiterate women who can't even be taken out of the house to go shopping and so on.

Editors: Since you are not very well-off economically, have you ever had sex with another man for money?

Holay: I have never thought of having sex for money. I'll never sleep with anyone unless I'm sexually attracted to him, even if he offers me money. Once I met a man in Pune and we went to a lodge where he lived. Later as I got ready to leave, he put some cash in my pocket. Say, about Rs 50. I didn't want it, but I took it all the same. This was the second time such a thing had happened. Once before too, I met a man in Pune, he took me to a lodge, and at the time of parting he gave me Rs 50, asking me to return the next day, which I did. We had a drink together. I used a condom for the first time as I had by then learnt all about AIDS. In fact, it was this guy who gave me a lecture on the need for condoms in the age of AIDS.

Editors: You talk about 'meeting' these men. Where did you meet them?

Holay: In public toilets. There are two kinds of public toilets—cruising toilets and non-cruising ones. One gets to know of all the cruising toilets in the city from the underground gay network. In my case, I was initiated into this sordid space during the Ganesh festival one time. It so happened that I lost contact with my [straight] friends in the crowd, and stepped into this public loo for a leak. There were no lights inside, and there was tremendous erotic activity going on. Here was a live pornographic movie! I got so addicted to visiting this place that whenever I got a chance I saved money and went there. I continue to go there to this day.

Editors: How do you identify yourself? Are you familiar with some of the words that help us determine our identity? Words such as *koti/panthi*, active/passive, gay/bisexual, etc.?

Holay: I'm not a college educated guy and I don't know English. Yet, I'm familiar with some of the words you mention, like active, passive and gay. I told you, when you asked if I ever have sex for money, that I'm active in bed. Which itself prevents me from selling sex, because I guess for that you have to be passive. But I didn't know until recently, what the words *koti* and *panthi* mean. I tried to figure it out on my own and got it all wrong. Once a man asked me if I was a *koti*. I said yes, and he just left. Although I'm not a *koti*, my ignorance, here, came in the way. The second time someone asked me this question, I was wiser. I asked him to explain to me what the words *koti* and *panthi* mean. Now I know.

Editors: Have you ever been gay-bashed, or been a victim of what is called homophobia—an irrational fear and hatred of homosexuals.

Holay: Yes. In Bombay, at Bhayander railway station. However hard I resisted going to Bombay, I landed up there all the same. I found myself in the washroom at Bhayander station at 9 p.m. one night. Don't ask me what I was doing there. There was a cop in plainclothes. He caught hold of an old man and slapped him hard. Then he held me by the collar too—kicking, slapping and abusing me. We came out of the loo. I was shit scared. There were three of us offenders, and he detained all of us. He took us to the police *chowkey*, asked the old man for his home phone number and threatened to call his wife. At this point, the other guy, the third one, started crying. I was trembling with fear, but I tried to keep my cool. Another cop in plain clothes joined us and took down our names. I gave them a false name and address. The cops then forcibly robbed the other two guys of all the cash they had in their pockets, say, Rs 300–400. I had just Rs 10 in my pocket. I gave it to them but they returned it with a warning: if they ever saw me in the loo again, they would finish me. I realised that these corrupt cops had made this highly profitable activity their nightly business. God knows how much illicit wealth they had amassed in this way, beating up and robbing poor people just for seeking sexual release, while big underworld dons went scot-free.

The second time I was gay-bashed, it wasn't by the police, but by *goondas*. And it wasn't in Bombay, but in Pune, in the heart of the old city. Again it was in a public loo, into which a group of about six to seven guys entered and caught us red-handed. Some of us managed to escape. But the hoodlums got me. They asked me what I was up to. One of them hit me in the testicles with his knees. I squealed in pain. The rogues claimed they were cops, but I knew they were *tapori* types, though they were smartly dressed. I wanted to ask them for their ID cards, but didn't have the courage. After all, they were so many and I was alone. So I apologised. They asked me for my address, and as usual I gave them a false one. They ordered me to come out of the toilet. On the street, they abused me and said I brought a bad name to Maharashtrians. Then they came to the point. They asked me how much cash I had on me. Well, as you know, I never have much cash on me; I'm usually flat broke. This time I had a measly Rs 20 in my pocket, which irritated them no end. They said they would get me thrown into the lock-up. I kept shielding my testicles with both hands, lest they assaulted me again. Since the pimps couldn't extract cash from me, they took away my watch and silver bracelet costing about Rs 250. It was a nice watch and I was sorry it was gone. To my surprise, the bastards told me as I was leaving that if I wanted my watch and bracelet back, I should meet them at a particular spot the next day with Rs 300. Then I could have my belongings back. After that, they let me off. At home, I fibbed about the watch and bracelet. Told my family members that I had misplaced them somewhere in the house itself. This is quite likely in village homes, where there is free entry and exit for all, and friends and neighbours keep popping in.

There was a third gay-bashing incident as well. Once again, it was in Pune in the Chandannagar area. A man who said he was a teacher gave me a ride on his two-wheeler to Chandannagar. We met at the Pune station toilet. Before starting out, we had a cup of tea, and I realised then that the guy was a bit drunk. On the way, we stopped for a leak at a deserted spot. That's when two cops came on a bike and asked us what we were up to. They confiscated our bike keys and went into the *maidan*—it was dark by then—to look for others like us. The teacher signalled to me to run for my life. I didn't run, but started to walk away as fast as I could. The cops saw me trying to escape and hailed out to me. They had caught a prostitute and her client in the *maidan*. They extorted cash from them, and then let them go. As for us, they took us to the Bund Garden police *chowkey* some distance away. They started whipping me with their leather belts. They said they would tell my folks what I did and ruin my life. Then they took me aside and whispered into my ear that they'd free me if I told them the truth about the other guy. But the teacher was brave. He gave them his phone number and called their bluff: he told them to call up his house. He said his wife was also a teacher and had full faith in him. He argued that we hadn't done anything wrong; all he did was to give me a lift and then we stopped at the open ground for a leak. He named some influential person, a politician maybe, whose daughter, he said, was his student. The cops began to lecture me on moral values. Adopting the teacher's line of defence, I reiterated that I had only asked for a lift, and we were only emptying our bladders. So they freed us. As soon as we were released, we went to another *maidan*, in the Viman Nagar area this time [close to the airport]. We were in a mood to defy.

Editors: That, then, was your hat-trick. You were beaten up thrice at different places, and each time you were lucky to be let off. But then, one day you landed in jail. Can you recount the circumstances that led to your arrest?

Holay: I could have evaded arrest if I had a full purse with which to bribe the cops. So you may say that I landed in jail as a punishment for roaming about with no money in my pocket. It happened like this. I met this young handsome guy at a railway station toilet in northern Pune. We went to a nearby bar and downed several glasses of beer. Soon, I was tipsy. The guy offered to give me a ride home (I was staying at a friend's place in the city) on his motorbike. We rode through the cantonment area, which was completely deserted, although it was only 11 p.m. Suddenly, we saw the headlights of an approaching police patrol van. It materialised out of thin air so suddenly that we were caught unawares. Before I could comprehend what was going on, my partner hopped on to his Splendor and zoomed off. There is a pattern here, isn't it? My partners always manage to escape, and it's me, the sucker, who gets caught. The cops wanted to know what I was doing there. They did not suspect it was sexual activity, but thought I was a *chor* (thief). It was a restricted area, they pointed out, and the time was past midnight. Since I couldn't reveal anything, and was drunk on top of that, they bundled me to the police station, where I was inter-rogated. The sub-inspectors there were kind. They assured me they would leave me if I spoke the truth. I fibbed about losing my way in the dark and sauntering into the restricted area purely inadvertently. However, my answer did not convince them. I was kept in the lock-up all night, and the next morning I was taken to court. I was very ner-vous and could not defend myself before the judge. My offence was bailable, I was told, but I could not furnish the bail amount, and I'd sooner die than inform my folks that I was picked up by the police. I had no option, therefore, but to accept the 45-day prison sentence that was awarded to me.

Editors: So, you were put in a well-known jail in Pune city. It's quite an infamous place, known to lodge dangerous animals. What was your jail experience like?

Holay: Oh, I could write an entire book on my jail experience. Though all prisoners are supposed to be equal, some are obviously more equal than others. Convicts virtually treat under-trials as their slaves, com-manding them to perform menial chores, threatening them with dire consequences if they refuse. Life can be nice in jail if one has the cash. You can order booze, fancy food or whatever you like. But for some-one like me, *kadka* (broke), it's hell. I had to be content with jail food, which, needless to say, was rotten. I had to grow my beard because I couldn't shave with a bare blade, and prisoners are not provided with shaving cream. Coming to sexual activity, there was ample scope for it, but I refrained. After all, it was my hunger for sex with men that had landed me in jail in the first place. But all that one hears about jails being hotbeds of homosexual sex is 100 per cent true. Dozens of guys are crammed together in a tiny cell, and they've been deprived of female company for months. Sex therefore, inevitably happens. It's one big orgy with men openly sodomising each other at night in full view of anyone who might be awake and watching. The jail wardens and guards can't do a thing about it. It's that rampant. Newcomers usually have to take on the passive role, while seniors penetrate them. Something weird happened to me in jail. I bumped into this guy from my village, who was also an under-trial like me. I was mortally scared. My folks had no clue I was here, and what if this guy spilled the beans when he was released? But thankfully, that did not happen. On the contrary, the guy was very helpful to me during my forty-five days in prison, offering me tips to survive my ordeal. At times, I seriously considered trying to escape. But the other prisoners advised me against it. I was so distressed that when I was finally released, I did not even bother to collect my wristwatch, which I had to deposit with the prison authorities at the time of my ar-rest. Funnily enough, after my release I began to miss jail life. I visited the place a couple of times with *beedies* for the friends I had made there. This was a precious commodity for them, who, like me, did not have a paisa in their pocket.

Editors: If your friends, relations, parents, family, employees and neigh-bours found out about your sexual life, do you think they would ostra-cise you?

Holay: They will not ostracise me, but will not accept me either. From my point of view, if any of these people you mention finds out about me, I will not be able to live in my house, in society. I will be so ashamed that I'll probably run away from home and go and live elsewhere—far away. But, no, I won't end my life? Why should I?

Editors: What are the sorts of support groups/systems that have helped you come to terms with your sexuality?

Holay: Once in Bombay, someone gave me the number of a gay support group, but I lost it. Support groups don't mean much to me. I'm more concerned about my immediate family and community. I would not want them to find out about me at any cost. I know that they'll never change their mindset and their attitudes. I don't think my own vision of homosexuality will change either—as I said, I still wish to get married and have kids. Sometimes I do feel I've got hopelessly addicted to gay sex, but I realise it's a bodily need that cannot be controlled. I'm eternally scared about being outed. What if my wife got to know about me and told her parents? That is why I never reveal my true name to any of my partners. I make up names. Ganesh is not my real name.

Editors: Have you tested for HIV? You should, isn't it, considering you've led a promiscuous life?

Holay: I avoided testing for HIV for a long time because I was scared the doctors would suspect that I was a *samlaingik*. And I was also scared of the results. What if I was positive? But then, one day, I mustered up the courage and went for a HIV test to the Samapathik Trust in Pune. And I was really relieved when the results came out negative.

Editors: Anything else you wish to share with us?

Holay: Just a few stray thoughts. I don't know why, but a lot of teachers are homosexual. There was this History teacher who once picked me up in a public loo. I didn't know then that he was a teacher. Afterwards, I was terribly embarrassed when I saw him in school. So was he. He pretended not to know me.

The perversity of high-society guys amuses me. I met a man in a cruising area whose fetish (as you call it) was to talk dirty on the phone. He would habitually talk about size and so on. I hated him, but put up with it in the hope that he would find me a job, as he was a high-level fellow. But, no, he was of no help.

I'm also intrigued by this business of paedophilia. A friend told me his cousin sodomised him at the age of twelve. Is this really possible? When his mother questioned him about the bloodstains on his shorts, he lied to her. He said he had shat in them.

I feel that if my mother were alive, I wouldn't have been the way I am—promiscuous and all that. She would put curbs on my movements, on my freedom, and not let me stay out of the house that long, sometimes for nights on end. My father, being a man, was busy with his own affairs and didn't have much time for us kids.

16
rajachandraratne

Editors: Please introduce yourself to us.

Raja Chandraratne: I'm Raja Chandraratne from Colombo, Sri Lanka. I'm a homosexual in my late twenties, with a postgraduate degree from the university and a job in a local newspaper. I live with my parents, close to Colombo city. I'm quite deeply into homosexuality and have led a somewhat debauched, promiscuous life so far. No, I'm not married and have not thought of marriage yet. In Sri Lanka, it's quite common for men to marry late. I believe I'm good-looking and handsome, and desirable to all the young men I make out with. Actually, I'm quite proud of my personality and even my sexuality.

Editors: When did you first become aware that you were homosexual?

Chandraratne: I first became aware of it in my teens. There were many others like me in school, in the neighbourhood, and so forth. We used to roam the beaches in search of older men who looked for boys. Most of these were Western tourists, and we heard that they paid young boys money to have sex with them. We ourselves hardly received any money from our parents who scarcely managed to make ends meet. The prospect of earning a bit of pocket money on the side seemed attractive. But it wasn't money that was the compelling factor. Our bodies burned with sexual passion and we sought an outlet for release. We turned to boys rather than girls because boys were accessible, whereas girls weren't. The only 'available' women we knew of were the prostitutes in the red-light areas, to whom we would have to pay money. That put us off. Money was one thing that was eternally in short supply. I also loved boys because I was in love with myself, and wanted to sleep with those who were like me, with penises that I was crazy about, rather than with those who were different, with boobs and cunts.

Editors: Since that time, have you mainly depended on casual encounters for gratification?

Chandraratne: Yes and no. I mean, I do have a lot of casual sex and spare no opportunity to have sex whenever I can, with whoever it is, provided the person is sexually attractive to me. But I have also had steady boyfriends. One of them was from the Netherlands and was a student at the university. We were classmates. But when I say we were steady boyfriends, I don't mean that we'd forfeited our freedom. I've cruised guys in front of him, but he did not have a problem with this. Rather, he encouraged me. He knew he was in Sri Lanka for a short time and would return to his country after receiving his degree. For the past couple of years, I've become addicted to cruising on the Internet and this works wonderfully for me. I also chat with men in India and frequently toy with the idea of travelling to India, which I can only do when I have the funds. I sometimes invite the Indians I know to Sri Lanka, but that too is easier said than done, because they're afraid to come here on account of the political situation. But all in all, I have a good time.

Editors: Why don't you ever see yourself as having a long-term relationship with a man?

Chandraratne: Gay sex is recreational sex. Why introduce tension into something that is enjoyable while it lasts, and comes with no strings attached? In Sri Lanka, many men turn to other men in order to escape the tyranny of marriage. An extramartial affair with a woman is different, because women by nature tend to be different. They want commitment. There is the fear of unwanted pregnancies. Gay sex is liberating precisely because it's free of these encumbrances. It's also transgressive sex and both the partners involved know this fully well. Where's the question, then, of entering into a long-term relationship, which goes against its very grain? Except for the activists, your average gay man does not want to come out of the closet. He's happy as he is. A long-term relationship may do just that—bring him out of the closet against his will, because people will notice and start gossiping about him. For me, personally, the best thing about gay friendships is that they are open-ended friendships, and when they end, they end without the mess that usually accompanies the break-up of a marriage or even an extramarital or premarital man–woman relationship. I've also observed that the above perception is shared by all straight-looking and straight-acting gay men like myself, whereas with the queers—no offence meant—it's the opposite. They tend to be more like women, and like lesbians, who prefer to enter into committed and long-term relationships with other men or women. I say this as a purely descriptive thing, and it isn't my intention to condemn the actions of the queers. It's also true that these things are complicated, and in the last analysis, one cannot generalise.

Editors: I guess marriage is compulsory in Sri Lanka, as it is in India. Do you plan to get married? If you don't wish to get married, will you be able to pull it off?

Chandraratne: Marriage, no doubt, is compulsory in Sri Lanka, but that is truer in the case of girls than boys. A boy can stay single all his life, and it will not be seen as odd. However, what makes you think I won't get married? As I said, gay sex is recreational sex. Marriage, on the other hand, is needed in order to settle down in life and put the brakes on one's wayward ways. Marriages are usually arranged by one's parents and we just comply. In my case, the choice will be entirely mine. When I'm ready for marriage, after I have a job and so on, I will say so to my parents and they'll do the needful. But they won't tell me *when* to get married, and if in the future I change my mind and decide to stay single all my life, that decision too will be mine and entirely mine, and no one, not even my parents, will have the right to interfere in my personal life and influence my decisions.

Editors: Will a day come when you might begin to see sexuality as a part of your personal politics?

Chandraratne: I can't say. One is of course influenced by one's environment, and there's a fair amount of gay activism in Sri Lanka that so far hasn't crept into my life, but who knows whether or not it will in the future, as I grow older. Right now, I'm not a member of any support group, some of whom have been holding international conferences on the island, and nor do I attend their meetings as a casual visitor. I guess for that to happen, one has to begin seeing one's sexuality as something that shapes one's identity. But right now, I see my sexual orientation only as a sexual preference and certainly not as something that shapes my identity, which is shaped by other things like the fact that I'm Sinhalese, Buddhist by religion, an urban Sri Lankan and a student. Maybe my homosexuality shapes it too, but to a relatively smaller extent. But it's possible that this will change in the future, and that I will begin to see my sexual orientation as something that defines my identity in a significant way, and then I might see the need to join the support groups, and make sexuality a part of my personal politics, as you put it. For that to happen, I must be convinced that I'm gay, totally unattached to the opposite sex, but even this is something of which I'm not entirely certain yet. I'm still trying to find out.

Editors: In your opinion, is it okay to lead a double life all one's life?

Chandraratne: It's okay as long as society continues to be what it is. We do not inhabit an ideal world. There are no utopias. So hypocrisy and deceit will naturally prevail. If I'm gay and closeted, I know I have to go round being on my guard at all times. To some, this may seem like a pain. They have to continue living their lie all their lives, and have to invest too much energy in ensuring that the cat is never out of the bag. This might prevent them from concentrating on other things, work, the family, etc., and might come in the way of their savouring life to the fullest. But, personally, I have quite come to enjoy the double life I lead. It's exciting and it's also a challenge because I'm like a chess player who has to plan my moves in such a way that I'm never checkmated. (Actually, I'm quite found of chess and play it whenever I have the chance.) What you must understand is that for most Sri Lankan and other gays, the trouble they might have to take to lead a double life is much less of a hassle than being outed as homosexuals. We need to respect their perceptions, given the circumstances in which we live, rather than sit in judgement. Everyone can't be like the activists and the leaders of the gay movement, who, no doubt, are very brave and are taking considerable risks to make life better for future generations of gays. But why should everyone be a leader? People have got to be practical. If tomorrow I stop leading a double life and announce from the rooftops that I'm gay, what do you think will happen? My family and I will be ostracised by our friends, relatives and neighbours. No one will come forward with a marriage proposal. I'll never get a job in a university or elsewhere. I'll become an object of ridicule whenever I go. I might also attract the law enforcing agencies like the police, who are perpetually on the look out for young men who service Western sex tourists, to be found in Sri Lanka in plenty.

Editors: Does the sex tourism in Sri Lanka make you unhappy?

Chandraratne: You know, I do not wish to take an overly moral view and condemn prostitution—all forms of it—as something that is despicable. Even if it is, it is after all a source of income, livelihood even, to many who are jobless and whose parents, having given them birth, have failed to do anything for them. What is the profile of the young men in Sri Lanka who service wealthy Western sex tourists? They are usually in the age group of eighteen to twenty-five. They may or may not be college educated. Always, they're from homes and families that are not economically well-off. They're mostly unemployed, having tried but failed to find employment, and nor has the government done anything for them. There is no unemployment allowance here as in many Western countries. Literally, these guys are pushed to the wall and turn to sex tourism out of sheer desperation. Of course, I don't mean to suggest that they don't enjoy the sex part of it. You must realise that most of them would be gay or bisexual to start with and, therefore, consider sex tourism as an option, which an exclusively straight guy may not, though you will be surprised to know that there are wealthy Western women too who want to be serviced by young men. The Western tourist is preferred to a native Sri Lankan because he's exotic to us, and all of us in the subcontinent, India included, still tend to fetishise white skin. He's rich and is able to pay us in cash and kind —what no Sri Lankan ever can. A lot of them even part with things like laptops in exchange for sexual gratification, massages, etc. The Western tourist is also safe because he's here for a short time, and there's no danger of his coming into contact with our family members and so on, more so as he speaks only English and doesn't know the local language. So there's no danger of our activities becoming public. For some of us luckier ones, it also becomes a means of escaping the tyrannies of the island, what with the political situation in Sri Lanka being forever so volatile, and emigrating to the West.

Editors: As a university student in Colombo, would you like to see sexuality studies acquire the status of an academic discipline, as it has in universities abroad?

Chandraratne: At this point, I have no likes or dislikes about the courses we are taught at the university. In my case, I've finished my M.A. and am about to register for my Ph.D. I simply don't know whether sexuality studies should be taught or not. Our professors are supposedly more learned and more experienced than us and it is for them to decide. Having said that, I must concede that if sexuality studies were a subject on the syllabus, I for one, would certainly opt for it. It is through education, after all, that awareness is generated, and the mindset of people undergoes a sea change. The introduction of a subject like sexuality studies in the M.A. syllabus might work wonders in terms of dispelling all the myths that people have about sexuality, homosexuality, and so on. In turn, it might help more and more young men and women, especially those who are queer, to come to terms with their sexuality, and eventually to come out of the closet. So the effects of introducing it can be far-reaching. However, we must ensure that we have qualified faculty to teach the subject, and also that we have enough funds to import books from abroad. Most faculty members in Sri Lankan universities are conservative to the core, and haven't bothered to update their knowledge since their own postgraduate days. I can't imagine them agreeing to teach a subject like sexuality studies with the sensitivity and the expertise that is required. Nor are university libraries well equipped and well stocked with the latest books and journals. Thus, introducing sexuality studies may remain only a pipe dream. Do Indian universities have it as a subject on the syllabus? I've gone through the syllabus of many of them on the internet, but can't remember seeing it listed. I know, of course, that the University of Pune offers two courses in alternative literature, one of which is lesbian and gay literature.

Editors: Have you read Shyam Selvadurai's *Funny Boy*? What do you think of the novel?

Chandraratne: This sounds like an exam question! But jokes aside, I like the novel very much. It's the first gay novel to come out of Sri Lanka and it has done us all proud. I regard Selvadurai as the Alan Hollinghurst of Sri Lanka. It's brilliant the way the author tries to bring the two things that marginalise and victimise his protagonist—his ethnicity and his homosexuality—together. More than all the activist and gay support groups, it is Shyam Selvadurai who is able to politicise sexuality through this novel. On reading it, I realised for the first time that sexuality too could be political. However, I cannot empathise with the protagonist Arjie entirely, because he, like author Selvadurai himself, belongs to the Tamil minority, whereas I am Sinhalese. So although I might go through the same things that he does on account of my sexual orientation, I won't be persecuted on account of my ethnicity, because here I am the persecutor, so to speak, for I'm part of the Sinhala majority. I must also confess that personally, I don't find myself sympathetic to the Tamil cause. I mean these guys are traitors because they seem to have greater affinities with the Tamils of Tamil Nadu in India, rather than with fellow Sri Lankans. They want to secede from the island and form their own independent Tamil Eelam. Tell me, are you sympathetic to the Kashmiris who want to break away from the Union of India? It's likewise with us in Sri Lanka. *Funny Boy*, of course, wants us to see the two things—the ethnic conflict and homosexuality—as no different from each other. But they are different, aren't they? As a literary strategy, it works, but in actual practice, I'm not sure if one's race and one's sexuality are, at the end of the day, the same thing.

Editors: Although you are Sinhalese, and not Tamil like Arjie, in *Funny Boy*, emigration to the West (Canada) liberates Arjie. Have you ever thought of emigrating to the West?

Chandraratne: Arjie and his family have to emigrate to Canada because they're a part of the Tamil minority. They go as refugees seeking asylum. I don't think that's a very dignified way to migrate—being hounded out of one's motherland on account of one's race and ethnicity. If you recall, Arjie has mixed feelings about leaving the island. His father too is apprehensive about living as what he calls a second-class citizen in a foreign country. Only his mother is reconciled to the idea because as a woman in a patriarchal, male-dominated society, it doesn't matter to her where she is, for her lot will be the same no matter where she lives; she will forever be the oppressed victim. In my case, I'm aware that my ethnicity and my sexuality are in conflict. I mean, as someone who's a part of the Sinhala majority, I have no need to leave the country. But as someone who is gay, yes, I can seek asylum in the West in order to escape persecution at home. I can live an openly gay life there, the way Shyam Selvadurai has been able to do. However, the West is no unmixed blessing. What about the racial prejudice that exists there? What if I become a target of racism? Isn't it like going from the frying pan to the fire, or from the devil to the deep blue sea? Besides, visas are no longer that easy to obtain for Sri Lankans in particular, and for South Asians in general, as it was in Selvadurai's time in the early 1980s. And what do I do once I get there? I can study, provided I get a scholarship, but after that what? Can I be guaranteed employment? Shyam Selvadurai is able to live by his pen because he's a gifted writer. I'm pretty average. I might just have to live selling my body to white folks. That I can do right here in Sri Lanka anyways, to, say, the North American Man Boy Love Association (NAMBLA) guys. So why take the trouble of packing my bags?

Editors: Is it easier for you to be gay because you are Buddhist by religion, than it would be if you were, say, Christian or Muslim?

Chandraratne: Buddhism, as far as I know, is silent on the subject of homosexuality, and unlike Islam and Christianity, doesn't prescribe a set of moral dos and don'ts for its followers. To that extent, it is easier. But that doesn't mean that either Mahayana or Hinayana Buddhism lend their tacit support to any kind of deviant sexual behaviour. I guess any religion, no matter which one, is in the last analysis opposed to homosexuality because it does not lead to the birth of children. Even Hinduism is no exception to this rule, though it outwardly pretends to be more liberal and more tolerant than most other religions. Personally, I'm not very orthodox. Like many young people all over the world today,

I'm born into a certain religion, but beyond that it doesn't assume too much significance in my day-to-day life.

Editors: In your emails to us, you are usually very guarded. Why?

Chandraratne: Sri Lanka's sex tourism has alerted the police, etc., who are forever on the lookout for foreigners as well as the locals who pander to their fantasies. The internet is not foolproof. Email accounts can be accessed, and the mails one has sent and received can be read and used as evidence against oneself. I've heard of instances where this has happened, and I'm scared. True, as I told you earlier, I cruise a lot on the internet. But we use a guarded, coded language understood only by us. We follow this approach even in the chat rooms. Your emails, on the other hand, used standard language understood by all. Your questions were very direct. They had to be, considering that it was an interview for a book. But they got me worried. Many a times, I did not respond to your emails for this reason, and thought you would get the hint. Candid interviews of the kind you are doing can only happen when we meet face-to-face. Any other means like letters, phone calls or emails are fraught with risk.

Editors: Has AIDS made any difference to gay people's sexual lives in Sri Lanka?

Chandraratne: The sex tourism may have come down a bit because of the fear of AIDS. I don't know and can't say for sure. There are no surveys that have been conducted. My impression is that people in the West today are not really that scared of AIDS as they used to be when the disease first broke out some thirty years ago. Although there's no definitive cure for AIDS, people can go on living endlessly with Anti-retroviral Therapy (ART). Of course, they take the basic precautions, like using condoms, etc. With Sri Lankans, on the other hand, there is still a lot of ignorance. There may be a new generation of gay guys that is aware of the dangers of AIDS and has only protected sex. But there are many older fellows who cruise the beaches and other gay hot spots, who dislike using condoms, because, as one of them once put it, 'they come in the way'. At the same time, I have never personally met anyone who has actually died of AIDS. I'm not suggesting that there are no AIDS related deaths in Sri Lanka, but the problem isn't as grave in a small country as it is in some parts of India—in your state (Maharashtra) for example, and also in some southern states like Andhra Pradesh. Isn't that so? AIDS in Sri Lanka would have been a much bigger problem if people from India visited the island in large numbers. Many gay Indians would have come as sex tourists too, because, what with your globalisation, people now have the cash. But because that isn't happening, given the political situation, the statistics aren't that alarming. Do I personally use a condom? Yes, I do now, though I never used them before. But I'm more into non-penetrative sex which is less risky from the point of view of being infected with the virus. The gay support groups here constantly advocate the use of condoms and even distribute them among their members and others. There are now a whole lot of fancy, flavoured condoms available in the market that makes sexual activity seem like a visit to an ice cream parlour! But I'm not sure we make condoms in this part of the world that are really suitable for anal sex. If a condom breaks midway, it isn't serving its purpose, and then it's only a myth that the use of a condom can save one from HIV and AIDS.

Editors: Is there anything else you would like to say by way of conclusion?

Chandraratne: I guess I've said it all. I wish you luck with your book. I would like to visit India some day in the near future, and come to Pune to meet the members of the QSC. We need to have more of a dialogue and more channels of communication opened between gays in India and Sri Lanka. Right now such communication is restricted to cruising on the internet, in chat rooms, and so on. But I would like to see serious issues relating to health, the laws, etc., being discussed, and not just among the activists. This interview with you has suddenly made me see the serious side of sex. I've never ever talked about sex as seriously as I've done here. You never know, after you leave, I might just about decide to go and become a member of one of the gay support groups! Then you can take the credit for opening my eyes, as it were. I would like to thank you for interviewing me for your book and for thus representing Sri Lanka. Please tell your publishers to send me a copy of the book when it's out. Thanks once again and have a safe flight back to India.

17

dariusankleshwaria

Editors: Please introduce yourself to us.

Darius Ankleshwaria: I'm Darius Ankleshwaria, about fifty-five years old. I'm a musician by vocation, the piano being my forte. I earn my living teaching music to schoolchildren in English-medium convent schools. I've been doing this for donkey's years; although I don't have a regular job in any school, I freelance in different schools instead. This brings me the same salary, if not more, that regular schoolteachers earn. I like my work in the schools and am a hard taskmaster. I must tell you that I have a great reputation as a music teacher in the schools, and parents seek me out to train their kids, even though I'm notorious for inflicting corporal punishment on my students, the mischievous ones especially. I have another facet too. I'm a train enthusiast. Since my younger days, I have been building electrically-operated, scaled model railway locomotives and railway cars that run on scaled model railway tracks. It's much more than a mere hobby, and I spend much of my income on this pastime, which is expensive, since many of the scaled model cars and locomotives have to be imported from abroad. In my flat, an entire room is devoted to these scale model trains, which I've modified to resemble the Indian trains like the Deccan Queen or the Rajdhani, and even the Electric Motor Unit (EMU) locals. It's permanently set up, and all I have to do is press a button and the trains come to life. Children enjoy the spectacle a great deal, though the irony is that there are no kids in my house because I'm single and not heterosexually inclined. So that's the other thing about me. I'm gay, and have been so for as long as I know. I have a fairly active sexual life even at my age. However, I don't consider my sexual orientation to be something that shapes my identity, and that is why I have mentioned it at the end of the question and not at the beginning.

Editors: So homosexuality for you is merely a sexual preference, nothing less, nothing more.

Ankleshwaria: That's how it should be, isn't it? I mean sex, of whatever kind, whether heterosexual or homosexual, is an entirely private thing between two consenting adults that happens within the confines of one's bedroom. To talk about it in conferences and seminars, to run support groups that advocate gay rights, to write books of the kind that you guys do; I mean, I'm squeamish about all of that. The only people who have any right to know about my sexual life are my sexual partners themselves, and maybe a few other gay men. Beyond that, I don't see the need to shout about my sexual orientation from the rooftops. You may call me reactionary, but I'd rather see myself as Victorian and Classical in my values. I can never bring myself to view sex as anything but a strictly private affair.

Editors: But times have changed. There's a burgeoning gay movement in India. You are not alone in this. Why, then, do you still feel the need to be in the closet?

Ankleshwaria: Let's say I'm not sure that in spite of all the gay activism that exists in India and the West, any real change can be brought about in the attitudes and mindset of the people. People, anywhere, are essentially conservative and status quoist and revolutions are bookish things. So why should I make myself the martyr by going public about my sexuality in the hope that I will serve as a catalyst and make things better for the next generation of gay men and women, while my own everyday life is jeopardised by my coming out?

One has got to be a little selfish and think of oneself first. Besides, don't forget that I'm a schoolteacher. I'm in a profession that makes me especially vulnerable because I'm dealing with young children. If I'm open about my sexuality, will schools employ me? Will parents seek me out to impart music education to their kids? You see it's also a question of my bread and butter. Discretion, as they say, is the better part of valour.

Editors: Right now, are you single or in a relationship?

Ankleshwaria: I've had steady committed partners off and on. One or two have even been live-in lovers. But these things have a way of ending quickly, because familiarity can breed contempt. Right now I'm not seeing anyone on a regular basis and I prefer it that way. As a creative person, I guess I'm an individual with a strong ego. Compatibility is harder to find among artists than among ordinary people, whether gay or straight. That is why so many poets, writers, painters, singers, composers, filmmakers, etc., have had strong and turbulent personal lives, and romantic involvements that have gone awry. Also, there is the factor of jobs separating people by forcing them to live in different towns. This has happened to me too. A lover and I had to sort of split because we couldn't find jobs in the same city. But I have a panel of lovers who still visit me from time to time. As I live by myself in a nice flat, I have the entire infrastructure.

Editors: You are in your mid-fifties. Are you afraid of leading a lonely life in your old age?

Ankleshwaria: Maybe I am afraid of old age and the loneliness that it brings in its wake. But what choice do I have? Loneliness is a more affordable price to pay than adjusting with someone whom you've invited to your house to permanently live with you. Ideally, everyone would like to have a lover of his choice with whom he sets up home and lives happily ever after, till death does him or her apart, so to speak. But in reality it doesn't happen that way, does it? There is also the other side, which is that we in India tend to make too much about loneliness. In the West, many people live by themselves and do not complain. I dislike wallowing in self-pity just because I live alone. Solitude, which is positive, as opposed to loneliness, which is negative, has its uses, especially for an artist. One can think and work better. One's vocal cords are not overly taxed because there's no one in the house to talk to. This is of tremendous importance to a singer. The thing about relationships especially in India is that they deprive the partners concerned of personal space, which is so important for peace of mind. In that sense, I think I'm much better off, because I can live and do as I please. That is why, over the years, I have come to see myself, not as lonely, but as solitary. And I love my solitude. And again, what gives you the impression that I do not have good friends who are willing to stand by me, come what may. They may not live with me under the same roof, but they're always there for me, and they ensure that I never think of myself as lonely.

Editors: Stereotypically, gay men are accused of promiscuity, of preferring multiple sexual partners to the stability of relationships. From what you say above, about having a panel of lovers and so on, do you think you might be perpetuating the stereotype?

Ankleshwaria: Those who accuse us of perpetuating stereotypes must go into the reasons, before opening their big mouths. It's a chicken and egg argument, because it's hard to say which precedes the other. I mean, do heterosexuals accuse us [of perpetuating stereotypes] because we opt for multiple partners, where the emphasis seems to be on sexual activity alone, or do we lead supposedly promiscuous lifestyles because mainstream heterosexual society is hostile and unsympathetic to our cause, and will not permit us to have the same institutions, such as marriage, that they have enjoyed for centuries? I don't think anyone has the answer.

You are aware that when the Naz Foundation's PIL against Section 377 of the IPC was heard in the Delhi High Court, and the government was asked to comment on the matter; its view was that the Indian society (whatever that monstrous entity is) is opposed to legalising homosexuality because it is against Indian culture. So the accusations are not in order, and I wouldn't pay any heed to them. I'd much rather live my life as I want, and do my own thing. It's my life, after all, and you only live once.

Editors: Do you ever pay young men to have sex with them?

Ankleshwaria: No. Because the moment money changes hands, the implications are completely different. Having sex for money amounts to prostitution, and apart from prostitution being a social and a moral ill, I'm personally put off by it too. You know, we all want to live a lie. All of us want to believe that it is love that leads to sex, and not purely animal or commercial considerations. If I pay someone to have sex with him, I know throughout, even when I'm with him in bed, that his performance, no matter how satisfactory, is only a service he's providing for the money he's going to receive at the end of it. This can ruin the entire act for me. Young men, especially those of the lower middle-class, sometimes ask me for money as a loan. Even this I flatly refuse, because I know it's never going to be returned. On the couple of occasions that I have taken pity on them and lent them the money, I've had hell trying to recover it. I've had to make repeated phone calls to them and so on, which needlessly leads to tension and heartburn. Also, I'm not very rich, and have to watch my expenses and save for my old age. Spending for sex, according to me, is a completely needless and wasteful expenditure. Both partners equally derive pleasure from the encounter, so why does one have to pay the other?

Editors: You say your friends, colleagues, neighbours, the schools you work in, etc., mostly know about you. And yet you consider yourself closeted. Is there a contradiction here?

Ankleshwaria: They know about me through hearsay. Now that's not the same as me openly declaring at meetings or wherever, that I'm gay. The thing about a rumour is that it always gives you the benefit of doubt. Whereas if you've talked about your sexual orientation in so many words, there's no way you can retract your statement later. Rumours and gossip are hard to prove, and maybe people don't take them that seriously and after a while they're forgotten. In my case, there's an ugly incident that took place in my life seven to eight years ago that generated these rumours. Suddenly, everyone seemed to be gunning for me. But before that it was fine. I don't think anyone except my partners and maybe some very close childhood friends of mine had any inkling about my sexual orientation and my sexual life. Another thing that feeds these rumours, undoubtedly, is the fact that I'm unmarried and live alone in my flat. This, of course, is a sort of occupational hazard that every single (I mean unmarried) person in India, gay or straight, man or woman, has to come to terms with. The moment someone is unmarried and lives by himself/herself, one of the rumours that does the rounds among neighbours in the housing society, and so on, is that the person concerned is gay or lesbian. Additionally in my case, they may see men ringing my doorbell from time to time, especially in the after-hours. However, I know something about human psychology. Unless and until one is actually caught red-handed in bed, no one can be entirely sure that the rumours are right, and they know fully well that at the end of the day, it's only speculation on their part. So, staying in the closet gives me that much needed alibi. If I came out of the closet, the alibi would be irrevocably lost.

Editors: You once attended the launch of a work of gay fiction at a well-known library, and were very uncomfortable while the reading went on. Why was that?

Ankleshwaria: It's like, as an adolescent, seeing a movie with explicit sex scenes, with your parents. That's exactly how I felt as I sat there in that room and heard the author read all the purple passages from his book that had to do with the homosexual escapades of his characters. I was embarrassed, especially as I did not know what per cent of the audience was gay and what per cent was straight. I imagined there were more straight people in the audience than gay, because this was a literary event where the emphasis was on literature, not on sexuality. And I assumed that these straight men and women were sure to come to the conclusion that whoever attended the reading, other than themselves of course, were gay. I tried to imagine the scorn and the moral disapproval with which they viewed us, and all this made me very uncomfortable; it made me perspire even though the weather outside was cool and I wanted to leave the reading as soon as possible. Still, I stuck it out till the reading was over, but after that I just made for the door, certainly not wanting to come face-to-face with anyone of these chaps from the audience during the cocktails that were to follow. I admit I was a bit paranoid, but this was in the aftermath of that ugly incident I referred to earlier, and I think I was justified in being paranoid. I guess it all boils down to what I said earlier, namely, that for me sex is a private matter between two consenting adults that happens within closed doors and any attempt to reverse that through literature, art, cinema or activism makes me uncomfortable.

Editors: Do you have any gay role models in India or elsewhere?

Ankleshwaria: Gay role models? You must be joking. I detest thinking of myself as gay except during sex, which is inevitable. I don't like to wear my sexuality on my sleeve. Does that imply that I'm homophobic? I don't know. Maybe I am homophobic. Maybe I'm irresponsible from your point of view, because I want to have my cake and eat it too. But above all, I'm human, and to be human is to be imperfect. I'm happy with the world the way it is, and I do not wish to change it, because I know that it cannot be changed.

Editors: Do you see homosexuality as a perversion and an abnormality?

Ankleshwaria: I certainly don't equate it to heterosexuality. I'm not one of those who can bring myself to say that there's no difference between a straight man and me, because just as he's sexually attracted to the opposite sex, I'm sexually attracted to my own sex. Society doesn't view us in the same way. The straight man is legitimate in their eyes, while we are bastards. Society respects the straight man's sexuality, while it abuses us for ours. Nature too, is entirely on the side of heterosexuality, which fosters procreation and keeps the race going. Homosexuality has no such chance. If god asked me, before sending me into this world, whether I wanted to be gay or straight, I'd definitely opt for the latter. I've heard people say that even if there were a cure for homosexuality, they'd never go for it because they are happy and contended the way they are and wouldn't trade it off for anything else. But I'm not one of those types. If there were therapies that could cure or rid me of my homosexuality, I'd be the first one to enrol for the treatment. Being a homosexual is messy. It leads to unnecessary problems, and to needless pain and suffering for all concerned. It's a curse to be born homosexual, and I wouldn't wish it for anyone.

Editors: How do you find your partners? Do you surf the internet?

Ankleshwaria: No, I don't surf the internet. At least not too often. At my age, I can't be the active man-hunter who goes out to the parks and loos to hunt for meat. I sowed my wild oats when I was much younger, but not any more. Since most of my sexual activity today is casual, I have trusted gay friends, closeted like myself, some into toy trains like me, who pass on the guys they've picked up here and there to me. Since these friends are in the picture, I know I'm relatively safe; the guys I sleep with won't do any hanky–panky. You may say I'm like a jackal or hyena—other animals do the hunting and I feast on the leftovers, though 'leftovers' in this case is an inappropriate word. I also have old ex-flames who might call up and visit me for old time's sake, though once a relationship ends it rarely becomes sexual again. Like this lover in the north-east who will see and entertain me, but refuse to let me touch him anymore, because, he says, he has grown out of it, though he's still unmarried.

Editors: You say your father may also have been homosexual. Can sexual orientation be genetically transmitted?

Ankleshwaria: You know, like most homosexually inclined men, I had a very unsatisfactory relationship with my father. He was a tyrant who made the life of my mother and me hell. After his death, people would sometimes come home and describe my father as a noble soul. At such times, my mother and I would exchange glances and smile. For we alone knew the truth—we who were victims of his tyranny. My father used to have sex with the cleaning women and so on, and with boys as well. I've caught him red-handed once or twice. I think I became gay because of him. If he was interested in boys, I sometimes wonder why he got married and had kids, and made all our lives miserable. But he was probably not gay, but bisexual, for as I said, he enjoyed sex with women too. Maybe homosexuality is genetic, and I was born a homosexual because of my father. I know of families where all the brothers are homosexual. But unlike my father, I'm not a hypocrite. I know how to deal with my homosexuality at a personal level. I have never thought of getting married, because I'm simply not attracted to women.

Editors: Did you ever think of coming out to your parents as a boy?

Ankleshwaria: Well, obviously, from the way I've described him above, you will gather that there was no question of coming out to my father. He was a beast who would never understand, and would probably thrash me black and blue if I told him, in so many words, that I was a homosexual. My mother, by contrast, was a gem of human being. I miss her terribly. As you know, she died recently of Alzheimer's disease. To this day, I'm moved to tears when I think of how she came into my room one morning, I must have been only twenty then, and asked me what was wrong in my life. She wanted to know why I looked so depressed. Then, she stunned me by saying she knew what was wrong! When I admitted to her that I was gay, she said,

> Just because you're gay, doesn't make you any the less my son. However, I would like to advice you to be careful about the way you conduct your life. Please don't do anything that will land you in trouble, or earn our family a bad name.

Such kindness, that. Coming out to one's parents and immediate family is a major concern for most gay people. But one cannot generalise here, or speak in terms of yes or no. One cannot say, for example, that coming out is universally good and not coming out is universally bad. It all depends on the circumstances, and on one's assessment of the readiness of one's parents to understand and accept their son's sexuality for what it is. In my case, as it turns out, I had one sympathetic and sensitive parent (mother), and one unsympathetic and insensitive one (father). It enabled me to see both the pros and cons of coming out.

Editors: Now, coming to that ugly incident in your life, which you referred to earlier—some years ago you were accused of paedophilia. Would you like to tell us about it?

Ankleshwaria: I'm truly repentant about the incident that happened with that twelve-year-old boy, six years ago. I don't know what came over me then. But, believe me, the boy, who was quite well built, led me on. He was after me for long. That day, he came home with me after my music class with him, and wanted one of my steam locomotives, which I refused because it's expensive and part of a set. That's when he probably decided to make a turnaround. He went home and complained about me to his folks, when they asked him why he was late. He made me out to be someone who had molested him. His dad, who is a sepoy in the army, then caught hold of me and beat me up. It's just as well that they did not go to the police, or things could have become worse.

Who would believe my part of the story anyway? They would obviously give the boy the benefit of doubt. After this incident, people began to gossip about me a lot. It was nothing short of slander. I lost my job as music teacher in several of the schools I was teaching in, especially boys' schools. The press called me a paedophile, and the horrible label got stuck to me. Some vicious folks began spreading the rumour that I was a habitual offender who molested several underage boys and girls in Bombay, before moving to Pune. But believe me, all this is a pure lie. What happened with that boy is an isolated incident in my life. I'm not at all into young boys. My preference is for well-built hunks in their twenties and above. Besides, I think it's morally incorrect to have sex with minors, and I totally disapprove of anyone indulging in this kind of activity. If I come to know that anyone's having sex with a minor, it makes me very angry. It violates my sense of justice and propriety.

Editors: Is there anything else you want to say in your defence, vis-à-vis the subject of paedophilia?

Ankleshwaria: Many years ago when I was in Bombay, I met a chap called O.D. I was in a public garden at Shivaji Park with a fifteen-year-old boy, who was the son of a cousin of mine, who had kept him in my charge as she was to go out of town. O.D. came up to me and said we'd met before, and asked if I could place him. But frankly I couldn't remember having met him at all. Anyway, we exchanged telephone numbers and addresses. I couldn't help noticing the lustful glances he made at my young nephew. He asked him his name, and so on. A few weeks later, I was horrified when my nephew reported to me that O.D. had called him up at home to chat him up. I confronted O.D. immediately, and ordered him to keep off my nephew, or things could turn disastrous for him. He confessed to me that he was gay and had a weakness for very young boys, sometimes as young as ten years old! I got the impression he was testing me to see if I could become a paedophile like him. But I was genuinely disgusted by what he disclosed to me, and before we parted, I advised him to stop his activities immediately, if he did not want to end up in jail. A few years later I happened to be in Bombay again, and was shocked to see O.D.'s name in the newspapers one morning. It was a news item in which the reporter cautioned people against O.D., especially people with young male kids, because he was a confirmed paedophile and homosexual. So many young boys had become his victims. I remembered my young nephew, and thought of how lucky we had been to escape the beastly, carnal instincts of this sexual pervert. There are people who, after the incident with the twelve-year-old boy, started to think of me as a sort of O.D. But I cross my heart, it's not the truth. I abhor people like O.D. and also hate myself for temporarily getting carried a way by the charms of that cunning kid. I had never done anything like that before, and never since. Does that still make me a paedophile?

Editors: You are a train aficionado and your hobby is to make and run model trains. To the extent that this is a childish or adolescent pastime—playing with toys—are homosexuals frequently men who have remained trapped in their adolescence, and not grown up?

Ankleshwaria: People laugh at my hobby. They tell me that playing with trains implies I've never grown up. Now you go and link that to my gayness! So what you're saying is that all adolescents go through a homosexual phase, and in my case, since my adolescence lingered on to becomes a chronic condition, so did my homosexuality. Who do you think you are, Freud the second?

Editors: Another essentialist question. You are an accomplished pianist. Do creative people, rather than non-creative people, tend to be gay?

Ankleshwaria: Well certainly, some of the world's most legendary musicians, poets, pianists, painters, etc., were gay. Michelangelo was gay, and so was Shakespeare, also the singer George Michael. But that doesn't mean, of course, that homosexuality is restricted only to creative geniuses. There are any number of down-market, non-creative people who are homosexual. A visit to an internet site, or a public park, or a cruising loo will establish that without doubt. Equally, lots of creative people in all fields are straight. One cannot generalise. However, in my own case, I do see a distinct link between my creativity and my sexual orientation. What that link is I can't exactly say, but I know at an intuitive level that it exists. I know that I'm attracted to members of my own sex, rather than the opposite sex, because I'm artistically inclined. Even my obsession with trains, come to think of it, is transformed into a creative pursuit when I build scaled models of them. Rather than an adolescent thing, therefore, I see it more as proof of my creativity.

Editors: You distance yourself from gay activism. And yet, when you were accused of paedophilia and ostracised by society, it is these very gay support groups you turned to for succour.

Ankleshwaria: I'm not opposed to gay activism per se. It's just that I do not wish to be involved in it, because as I said earlier, there's too much at stake. LGBT activists are brave souls, and I admit that I'm not brave. But I'm not ungrateful either. I acknowledge the help provided to me by some gay groups during those difficult times in the aftermath of the paedophilia charge. In return, I'm willing to do anything for these groups in my personal capacity. It's just that I do not wish to be recognised as a gay man, which membership of any of these groups instantly assures. You may call me a hypocrite if you like, but that's how it is.

Editors: Because of your light skin, you are often mistaken for a foreigner. What are the personal and political implications of this?

Ankleshwaria: I have no clue what the political implications are. That is for intellectuals like you to figure out. I guess you'll call me colonial and all that. Personally, resembling a foreigner, since I'm very fair, is beneficial because it ensures that I'm never without company whenever I need it. We in India, as you know, tend to exoticise, eroticise and fetishise foreigners. Straight men might do this to foreign women, and gays to foreign men. A lot of young men in India, especially from the working class, but others as well, chat me up because of my mistaken identity. They think they're talking to a European, and are surprised when I speak to them in Hindi. As someone they believe is a foreigner, I am to them the other, the outsider. Being the other is a prerequisite for romance as you [R. Raj Rao] once said. I cash in on this because I'm certainly not the one to look a gift horse in the mouth. The lord be praised for giving me light skin.

Editors: You particularly fancy men from the north-east of India, and have had one or two serious relationships with men from this part of the country. Why didn't any of them blossom into something permanent?

Ankleshwaria: I answered this question earlier, didn't I? I mean, the one about relationships. As for this guy from the north-east, well, he just turned fickle. We were in a great relationship while we lived in the same city, but god knows what came over him once he returned to his home-town. A few years after he went back, I happened to be in the north-east and I visited him. But there was a complete volte-face on his part. He emphasised that we were friends, but as far as the sexual thing went, he simply did not want it anymore. Nor did he give me any reasons for the turnaround. And mind you, it's not as if he was married and suddenly decided that enough was enough, as far as homosexuality was concerned. He was single, and I know for sure that he's exclusively homosexual, not bisexual like so many others. It wasn't likely that he had found another partner either. But this sort of fickleness, in my experience, is common among gay men. They're suddenly seized by guilt, or something that makes them see what they've been doing as sinful and immoral. Society, religion, the family, etc., are to blame for the self-doubt that homosexuals often feel.

Editors: You have many straight friends too. What is their attitude to you? Is it one of respect and admiration, or do they make fun of you behind your back?

Ankleshwaria: Like anyone else, I have a few trusted friends, several of them family or childhood friends, who will stand by me come what may. They were a pillar of strength and support to me when the whole world started to call me a paedophile. Had it not been for them, I might have even contemplated suicide. To these people, my sexuality is of no concern—it's me as a person that they care for. I'm not suggesting they're liberated. They may or may not approve of homosexuality in general, but in my case it doesn't matter to them, because it's me who's more important, not my sexual orientation. Then there are many others whom I may meet at the work place and so on, who might pretend to be my friends, but who might bitch about me behind my back. Such people are not real friends, but colleagues, professional acquaintances, etc., who are good to you on your face merely out of politeness. But I'm not the only homosexual to experience this sort of hypocrisy. I guess every single homosexual or lesbian anywhere in the world experiences it all the time. We've grown used to it and have taken it in our stride.

18

dilipsheth

Editors: Dilip Sheth, we would like to know something about your background.

Dilip Sheth: I am a lower middle-class Gujarati speaking guy living in the state of Maharashtra. I am over forty years old, though I look much younger than that because I am slim. I am unmarried. Usually, people do not associate those from the lower middle-class with higher education, but it is different in my case. I have an M.Com. degree, which enabled me to get a clerical job in the accounts section of a well-known college. I got the job on my own merit, without any influence and things like that. It is a regular ten to five job. You may say there are two unusual things about me, given my social background. One is the fact that I am a postgraduate, and the other is that I am unmarried, though I have crossed forty years of age. I live with my mother, my two sisters being married and away at their husband's homes.

Editors: You are over forty and unmarried still. How did you resist the pressure to get married? Does your mother think of you as a confirmed bachelor?

Sheth: I am lucky to have parents who are mild and docile. Maybe I have inherited my own mild nature from them, especially from my mother. My parents were never aggressive. When it came to my marriage, I simply let them know that I was not interested. Of course, I did not tell them about my sexual orientation. Does one discuss these things with one's parents? But in middle-class Indian families, one's financial and economic position provides an excellent alibi for avoiding marriage. I kept putting off my marriage by arguing that I was not earning enough, and that I wished to pursue my postgraduate education. I said that I did not wish to ruin the life of a young girl by bringing her into a home that did not have enough to give her a comfortable life. This convinced my parents, who initially saw it as a temporary thing, and believed that I would one day get married, as everybody does. Then I crossed thirty-five years of age. My father passed away, and it slowly dawned on my mother that I would stay single for life. To this day, she broaches the subject of my marriage from time to time, but I always find an excuse and put an end to the topic without losing my cool.

Editors: The clerical job at the college is your main source of livelihood. But you make money by doubling up as a masseur as well.

Sheth: Yes. But it does not bring me that much of an additional income. I am not one of those five-star masseurs who work in saloons and gents parlours attached to five-star hotels, though I once went to Hotel Blue Diamond in Pune to look for customers. You may call me a freelancer who caters more to the middle class. Nor do I advertise my services in the newspapers, etc. My clients get to know about me through word of mouth. People who have been massaged by me recommend me to their friends if they are satisfied. But I do not have too many clients. It is not as if I am busy every single evening massaging people. Sometimes, no one calls me up for weeks on end and it is me who has to call them to inquire if they would like a massage. I now have a mobile that makes it a little easier, but until recently I could not afford one, and there is no telephone at home either. So the college was the only place where my clients could contact me, and here, for obvious reasons, we had to speak in a guarded way. I could not openly use the word 'massage' while speaking to them on the office phone, because no one among the staff knows that massaging is my part-time job. You see there is a stigma attached to massaging which makes me want to hide the fact that I am a masseur. That may be slowly changing in upper-class society, but in the middle class, being a masseur is considered unrespectable. In my case, my colleagues may also link it to my homosexuality about which they may have a suspicion, given my slightly effeminate way of walking and talking. Hence, I have succeeded in keeping it a secret.

Editors: How much do you make from massaging in the course of a month?

Sheth: I charge Rs 200–250 for a massage. Earlier, it was less, says Rs 150, but I have finally hiked my rates. I massage about five to ten people in a month, so work that out for yourself. It barely comes to Rs 1,000–2,000. Plus, you must deduct what I spend on oils—the customers do not provide the oil. All said and done, I do not make much. Yet I continue. I like massaging men. Everything cannot be measured merely in terms of money. If something makes us happy, we do it even if it is not very profitable financially.

Editors: What drew you to massage in the first place?

Sheth: I think *samlaingik* men are naturally drawn to occupations like massaging and hairdressing because these jobs are physical in nature.

Of course, this does not mean that all masseurs and hairdressers are homosexuals. In my case, I will be lying if I say that the opportunity massaging provides me to touch men's bodies is not one of the reasons that I took to it. I am quite a physical person by nature, and need the comfort of human touch to feel secure, to feel loved. I have been this way since childhood. That is why I always look forward to massaging a client even after a hard days' work. I do not see it as a chore. You may say that giving a favourite client a good massage is as relaxing to me as it is to him, although it is me and not him who is expending energy. The client's warmth is transmitted to me as I rub oil on his body and massage him for close to an hour.

Editors: Did you train to be a masseur or did you just pick up the art on the job?

Sheth: I took a course in ayurvedic massage at an institute in Pune city. It was not a big, fancy place, but my instructor was good and I learned quickly. Nowadays, professional massaging has become a prestigious thing because it has been linked to yoga, ayurveda, etc., and is sought after by foreigners. It is a bit like being a chef. Some masseurs, especially those attached to five-star hotels, charge Rs 1,000 or more for a single massage. I too have a couple of foreigners as my clients, but I do not charge them fancy prices. I am serious about my work as a masseur and I want to learn more about it and improve my performance. Professional training is only one aspect of it. As in any other job, here too one begins to excel in one's work with practice. The more clients one has, the better he becomes in his trade. That is the other reason I am constantly on the lookout for new clients. I am afraid of losing practice and feel wretched when I have not massaged anyone for long. I even resort to sales pitch. While massaging a client, I often discuss the benefits of a good massage with him, and point out how it is as important as a good diet, because it has the capability of relieving him of stress, relaxing every nerve and muscle in his body, and so on. Most people are quite ignorant about the advantages of a good massage, especially in India.

Abroad, they understand this much better. Hence, few Indians take a massage on a regular basis, say, once or twice every month. For most of them, it is a once-in-a-while thing. I have also noticed that as compared to foreigners, Indians are averse to their bodies being touched. I do not know why this is so.

Editors: What is the sexual profile of your clients generally? Are there both gay and straight men? Have you ever massaged women?

Sheth: I have massaged women, but very few of them. In my experience, Indian women are even less comfortable with the idea of being massaged than Indian men. If they do decide to take a message, they prefer women masseurs to us men. The quality of the massage is less important to them than the fact of who is touching them! For many men and women who do not know much about massaging, all massage is the same. They are unable to tell the difference between a good and a bad massage. So what becomes important is who the masseur is, not how he does his job. As for your question about the sexual profile of my clients, well, let me say that my clients are made up of both gay and straight men. However, the gay ones are the majority. I guess this is inevitable, considering I'm a homosexual myself. A gay guy who has been massaged by me will naturally recommend me to other gays. It is highly unlikely that he will recommend me to someone who is straight. Another thing that I have observed, over the years, is that heterosexual men are very particular about making sure that a straight and not a gay masseur massages them. This may be due to what you call—what is the word, yes—homophobia. Somehow, there is this comical impression among them that if the masseur is gay, or even bisexual, they are at risk of being raped or molested! How foolish such an assumption is! What these people do not understand is that the masseur's trade is as professional a job as their own jobs are, and like any other profession, or perhaps even more, there are professional ethics here as well. Any masseur, whether gay or straight, will simply do what his client instructs him to, if he is serious about staying in the profession. He is not going to put his reputation at stake. Besides, if a masseur is gay, he is likely to be less inhibited while massaging men, not hindered by the natural resistance a heterosexual masseur might feel while massaging a heterosexual client. That is my take on the subject.

Editors: For a gay masseur like you, does a massage often lead to sex? Can it be an excuse for getting into bed?

Sheth: As I said, if one is serious about one's work as a masseur, one leaves it entirely to the client to decide what type of massage he wants—a regular massage or a sexual massage. I never initiate anything myself, even if the client is sexually attractive to me. For most gay customers, the line between a *tel malish* (oil massage) and sex is indeed very thin. For many of them, the word 'massage' is merely an euphemism, for sexual activity. I know this and am fully prepared for any eventuality and play it by ear. The situation can get tricky if the client is attracted to me, but I am not attracted to him. But even if he is old and unattractive to me, I have to pretend I am turned on by him and yield, if that is want he wants. It is the occupational hazard of the masseur's trade. One knows early during the massage where it is leading to, from the way the client speaks, undresses, etc. Some may come to the point directly, especially those who have been recommended by previous clients who know that I am open to anything. Some are voyeurs. They want to see me massaging a friend of theirs, and talk dirty during the massage or ask embarrassing questions. I take all this in my stride. I am anything but prudish. Do I charge extra for a sexual massage? Well, it depends. If the sexual activity that follows the massage, either superficial or full-fledged, is enjoyable to me as well, I may not charge extra in order to build up a sort of goodwill with my client. If it is not, I may. There are no hard and fast rules, and, like I said, I play it all by ear. And what you must not forget is that I am a human being too, with a sexual nature, like any other human being, and god has made me a homosexual. I need sex, just like anyone else, and that is one of the reasons, maybe, why I chose to become a masseur. It is not just the client who is getting something out of me. Equally, I am getting something out of him.

Editors: Is the masseur's trade, then, especially for a gay masseur, an alibi, and a euphemism, for say, male prostitution?

Sheth: Perhaps, if that is how you want to see it. But no one likes to be called a prostitute. I do not see myself as a male prostitute. A prostitute—male or female—makes a living entirely from sexual activity. For me, massaging is my source of livelihood, not sex. The sex is incidental. Moreover, as I told you, I do not always charge for sex. What my clients pay me is for massaging them, not for sex. I am sure no gay masseur anywhere in India will agree to being called a prostitute.

Editors: Does your family know that you are a masseur?

Sheth: Actually, they do not. I told you earlier that there is a stigma attached to this business of massaging. I am also worried that if the family gets to know, they may put two and two together, and find out that I am gay. So just as I have kept it hidden from my office colleagues, I keep it hidden from my family members as well.

Editors: Are you attracted to women at all, or are you exclusively homosexual?

Sheth: No, I am not exclusively homosexual. Let us say three-fourths of me is homosexual, and one-fourths of me is heterosexual. If the percentages were any different, if they were tilted, that is, in favour of heterosexuality, would I not be a married man with kids? I must tell you that I do not exactly like this sort of a lonely existence, with no one to welcome me home after a hard day's work at the office and then with clients. True, my mother is there today, but she is old, and may not be there for me tomorrow. Sometimes, I just cry out, and then the realisation dawns on me that it is after all my karma, my destiny, to be born a homosexual, and nothing can change that.

Editors: Do you have a steady boyfriend?

Sheth: How does one go about looking for a steady boyfriend? In our strata of society, even marriage partners are found out for us by our parents and family members. That is to say, we have arranged and not love marriages. It is a cultural thing, and we grow up sans the ability to choose our own life partners, as they do in the West. In the circumstances, finding a steady boyfriend seems like an impossibility. I mean, where do I go around looking for him. I am not internet savvy, though I am somewhat computer literate—my clerical job at the college requires me to be so—and I am too scared to cruise in all the usual places like public toilets and *maidans* (grounds), because I have heard terrible stories of people being picked up by the police, or beaten up by *goondas*, though, by the grace of god, I have never experienced any of this myself. Also, if I have a steady boyfriend, where do I take him? Indian homes have no privacy with the houses being small and parents and family members always being around. Nor can I afford to go to beer bars and lodges, and besides I do not drink much, just an occasional beer maybe. Ideally, I would like to become the steady boyfriend of a rich man whom I fancy and who fancies me equally. But that has not happened so far, and time is running out because I am already over forty. Please pray for me so that I find Mr Right before it is too late.

Editors: Although you are in your mid-forties, you look much younger. How important is it to you to look physically fit and attractive?

Sheth: I do not think anyone likes to be massaged by an old and ugly masseur. I mean there are several masseurs exactly like that, including the ones that, until a few years ago, used to roam about in Bombay's Chowpatty beach. But I have conducted my own silent surveys and found that particularly with gay clientele, the appearance of the masseur is as important as the quality of the massage he provides. For heterosexuals, for whom it is chiefly the massage and nothing else that matters, an unappealing masseur may do. But not for homosexuals. Having said that, however, I must clarify that I do not spend much on my appearance. I simply cannot afford to. My youthful looks are natural, god's gift maybe, and I am blessed with a slim and taut body, which is constitutional. As for clothes, I wear well-fitting shirts and trousers, no doubt, but these are bought from places like Fashion Street; they are not branded clothes manufactured by international companies. Personal hygiene also matters to a masseur, and so I use perfumes and deodorants. In the past, masseurs, especially the Chowpatty masseurs, may have ignored these aspects of personal appearance and hygiene, but things are changing. I also do a little bit of yoga, which I picked up at the same ayurvedic institute where I learnt how to massage. And at home, we are vegetarians by diet. I guess all this, plus the fact that I am unmarried, helps me stay in shape and look younger than my years, and I hope I always remain that way. At the back of my mind, there may also be this thought that unless I look good and look smart, I will not find clients and partners.

Editors: Where do you see yourself, say, ten years from now?

Sheth: Ten years from now, I will be over fifty. That is old, isn't it? I may not have the strength to continue massaging and may have to retire from the job. My clerical job, of course, will continue because the retirement age for government employees is sixty. But ten years from now I will still be unmarried. If I have successfully been able to resist the pressures to get married until now, there is no reason why I should tie the knot when I am older. No, loneliness does not bother me—I have not begun to think of it yet. However, ten years from now, I hope to be living with my dream lover who will look after me and make my life worth living. This, of course, is only a dream, so there is no guarantee it will come true, for dreams rarely materialise. Of course, I say all this only because you ask. I do not think much about the future. We in India are accustomed to living in the present, and not worrying too much about what the future has in store.

Editors: Why do you function in isolation, rather than as part of the queer community?

Sheth: I am completely unaware of the existence of any queer community. It is news to me that there are what you call gay support groups that address the problems of homosexuals. If you give me their address, I promise to get in touch with them. Alright, go ahead and call me ignorant. It is your prerogative as editor. But I am what I am. I am an M.Com., no doubt, but my life so far has revolved around my college job by day and my massaging by night. I am a simple guy. Other than yourselves, I have never come across anyone—and I have massaged quite a few gay men—who have told me anything about these support groups. In all likelihood, they did not know anything about it themselves. But I am glad you have enlightened me, and thank you so much for that. I will make the time some day to attend the meetings of some of these groups that, hopefully, will change my life for the better.

Editors: As you say, you have a somewhat effeminate manner. Does that give you away in your workplace, at home, etc.?

Sheth: At home there is only my mother now, and she is a simple soul who does not understand these things. My sisters and their husbands are decent people too, and would not bitch about me. In office I have heard the [derogatory] word *chakha* (eunuch) used behind my back on occasion. But this happens very rarely. Nowadays, there is an increasing awareness of homosexuality, thanks to the media, especially the private TV channels. So people in the college, especially the students I have to deal with when they come to pay their fees, etc., might guess. But no one ever says anything to my face. I am constantly nagged by this suspicion, however, that they are gossiping and bitching about me behind my back. I hate it, but there is nothing I can do about it. So I have just learned to live with it, and I console myself by reasoning that since I have no proof that people are saying all these thing about me behind my back, it is possible that it is nothing other than a figment of my imagination.

Editors: If there were a cure for homosexuality, would you go for it?

Sheth: I have not thought of it at all. Never in my life have I imagined that one's sexual nature could be changed by therapy. So how can I answer your question? You will have to give me time to think about it. My answer, probably, will be no. Not because I am happy being the way I am, or proud of my sexual preference, as you say many highly educated men and women today are, but because I have got used to being what I am, and used to living the way I do, and it is too late now to change. I am okay the way I am.

19

shivjipanikkar

Editors: Could you give us a brief personal history of yourself?

Shivji Panikkar: I was born in June 1954 in a small village (Kavalam) in central Kerala and was brought up there until I passed the tenth standard. I spent the next seven years doing my college (pre-degree and degree in Economics and History) in small towns (Changanachery and Alleppy) near the village, travelling back and forth between the towns and the village. At the age of twenty-one, I developed my interest in painting through self-training and did a six-month course in an evening class, three days a week, in a city (Cochin), travelling back and forth between the small town (Alleppy) and the city. During those years, I also grew interested in acting in plays, and I experimented in that direction. At the age of twenty-two, in 1976, I reached Baroda to do my B.A. (Fine Arts) in painting at the M.S. University (MSU). I did that for one year and then shifted to M.A. (Fine Arts) in Art History in the same university. I have been living in Baroda since. I did a Ph.D. in Art History and B.Mus. in *Bharata Natyam* (both in MSU), and have been teaching Art History in the same University since 1984. I quit dancing in the early 1990s, and concentrated on Art History, and since then I have published a few books and many articles in research journals. Since 2001, I am the head of the department of art history and aesthetics at the faculty of fine arts (MSU).

I am the middle child to my parents, with an elder brother and younger sister. The age difference between the three of us is less than two years. My father was educated in Delhi and has travelled and lived in other parts of north India. He was well read and well aware of the world; my mother had less education and grew in the same village as my father, but in a less privileged family. My father's family owned a lot of agricultural land, and so we grew up in close proximity to the soil, and within the dwindling and fast changing feudal social set-up of Kerala. My father had been a very intense and dynamic person, often verging on the violent, whose macho, romantic outlook and bizarre visionary traits, I suppose, remained edgy due to his excessive drinking habit. Transition from the village to small town to city was not too shocking, since our father used to take us for long summer tours to other parts of the country, in the south, north and east of the country. The most memorable of those trips was when the whole family travelled to Srinagar through Delhi, Agra and Jammu in 1972. My father loved music and reading English novels, crime thrillers and detective novels like those by Perry Mason and P.G. Woodhouse. But none of us developed an interest in reading, though we grew up with the music of K.L. Saigal, Pankaj Mallick, C.H. Atma, the early Lata Mangeshkar, Jim Reeves, the songs of the film *Sound of Music* and Malayalam film songs. My father took my brother and me with him to the Sabarimala temple for the annual pilgrimage several times. The village sponsored the annual temple festival, the Kerala Hindu festivals like *Onam* and *Vishu*, the boat race, an occasional movie in the local theatre or in the town, and once, a small circus group's performance and a cycle-*yajna* (a guy riding bicycle for a week at a stretch). In the last three years of school at the village, I participated in various cultural activities; won the first prize thrice in fancy dress competitions and took part in a play impersonating a woman. Possibly, this grew out of my cross-dressing habit at home from a very early age along with my sister, entertaining ourselves and a small audience of house servants. Once, my father took me in his arms and lifted me high because I was dancing away to some songs played by him (deep inside I knew that I was performing for him); later, he praised me a great deal for a little painting I had done of a Christian woman. Life in the village was full of things to do: rowing boats and swimming in the river, catching fish, playing hide-and-seek, etc. I loved playing with the girls, (games like 'house-house') much more than with the boys. Several times, I had been severely beaten up by parents for being naughty. My secret sex life began quite early, much before teenage, and those early memories are peopled with older household servants, friends at school, older cousins and teachers.

What helped me to grow into adulthood was my two-year stay at the boys' hostel for my pre-degree. I moved among boys who were intellectually oriented, and among those with whom I shared pure physical love. It is from the intellectually oriented that I developed the reading habit; I used to read Malayalam periodicals and novels. This helped me enlarge my world. Also my imagination. I began seeing myself as an individual with distinct traits and qualities. I had been very poor in studies throughout, until I did my M.A. in Art History. Before that, I even failed twice in the examinations, in pre-degree and B.A. It is the need to shape my identity, I suppose, that motivated me to begin to paint seriously. During those years, I romantically related to women as friends, although nothing happened in physical terms, for I was not attracted to them sexually.

I got married in 1982 to a woman whom I knew for five years and loved very much. She was a sister of one of my hostel mates in Baroda and a long time sexual partner. It was he, who introduced me to her, and soon we were in a relationship, and we commenced our sexual life together much before we actually got married. Our first child, a boy, was born in mid-1983, and the second child, a girl, three years later. All of us lived together till 1997.

Excessive religiosity and an interest in homosexual pleasure since childhood, through teenage and adulthood, was probably a way of escaping from the harsh realities of life. I loved the friendship of older men, for they gave me a sense of support and self-confidence. Or, was it merely a matter of seeking pleasure? I don't know. I became more self-aware and rationalised about these things around the age of nineteen, and since then I became an atheist and also grew self-critical. I was torn by self-doubt: was I a prostitute, a promiscuous slut who slept around? I used to curse myself for what I was, but could never control my hunger for men. It took me some time to understand that I was only seeking love, care, and pure sexual pleasure, and that I was not doing these things for money or other monetary benefits.

Moving beyond religious beliefs and temple-going, I started reading religious books and this led me to consider spiritualism, which I cultivate today as a matter of feeding my inner-self. And I believe that there is much to learn from various schools of Yoga—both in terms of physical and spiritual self-maintenance, or what Foucault calls self-engineering. But, it is the cultural/artistic expression of human beings that has interested me most throughout the past years. But it is not as if I am not interested in other aspects of life, such as politics, society, religion, history and sciences. Yet, primarily, it is art/culture that connects me to others. Among other things, I am most interested in the potential of communication through art.

Editors: Unlike Western women, Indian women don't seem to have that much of a problem with their husband's homosexuality or male lovers. They don't even understand it fully. However, this is not borne out in your own case. Would you like to comment?

Panikkar: Who is *the* Indian or *the* Western woman? Like men, they too cannot be lumped together, having no or less individuality. Each woman I have known is different. This is understandable if you see them through the frame of their location, of caste, class, ethnicity, sexuality, education, profession, etc.

No one, including women, can understand anything unless there is clear and focused communication with a definitive purpose. In my case, I suppose I kept many things open for the other person to understand in his or her own ways. This was also because for long, I was quite unsure about my own sexual preference. In fact, many women (Indian and Western) have loved me, including the woman I was married to. Invariably, they all knew that I have a gay side to my life. Either they showed a certain audacity, assuming that they could win over and change me because they naturally possess the charms to conquer a man, or they believed that gayness is inconsequential, temporary, while heterosexuality was the legitimate form of sexuality. Or, maybe they loved me for purely selfish, sexual reasons. It is true that love is blind, it doesn't see anything else but its own goal, once it realises that it has achieved or that it cannot achieve what it is aiming at, it withdraws. The woman who was my wife decided to marry me, although she knew of my bisexual orientation, because she blindly loved me. She broke off with me in a state of desperation, and by then her love for me was possibly exhausted. When she did that, she had several other valid reasons too to do what she did. One reason was that I was intensely relating to another woman apart from my male lovers. Besides, my health was in a critical state for a long time, and above all, the job she was doing was over.

Editors: You have two kids. Do you love kids? Why didn't you keep at least one of them with you? Can you describe your feelings when your family walked out on you?

Panikkar: On 7 July 1997, I entered an empty home in the early afternoon; I didn't know that something had happened, since most things were in place. But there was no food; instead, there was a note on the table saying that the maid was being sent away. I ate some leftovers in the fridge, and relaxed for a while, but soon realised that something was wrong; the fear was building up. Before I left to pick the kids up from the place where their school bus deposited them, my neighbour gave me a letter which said,

> I have resorted to the last resort. I am fleeing from you with the children...
> If you have any little love for the children, my only request to you is PLEASE
> LEAVE US ALONE... That is the only way you can get any respect from
> the kids.

That was the end of the heterosexual family life for me. Within a year, we got separated legally. I knew that I will not kill myself if the marriage had to end, but I was terribly afraid of the shame. I was worried for my parents, especially my mother, and my sister too had been always in my heart.

I always loved kids, and that was one the reasons I got married. I loved my kids, and I gave them the best I could afford. But when my wife walked away, she claimed both my/our kids. While arguing in favour of keeping both the kids, she threatened to out me to the kids (as a homosexual), which would go against me, against my worth as a parent. She left home with the kids without telling me; the kids had been cajoled to do that. The boy was even told that I am gay (he was just thirteen years old), and the little one was more interested in the thrills of the travel, like getting onto an airplane, and she was too young to realise the seriousness of the situation.

Further, I didn't want to make a claim on them; how could I? I didn't want to hurt my wife anymore—I decided to let her be at least happy having the kids and I also believed that it is not good to separate the kids from each other. Of course, I suffered a lot of pain. I terribly missed my kids. Initially, it was unbearable; the things left behind by them constantly laughed at me, and I knew that I couldn't make any claim on them. I tried several times to contact them—initially through letters and phone calls. But I was not even allowed to wish them on their birthdays. Though I succeeded in meeting them a couple of times, the parting was painful, especially for my daughter. Once I got very violent in front of them, and that too in public, for their mother reasoned out to them that I was an unreliable, violent, barbaric and unworthy person.

More recently, there had been occasions to communicate with both of them through emails and telephone calls. I have even met my daughter in person; things have changed, they have grown up now, but I painfully realise that they hate me and have become unbearably abusive towards me. So I don't try to relate to them or even think of them. Still, in the early years, I missed them terribly. For long I couldn't even look at any children, for I used to become uncontrollably emotional.

To begin life anew was tough. People who were friends when the family was together turned their heads away from me, and I suffered terrible isolation, shame and loneliness. However, I had some friends with whom I could share my pain. But, meanwhile, I was meeting many gay men, and all of us used to occasionally socialise, and for the first time in my life, I began enjoying my gayness freely without anything to fear.

Editors: You were aware of your homosexuality/bisexuality when you got married? Why did you still go ahead with marriage? Does staying single seem odd to you? And, as a highly educated man, did you ever toy with the idea of coming out to your wife?

Panikkar: I surely knew about my homosexuality when I got married. I was not too comfortable about the heterosexual marriage, and was not even economically independent. I did speak about my homosexuality to the woman I was going to marry, so that she could reconsider her decision. But from her side, for various reasons, there was a great hurry to get married. As I said earlier, she possibly thought that my gayness was a passing phase, you know, the sort of things men do before marriage. She was more upset when I told to her about the brief heterosexual affair I had had before meeting her, which was a disastrous experience to share with her, since it had led to pregnancy and abortion. She was very sad and disturbed, but she reconciled with it soon. Moreover, her brother too knew me as a homosexual, and in fact he had encouraged me to relate to this woman acquaintance with whom I had developed a certain intimacy. He used to say that I would get over my homosexual tendencies once I began relating to women. It was the late 1970s and early 1980s, a period just before people began speaking about gay liberation or gayness as such in public in India. I had no access to the international scene. All those men who had sex with men, including myself, were married or were going to get married sooner or later. Gay marriages, permanent partnerships or living together was unheard of, and all gay relations ended in physical gratification, or sometimes a friendship of convenience. I didn't know a single person who opted to be single because he was gay. On the contrary, I naively believed that my love of sex with men would automatically disappear after marriage. I realised through the 1980s that I was wrong; the desire for men was irrepressible, despite a happy married life, a busy work schedule, and above all, two lovely kids and a caring wife. This eventually led me to seek psychiatric help.

After my initial disclosure before marriage, I had shared with my wife my 'problem' of getting mentally affected by certain men who used to frequent our house as friends. It was after I began seeking psychiatric help, and she too had a sitting with the doctor. However, I could not confess my hidden physical relations with men to her. I thought it unnecessary, and moreover, I didn't want to hurt her. She had no clue about my double life of those years, one lived with a sense of guilt and inadequacy.

Editors: How did she finally get to know about you? Was it bizarre?

Panikkar: As per the suggestion of my psychiatrist, since the late 1980s, I used to write my diary, to keep tabs on my mind. I think she was unhappy to realise that I had a problem, but I don't think she bothered to spy on my jottings of those years. But she did that in 1997. 1996–97 was a very bad time for me. I had developed an intense friendship with a woman, which, led to sex a couple of times. But, at that point, what my wife couldn't bear was that I shared a deep intimacy with this female friend. The intimacy was valuable to me because I could freely open out to her and I was still accepted. My wife tolerated much of it, but when she came to know about my physical relations with a younger male cousin of mine, she was determined to leave me. Meanwhile, she also began to spy upon my diary. She got to know that I was psychologically affected by, and deeply attracted to this younger cousin with whom I shared my adventures with women. My wife too was close to him and eventually he spilled the beans.

It was bizarre in the sense that coming out to my wife was not easy. I was by then more open about my gayness in public—I shared my experiences with friends, who were also friends of my wife. My wife apparently hated it for obvious reasons—the prestige of the family. My anxiety to express my gayness also took very bizarre shapes; for instance, during an auditorium performance, when Bhupen Khakhar and his boyfriend walked in, I enthusiastically told my son that this was so-and-so with his boyfriend, which my wife rightly didn't like, since the boy was still young. I think my purpose was to come out, but there was no way, and so it took unusual forms, and it was all bizarre.

Editors: Were you already in a committed relationship with a man when your wife left? If so, how did your boyfriend view the whole thing? And did you move in with your boyfriend soon after? And have you been with the same man ever since?

Panikkar: I had no committed gay relationship when my wife and kids walked out of my life, although there had been a couple of purely casual relationships. But soon, I met a lovely, handsome young man; we spent many lovely evenings and nights together, but on our second meeting itself, he showed me the photograph of his fiancé to whom he was to get married. We maintained friendship and sexual companionship for a year or so. I even attended his wedding with lots of pain, but I understood him, and didn't try to persuade him to change his mind. Other gay friends sympathised with me for the loss of my family; a few thought that I should have acted more discreetly; one even said that if he had to face a similar situation, he would have committed suicide!

The intimate woman friend whom I referred to above had been living with another man. A few other women were very keen on me and

I gave myself to each one of them as much as I could. At the end of it, I was really tired. I began to come out to each one of them, and since the night I met my first-ever committed male lover, I decided to be gay, and not bisexual. This was in December 2000. With him, I managed a live-in relationship for more than two years. But then, he had to take up a job in another city. We maintained our relationship for two more years, meeting once in two or three weeks, but I had to end it, and had to move on.

Since the last two years, I have my present live-in lover. Nothing is certain about our future. He is much younger to me, but we love each other and live a happy life. Who knows what is in store for the future?

Editors: We believe your current boyfriend was a former student of yours at MSU? But after moving in with you, he discontinued his course because both of you thought it wouldn't be prudent if he continued to be a university student. Is this true?

Panikkar: Our relationship is only two years old. Yet, both of us don't need anyone else; we live as a family; we love and support each other. Initially, when we began dating, there had been questions and doubts raised by some faculty members, and we cleared them then and there. His leaving the course has nothing to do with our relationship. I still don't have one answer as to why he quit studying in the department. He is confident of becoming an artist without having to go through the elaborate procedures of examinations and so on. He is mature enough to understand art and how to create it. Maybe it is his inability to be a student in a department where his lover occupies an important position, maybe he doesn't want to be one among a herd of other students, maybe he is not sociable enough, or maybe he finds a lot of mediocrity around and doesn't expect anything from anyone, but simply wants to worry about his art.

Editors: Now tell us, this child you have adopted—how old is he? How did he come into your life? We are told that the child's parents are very much alive and live in the same city as you. Then, how did they let you adopt him?

Panikkar: The boy, Santosh, lives with me and my lover; I am only a guardian to him. I couldn't adopt him, since there was no one from whom he could be adopted. He came into my life accidentally. His biological age now must be about thirteen.

It happened like this: On 1 July 2002, at about 7 a.m., I was on my regular stroll, along with my dog Masti, in the university campus. A little boy was hurriedly walking behind me, and we looked at each other. At first, I thought he was fascinated by the dog, but soon he came closer and asked if I could buy him tea, and not much later he asked me if I could keep him with me. It took me about ten minutes to decide whether or not to take him home and feed him. Meanwhile, I also found out that Santosh was staying on the pavement with his father who was sick, who compelled him to beg, and generally ill-treated him. The previous night, his father had kicked him badly and had not given him any food, and now he was fleeing from him. His mother had already fled earlier with a sister of his, while two other sisters were dead. Santosh also told me about a *mama*, who was living in a nearby part of the city, and who had driven them out of his house. He was very dirty and full of wounds, so, as soon as I brought him home, I washed him thoroughly. He was wearing only a pair of dirty shorts. I gave him the smallest T-shirt I had with me, and then I fed him. He was really hungry, and there were lots of leftover *chappattis*, which he gobbled up with some *achar* (pickle). I also gave him a glass of milk. After that, he came to the sofa and slept off, while I worked on my computer in the same room.

By about 8.30 a.m., I was terribly confused, because I realised that by then I had developed an attachment to him. I missed my kids so badly all those years, and as such I had been wanting to adopt a child. I had been told that a single man, over forty years old, could legally adopt a child, and some friends were even trying to find a child, but I didn't want to adopt a very small kid for practical reasons, and I remained undecided on the matter.

After consulting my maidservant, who was surprised to see the kid (she thought that someone was playing a trick on me), I told the kid that

I was going to take him back to his father or uncle. When I insisted, he ran out of the house crying and said that he would not go back. He sat under a tree crying. The maid herself went and brought him back. I was very confused, and at around 9 a.m., I called my closest friend and told her the story. She called up an NGO (Shishumilap) and they came up with four options. First, I could take the boy to the police station and they would send him to a remand home, but eventually, he would return to the street. Second, I could convince the child to go back to his father. Third, I could hand him over to an orphanage, and fourth, I could keep the child with me without informing the police. I chose the fourth option, but decided to meet an official of the NGO. At 10.30 a.m., I bought the boy a pair of new clothes and took him to the NGO's office. After listening both to him and to me, they asked me to keep him with me, and said that if there was any complication they would stand witness at the court.

I had to go to work, so I took the boy with me to the university press and to my department, and later we had lunch at home and relaxed. At 4.30 p.m., an artist friend called from Bombay to inquire about a paper of hers that I was editing for a book. I narrated the story of Santosh to her and she insisted that I should inform the police. It made sense, and so I went to the police station and explained the situation. We had a tough time in there. To begin with, the kid didn't want to enter the police station. Later, a police woman asked him an insulting question about his mother, and he ran out of the place, and I brought him back with great difficulty. After about three hours of discussion, the guys agreed that I could keep the kid until there is a complaint. After that, I felt more confident to deal with the situation. Next day, I took the boy to a day care centre, and also had a doctor do a checkup. In a few days, I admitted him to a school.

Those days he used to eat intermittently, as if he feared that the food will escape. On the fourth day evening he told me, 'Uncle *aap ache hai* (you are nice)' and I said, '*Aap ko bhi acha hona hai* (you have to be nice too).' It took some time for Santosh and me to get adjusted to each other and to our respective schedules. My life certainly changed.

I took special care to introduce him to formal education, to discipline him and to attend to his health. He could do a lot of things by himself, and that was good. Of course, he demanded a lot of attention, which meant cutting down on my hours of work. Within a week, we had very precious moments. He used to cling to me at bed time. I used to sing for him, and soon he too sang a song for me. I had to confess to him, 'You are as important to me as I am for you.'

Two of my friends were very nice to him. They bought him clothes, toys and sweets. We went to their homes for their children's birthdays. On 1 July 2003, exactly a year after we had met, we celebrated Santosh's birthday—actually his rebirth day. Meanwhile, in the first year itself, I took him to Delhi once to introduce him to my brother and his family, and also to my parents, and my sister and her family. They wholeheartedly accepted him.

All along, our great worry was that Santosh's father might locate him and take him away. Once, as he was playing outside he came to face-to-face with a boy who knew him. Santosh ran back home and hid. I comforted him and assured him that nothing will go wrong, but actually, I was also anxious. Nothing happened, but sometime later Santosh accidentally came face-to-face with the same boy once again, and this time too he ran home and hid himself. Those were moments of great anxiety because the other kid was going around the house and calling out Santosh's name. But then, later on we came to know that the boy who was known to Santosh had left a message with other kids in the colony that his father was no more, and truly, I have not seen Santosh happier than that ever before. We were so relieved.

Editors: What were some of the other difficulties you had vis-à-vis the child?

Panikkar: I took Santosh to the doctor, got all checkups done, and also gave him some vaccinations. I also took him to a psychotherapist to find out if he has any learning impairments. My doctor and psychotherapist know that I am gay, but they don't have a problem, although my psychotherapist counselled me at my bidding about the things one should avoid while dealing with a kid.

I also met a lawyer, who advised me to make an application in the court for permission for guardianship, which I promptly did. All these things were done without much difficulty. But, I had to face real trouble arranging for Santosh's birth certificate. The school gave him a double promotion from LKG to first standard, on the express condition that I would produce a proper birth certificate. I had already made an affidavit stating his date of birth, which was not valid enough for their purpose. I contacted many people; one asked for Rs 15,000, which I couldn't afford at that point. A few said that they could manage a birth certificate from some remote village office, but later on I was told that it wasn't possible. Then I explored the possibility of getting a birth certificate from the municipal corporation. I went to their office with the kid many times, spending several hours, meeting everyone from the smallest officer to the top boss, and finally I was told that they couldn't issue a birth certificate to a guardian. Seeing that I meant business, they suggested I go to the civil hospital and get the kid examined there to determine his age. I did that too, and after several visits and several examinations, the doctor gave me a certificate stating that he is between eleven and twelve years old. That certificate was of no value to the school authorities, since they wanted a certificate showing his date of birth. Then I explained my plight to my maidservant, and asked her if she could pose as Santosh's mother at the municipal office and do the needful. She declined saying that she couldn't tell a lie, but luckily she said she knew of someone who would be willing to lie. And so, a lady was brought, but Santosh rejected her because she was not his mother! Anyway, this lady said she would manage things on her own, and indeed she did manage to obtain a birth certificate with the actual names of the parents in it, and I paid her the amount she asked for, and a big problem was thus solved.

I was with my previous boyfriend when Santosh came into my life—he used to visit us from another city, occasionally. I wanted the kid to call me by my name, but from the day one itself, a close student-friend made me Santosh's uncle. My lover, on the other hand, wanted the child to address him with respect, so *bhayya* (usually means elder brother) was suffixed to his name. My present lover is quite young and he too is Santosh's *bhayya*. So, you see, there is no question of him having two daddies, and this suits all three of us.

Editors: Does your child wonder how he is living with two men, instead of with two parents of opposite sexes? Has he ever asked you? When the time comes, how you do plan to reveal it all to him?

Panikkar: One thing I practised from the first day of his coming into the house was to occasionally make him remember his past. He remembers his father, mother and sisters; sometimes, he even shares his memories with us. He also knows that I had a wife and kids and that they left me. He knows too that I have changed my partner. Once in a way, I show him photographs of all of them. Things are very clear. By the way, my partner too had lost his parents in childhood, so he can empathise with Santosh. We often say to each other that we are three destitutes living together. We are now family while my real family lives far away from me.

About sexual matters, the kid is just beginning to understand. He knows about boyfriends and girlfriends, and I often tease him that sooner or later he'll find his own lover and get married. No, he has not asked me about the nature of my relationship with my partner. Santosh sleeps in his room, while my partner and I sleep in ours. Some day, the kid will grow up and figure it all out. I/we don't have a definite plan as to how to go about explaining it to him. My feeling is that I will be straightforward, plain and direct about it, and I am sure he will still love us and will be proud of us for what we are, for loving, caring and supporting each other.

Editors: We are reminded of Pooja Bhat's film *Tamanna*, where a child brought up by a *hijra* grows up to be repelled by him and rejects him when she finds out who he is. Have you worried about a similar scenario in your life?

Panikkar: Thank you for invoking such anxieties. That kind of situation may be possible in life, but in our case, I don't really think it will happen. In case he rejects me/us, I believe that it will be his loss rather than mine. That is exactly how I rationalised it when I lost my biological kids—in fact, a friend had said, 'They lost the window to the world.' Actually, I do feel that if my kids were with me, they would be better human beings. But I am not worried, because ultimately it is not others we are concerned about but merely ourselves.

Editors: Has Bhupen Khakhar been an influence on you in both your personal and professional lives? If so, please explain how.

Panikkar: Bhupen Khakhar has been very important to me, in my development both as a person and an art historian. It is not as if we shared a great friendship—we were good to each other whenever we met, I treated him as I would treat any other artist, and he too was polite, warm and serious in his dealings with me. He was already a big name when I was a student, but the first time I was struck by his work was when he exhibited *Two Men in Banaras*. Honestly, I was shocked. How could someone paint two men making love so un-beautifully. But, I was excited too. When I realised that there could be gay art, I preferred David Hackney, for he was romantic and lyrical, and his boys were painted more youthfully and attractively. I loved Khakhar's stories for their uncanny wit and simplicity, but many of his paintings were too uncouth or bizarre for my taste. But then, there was no one else in the Indian art scene to choose from. So, I wrote about Khakhar's art along with a feminist artist in 1991. At that point, I particularly liked his *Yayati*. In fact, it is after his death that I felt the need to write more about his art, although he was too caught up within his elite coteries. But I understood what entrapped him, and my present writings on him reject all the existing rationalisations, and demonstrate how he allowed himself to be consumed by the elite art sphere. I try to reclaim him as a gay subject, for purposes of the political activism. Now, I understand the underlying pain and celebration, and the ironical content in his art.

Editors: As a faculty member in an Indian university, do you face hostility/discrimination from your colleagues and students on account of your sexual orientation? I believe you are also the dean of the Fine Arts faculty at MSU.

Panikkar: No, I am not yet the dean, but soon I might be. Since the last five years, I have been the head of the department of art history and aesthetics. It is not hostility or discrimination that has bothered me, but it is the trivialising of gayness that I resist and deal with on a day-to-day basis. As far as possible, many of my colleagues and students want to keep the business of sexuality out of academic discussion—they almost seem to assert that sexuality is purely a personal matter. This may be true for heterosexuals for obvious reasons (normal, natural, etc.), but why should a sexual orientation that is normal and natural to me be considered as a matter of shame to you? However, it is my assertive, playful and persuasive nature, that insists on making others hear my 'stories' and my responses to theirs in my own quirky ways, that disarms them, I suppose. Among all my colleagues, I am one of the best in academics, planning, leadership and organisational skills. And it is this that has made my colleagues and students warm up to me. So, at the end of the day they have no option, but to love and respect me. Moreover, everyone knows that when there is a need to protest or even shout from the rooftop, I will do so without any hesitation.

Editors: Do you think things are improving for gays in India? I mean, there are several people like yourself (or Dr Hoshang Merchant or us) who continue to hold their jobs in spite of being open about their sexuality. Twenty years ago, it might have been different.

Panikkar: Surely, things are brighter for gays today than twenty years back. There is a greater visibility and awareness about it through books and the media. But of course, even today the nation's law prohibits it, there is a lack of support systems, heterosexual middle-class families resist and denounce it, and a large section of underprivileged people are oblivious of its existence. I am not sure if gays themselves are really addressing the issue of alternative modes of family, adoption and inheritance.

Editors: As an art historian and academic, would you accord greater importance to representation of homosexuality rather than gay activism? Or are both equally important to you? Several gay artists and writers seem to shy away when it comes to hardcore activism.

Panikkar: Varied gay representations in all possible mediums and gay activism, according to me, are two sides of the same coin, and both are equally important. I don't consider these as polarities, since both exist in the socio-political space, and both are complimentary to each other. Sure, if certain artists or writers shy away from hardcore activism, there could be various reasons for each one of them. For instance, Bhupen Khakhar kept out of activism, but it can hardly be held against him or his art, for his coming out of the closet through art at that particular point in history gave strength to so many others to be courageous. So, surely, he occupies a very important place in the formation of gay identity in the public sphere, and it is significant that his coming out predates the formation of any activist gay collective in India. I thoroughly agree with Rustom Bharucha, who wrote in a letter to me:

> Though Bhupen was not an activist as such—and his politics can be questioned at many levels—I think the so-called 'real' activists could do with some of his irreverence. Our activist culture is far too straight. A bit of queer energy could be an animating force.

But I do not agree with homosexuals who assert that their sexual life is a private matter and is not something that needs to concern society at large. To me, a sensitive and striking social representation of homosexuality, combined with an activist's purposiveness is what I would personally yearn to see in artists, writers, performers, etc.

Editors: Are you a member of any support group in Baroda? Do you attend the meetings of Lakshya? Has it changed or altered your perceptions in any way?

Panikkar: I am not a member of any support group, nor do I attend the meetings of Lakshya, but I do keep in touch with a few of them. This is so not because I don't support their aims and purpose, but it is because I prefer to spend most of my time in academic work, and also for the day-to-day functioning of my family. My belief is that the spirit of activism should permeate one's workplace, family and social transactions. About issues related to sexuality, I interact with openness; students, colleagues and others, within or outside the classroom, are free to come and engage and deal with various situations arising out of it. With this in mind, I have facilitated and wielded an interventional agency of being gay in the regular programmes of the Faculty of Fine Arts. I would like to give you two examples.

Chandni Bar, in the December 2003 Fine Arts Fair, was a mocktail bar, initiated by the postgraduate students, and it was styled like a popular art site with male performers dancing to popular Hindi music, which was interspersed with a choreographed HIV/AIDS awareness performance. For this, under my guidance, the students of the Department of Art History and Aesthetics had collaborated with Lakshya volunteers. Performing to popular Hindi music was an intrinsic part of the project, and since female students were reluctant to perform, we decided to have male performers instead. This led to problems with the authorities and the senior faculty.

As *Chandini Bar* was different from the usual performances in a Fine Arts Fair, the authorities assumed a holier-than-thou attitude in the true spirit of moral policing. The name *Chandni Bar* was changed to *Chandni Bahar,* fearing a negative reaction from the public. 'Bar', after all, suggests the sale of alcoholic beverages and '*Chandni Bar*' was thought to be inappropriate in a dry state! We were specifically instructed not to reveal the sexual identities of the performers from the Lakshya Trust, because homosexuality is a taboo subject. The practice sessions were conducted in the faculty and these sessions were constantly monitored. The choice of songs and dances were initially left to Lakshya. However, they were later told that certain movements would be objectionable and hence had to be avoided. During the final practice, when a dress rehearsal was underway, the students were told that the performers could not wear clothes suggestive of cross-dressing. They were told to dress either in male or unisex attire. Female mannerisms and movements, which were replicated from the original choreography of the songs, were termed vulgar. Thus, just two days before the show, the whole project came under threat. The students were warned that they had to abide by the rules laid down by the higher authorities, who in this case were the police. Or else, permission given for the Fair would be withdrawn. Songs such as *kaanta lagaa* and *choli ke peeche* were banned. We were told that depiction of these songs by male performers make them look vulgar.

Despite all these restrictions, the show was greatly educative for the students: it told them so much about homophobia and the vulnerability of sexual minorities. On the other hand, collaborating with an educational institution for an event such as this, gave Lakshya a platform to reach out to a larger audience; it afforded them an entry and an admittance into a larger heterosexual social space where they usually faced rejection. The performance thus turned out to be an assertion of gay identity and an interventional coming out strategy.

The second instance was a performance titled *Jism* during the December 2005 Fine Arts Fair, which, once again, was based on issues of gender, community, sexuality, identity, and individual experiences and choices. After month-long discussions and a few workshops, the students of Art History and Aesthetics came up with a script for a musical performance based on the experiences of five persons. These auto-referential texts based on actual people, were choreographed with elements drawn from fashion and dance shows. One of the segments was about the experience of a young man with a queer orientation. The script mixed Hindi and English and went like this:

Male voice: *Kal mere* hostel *mein ek ghatna ghati.* (Yesterday, an incident took place at my hostel.)

Male voice 1: *E, ye kya jab dekho tab kapdon ko leke baitha rehta hai, bada hoke darzi banega kya?* (Look at you, sitting with clothes all the time, do want to be tailor when you grow up?)

Male voice: *Han mai Paris jana chaahta hoon, wahan darziyon ko* fashion designer *kehte hain.* (Yes, I want to go to Paris, there tailors are called fashion designers.)

Male voice 1: *Abbe sissy, chod ye sab, mujhe dekh, mere paas jigar hai, tere paas agar jigar hota to tu ye sab Paris-varis chod kar mere saath* National Defence Academy *join karta.* (Hey, sissy. Forget all this. Look, I have the guts. If you had the guts, you would forget all this Paris stuff and join the National Defence Academy like me.)

Male voice: *Kaun kehta hai ke ladke kapde nahin bana sakte? Aadmi aur aurat mein* biology *ke siva kya farak hai?* (Who says that men cannot stitch clothing? There's no difference between a man and a woman except for the biology.)

Male voice 1: *Farak yeh hai ke* boys like girls and girls like boys. *Tere jaisa nahin.* (The difference is boys like girls and girls like boys. Not like you.)

Music: [the grand duel]

Male voice: [loud] …Maybe I'm different. Maybe I'm not normal. I still am. That is not going to change. I'm a boy who likes boys.
[Music gets louder and recedes…]

These two instances go on to prove that activism and representation are not to be understood in a limited sense. They involve pedagogy, intervention, and non-formal teaching and learning, and in relation to the reality that surrounds and concerns people, mapping it upon real life situations. Students like Nalini Kannegal and Niveditha Kuttiah, who were the two main organisers of *Chandni Bar* observe in their article:

Paradoxically, the curriculum that the Faculty generally, and the Department of Art History specifically, followed covered issue-based studies; here minority issues were openly discussed in the classrooms. Historical and Art Historical studies have always dealt with ancient and contemporary documents which show us that cross-dressing, same-sex representations in texts and visuals are aplenty…While on one hand these issues were part of theoretical studies, when it came to the practice and presentation of related works, there was a need for a sanitised and muted version of the issue. (Panikkar and Achar, forthcoming)

Editors: Recently, the Manvendrasinh Gohil story hit the headlines in newspapers and TV channels. What's your take on it? Is it difficult being gay in Gujarat more than elsewhere in the country, considering how notoriously right-wing the state is?

Panikkar: Lack of empathy, education and understanding of minoritarian issues and struggles is a national problem. Conventions and social prestige command greater importance than an individual's reality, truth and choices, within the largely tradition-based modernity of a nation like ours. The various incidents and experiences of previous years prove this, particularly with regard to the right-wing political agenda. The right-wing surely is oppressive, but possibly because their principal agenda is to victimise people belonging to minority religious communities, read Muslim; other minorities such as gays are relatively better off. The problem is experienced more as a problem, without too much open confrontation and violence. A case like that of Manvendrasinh Gohil can be seen as an average situation that prevails in any part of the country in most Indian families. It takes real courage to come out of the closet and speak up, and no one should underestimate or ignore the pain, anxiety and feelings of loss that such people suffer.

To my mind, gay liberation isn't possible until one becomes independent from one's paternal (or parental) family, economically, intellectually, and most of all, emotionally. Half the battle for empowerment is won if youth can be liberated from the tyranny of the family in these fronts, and are able to live on their own.

Reference

Kannegal, Nalini and Niveditha Kuttiah. Forthcoming. 'Chandni Ba(ha)r: Questions of Place, Space and Censorship', in Shivaji K. Panikkar and Deeptha Achar (eds), *Art and Activism: Articulating Resistance*. New Delhi: Tulika Books.

20

mohammadsoltani

Editors: A biographical sketch of yourself, please.

Mohammad Soltani: As the only child of my parents, I was born in the early 1970s, in an expanded family home in Tehran. After a couple of years, my immediate family, including my parents and I, shifted to a very small town almost one hour from Tehran. The cultural gap between my new classmates and me pushed me to growing up as an extreme introvert. As a child, I was quite talented in poetry and painting. This talent and my introvert characteristics gave me this idea of being a painter, and so it went.

Editors: How do you view sexual orientation, as fluid or in terms of fixed categories like gay or straight?

Soltani: What do we talk about when we talk of someone's sexual orientation? Do we talk about the way she/he handles her/his sexual behaviour, or do we talk about the lifestyle one adopts according to her/his gender identity?

Unfortunately, most of the terms centring on sexual identity and gender are very ambiguous and vague. For example, the very fashionable term 'queer' literally means bizarre and weird, and we use it happily to characterise our behaviour. I admit that there is a difference, but not to such an extent; this is insulting. There is nothing queer in my behaviour. But there is a gay spirit in the behaviour, opinion and point of view of people with an alternative sexuality, which can be considered gay, in the way that some characteristics are feminine, some are masculine, and others neutral.

Editors: How would you define your own sexuality?

Soltani: I am gay, but as I mentioned before I don't like bounding myself in these categories, and gaiety is not just about sexuality; so if we are going to talk about sexual behaviour, I prefer to consider myself as a person (in contrast to homo/hetero/bisexual) with alternative sexuality.

Editors: Back in Iran, are you completely closeted? Are there at least some trusted friends who know about you? Does your body language give you away?

Soltani: As the closet is not a pleasant place to be in, no one stays for long in the closet. Iran is an Islamic republic according to its constitution and its legislators believe in the rule of *Sharia* (there is a narrow difference between rules of Allah and the rules of *Sharia*). But common people are not like their legislators and most of them do not believe in the constitution. So a gay man can find a couple of people to rely on. I have disclosed my sexual orientation to most of my friends, but not to my parents.

Recently, I've heard about some discussion groups in Tehran that gay and lesbian people can join, and talk to others like themselves in an attempt to come out of the closet. These movements are exceptional, but they do help in changing the overall perspective of society in the long run.

Editors: How is Islamic law interpreted in Iran, in relation to gayness? In short, what will happen to a gay person who is found out? Did you know that last year, two teenagers were stoned to death somewhere in Iran because they loved each other?

Soltani: The story of same-sex love or alternative gender behaviour in the new Iran is a long story full of contradictions and dead ends. For example, as you know, according to Islamic *Sharia* (Islamic religious law), any act of sodomy should be awarded the death penalty. The actual act of sodomy according to *Sharia* is to be punished by stoning the person to death.

But after 1,400 years of Islamic history, one can find plenty of gay kings, poets and painters who were not stoned to death. And so in modern times, this sword of Damocles is always there, but is rarely used.

Editors: So does that mean that same-sex activity in the country is virtually invisible?

Soltani: There are places in Tehran (I have heard about similar places in some other major cities, such as Isfehan, Tabriz and Mahshad), where male sex-workers hang around for potential customers. Although the moral police attacks these places once in a while, they all know that this is not something serious. The numbers of couples (both lesbian and gay) who opt to live together are increasing, and there is also the controversial debate about transsexuals—legalising the sex-change operation according to the *Sharia* and the legislation. But simultaneously, transsexual and transgender people who apply for a legal slip of military service face a huge nightmare of insults, abuses and, most of the time, molestations.

Editors: Would two men or two women who opt to live together pretend, say, only to be friends?

Soltani: To give a vague estimation, I can say that personally, I know at least three lesbian couples and two gay couples who live together, albeit as room-mates or relatives. These couples have to be very careful about not letting their neighbours know of the exact nature of their relationship. To give you a better idea, let me tell you a story I recently heard from a friend. She said that they used to have a neighbour who was single. He was living with his nephew on the same floor of their building. The guy and my friend's parents were good friends and compatible neighbours. Until one night, her parents heard the neighbour and his nephew making love. Immediately after that, they cut off their friendship with the neighbour and soon after that the poor guy and his lover had to leave the neighbourhood. This shows how intolerant Iranian society is to same-sex love.

Editors: Are there any underground gay support groups in your country that you know of?

Soltani: There are some electronic newspapers such as *Hooman* and *Bidari*, which I guess have all been censored nowadays. But, as I earlier said, very recently, I heard about some discussion groups that gay or lesbian people can go to and talk about their needs and problems, and make friends and help each other. Obviously, this is happening on a very small scale and as you suggest, clandestinely.

Editors: When you chose to come to India for your education, were you really seeking asylum from your hostile country?

Soltani: Absolutely.

Editors: What has been your experience in India, as far as gayness is concerned? Do you think the situation in India is better than that in Iran in spite of laws like Section 377 of the Indian Penal Code?

Soltani: The situation in India is much better than in Iran. In spite of Section 377, you have freedom of speech. You can talk about the issue, both at the institutional level as well as in public. I have attended plenty of seminars in India about sexuality and gender, some of them with an emphasis on queer theory and homosexuality. So, if you are allowed to have workshops and seminars about these issues, it means that you can increase the society's awareness about these subjects, and more awareness is equal to more understanding, and more tolerance towards the people who consider themselves a part of these minority communities.

In my opinion, the most important difference between Iran and India is about how you can gain knowledge about the issue. Here, you don't have the problem of censoring the net and other mass media, you have workshops and seminars and lots of people discuss the subject in public. A quick glance at a recent book dealing with thirty years of sexuality and homosexuality in India shows not a perfect, but an enthusiastic attempt by intellectuals to bring the debate to the public sphere.

I've read *Yaraana*, edited by Hoshang Merchant, which was very explicit about the history of homosexuality in modern Indian literature. A couple of years ago, Sirus Shamisa published a book called *Shahed Baazi Dar Adabiate Farsi* that was about same-sex love and intimacy in old Iranian poetry. This is a very well-known issue but the book itself was not that explicit. What happened to the book is that the governors and the censorship system banned it and destroyed all the existing copies. Fortunately, some copies escaped this doomed fate, and people who were eager to read the book succeeded in procuring underground copies.

So, you can see that in contrast to India, there is no hope for the Iranian society to increase its awareness, at least not in a direct and healthy way. And, as mentioned earlier, there is even no access to any websites, so we live in perfect ignorance, which is not conducive to progress.

Editors: Now let us talk about your work as a painter. Is much of it gay themed?

Soltani: No. I can say for sure that there is nothing explicitly gay in my painting. I accept that there is a gay sprit in my painting, but I'm not going to push it too far. This sense—I insist it's only a sense and not theme—is there because it is a part of me. It is a part of my life. I'm gay, so there is something gay in my paintings, but I don't intend to represent only gayness in my paintings. My nationality, the beautiful language that I speak, my parents, my education and a thousand other things are depicted in my painting. I very rarely make same-sex love the subject of my painting, unless I absolutely feel the need for it.

Editors: Would you be able to have an exhibition of your work in the Iran of today? Would it be any different in the distant past?

Soltani: I can't exhibit all my paintings in Iran. Sometimes, that spirit that I talked about, makes my paintings break some very inflexible Islamic republic red-lines. Artists and authors have a tough time out there in Iran.

Editors: Does representation partially become a substitute for the real in your case? A sort of sublimation of your same-sex interests?

Soltani: Sublimation? It sounds a little odd to me…Why should I try to sublimate my sexual life? Why should I not just let it be where it belongs, or at least let it go where it 'normally' is supposed to?

By representing my imagination and my fantasies, I try to make the world a little more perfect and easier to live in, at least for myself. I don't try to substitute anything with anything else. This is schizophrenia, and I don't want to be schizophrenic. I know exactly where the real world ends and my painting begins. A painting, a poem and a good movie are transcendental because they come from a sublime and elegant source somewhere inside the mind of creator; so no matter what their subject is, they will be sublime, pure and spiritually beautiful.

Editors: Would you say your paintings come from your imagination or from your fantasy?

Soltani: From both I guess. I have fantasies about what I see and I can't (or barely can) have, and I depict them. And I imagine things that I want and I depict them too. Most of the time I'm not conscious about the source of my creativity. I just do it.

Editors: Several of the world's best-known painters were gay. Have any of them influenced you? What school of painting do you adhere to?

Soltani: David Hackney for sure had a big influence on me, but it is not just because he is gay (which manifests itself in his work openly). It is because he is the best painter I have ever encountered.

I'm very enthusiastic about new currents in Fine Art. I love to experience almost everything happening all around the world after pop art. But simultaneously, I'm very fastidious about the medium. I really believe painting is brush and colour, that comes out of a tube. The new mediums such as video, installation and so on, don't attract my artistic sense. They don't move me towards creativity.

Editors: If one were to describe you as a gay painter, what should assume greater significance—your gayness or your painting? Why?

Soltani: What is the exact definition of this term, gay painter… Does it refer to a gay person who also is a painter or is it a painter who depicts gayness in his work?

This superficial and artificial system of labeling people by just one of their characteristics sounds a little odd and problematic to me. My gayness is just one of the many aspects which make me who I am. It can affect my creative processes just as much it can affect my taste in food or clothing. I don't want to deny its importance in the construction of my 'self', but beyond this I do not wish to go.

Sometimes, my paintings represent my inner feelings, one part of which is my gayness. At other times, I try to show my grief and my anxiety in my paintings, my problems with society that ignores my queer desires and labels them as abnormal. In this case, my gayness will become the subject of my paintings. And of course, if I'm going to make a picture about my love life or my sexual desires, it will be very gay.

Editors: Gay art often runs the risk of looking obscene or pornographic. Does this matter to you? If so, where would you draw the line between art and pornography?

Soltani: Art lies in the eyes of the beholder, so there is nothing obscene or immoral in pornography as it has its own admirers. Creating porn and watching or reading porn is a need, and any need, if it does not cause pain or harm to others, should be satisfied. On the other hand, talking about sex, or depicting the genitals or sexual intercourse is not necessarily pornography. In short, I mean pornography is something that can't be categorised as Fine Art. They are different things. There is the aim and the genre of the work which leads us to call a thing either art or porn. To whom has it been addressed and what need is it supposed to satisfy?

Editors: Has your personal life, including your sexual and romantic life, registered a change after you came to India? If so, what fostered this change?

Soltani: Yes, it has changed. The food that I'm eating here is different, the language I'm communicating in with people is different, and so is everything else. But the most significant change is happening inside me.

I'm not scared anymore, or at least I'm less scared than I used to be. And I'm more aware about who I am.

Editors: So where do you see yourself heading from here—back to Iran or anywhere else in the world, like the West?

Soltani: I don't have any plans of returning to Iran. After finishing my studies here in Pune, I'll apply for some jobs or teaching positions somewhere in this world. Somewhere freer and more tolerable, to go on with my career and my painting, as well as my life.

21

bindumadhavkhire

Editors: Bindu, if we say Bindumadhav Khire needs no introduction, would that be accurate?

Bindumadhav Khire: No, it won't be accurate. Just because I run a gay support organisation and have written a couple of books, it doesn't make me famous.

Editors: You started out as a software engineer in the Bay Area, US. Please tell us something about that phase of your life.

Khire: Well, I went to the US on a work permit (H1-B visa). Initially through TekEdge (Sunnyvale, CA), I worked as a consultant to Informix (at Menlo Park), after which I joined Informix. Since then, I stayed with that company, till I decided to come to India for good (in the beginning of 2000). After I came back, I joined Informix, India (in Mumbai).

Editors: We believe, you were a much-married man before you went to the US. Would you like to talk about your marriage and eventual divorce?

Khire: That is the biggest mistake of my life. I will feel ashamed of that all my life. That one year, till I got the divorce, was a nightmare.

Editors: Are we right in inferring that it was in America that you first became aware of your gayness?

Khire: I have known that I was gay since I was in the seventh standard (twelve years old). It's just that I did not know any words for what I was feeling for one of my handsome classmates. I was disgusted viewing half-naked women in *Debonair* magazine, over whom my classmates used to drool. But I had to pretend that I was just like them, as I was afraid of being ragged. I used to try to masturbate thinking of women and was never able to do so. I would always get sexual satisfaction fantasising about having sex with a handsome classmate or an actor. I would fantasise loving a classmate/a male friend and living with him forever. At that time, there were hardly any articles about homosexuality in the newspapers, there was no internet, and hence, there was no way for me to know who I was. I just knew I was different.

When I found out in college that what I feel is considered a disorder (by reading books on psychiatry at the British Council Library in Pune), I was very depressed. I felt, 'Why me? What have I done to deserve this?' I prayed to God to make me just like others. I started wondering whether I was the only Indian who was 'like this'. If there were others, where were they? How would I come to know who they are? Whom can I talk to? All this depressed me, gave me suicidal thoughts, and a feeling that I am bad, I am a sinner, and I deserve nothing but punishment for my 'bad' desires all my life. I lost interest in studies and my sexuality became the only focal point in my life.

I started hating myself and hating society, which did not understand me (and accept me).

Editors: One of the stereotypes of Indian gayness is coming out to the white man. Although you are not stereotypical by any means, would you say this is true in your case?

Khire: Well, I came out to a bunch of Indians (at the Trikone organisation) in the US, not to a white man. In fact, it was some time before I got introduced to a white man who was gay. He was a boyfriend of one of my Indian friends.

As far as the stereotypes are concerned, all of us (straight or gay) confirm to society's idea of a stereotype in some ways, and not so in other ways. If I look at the stereotypical traits in me—I was an introvert, I was bad at games, and I was emotional. If I look at the non-stereotypical traits—I was not feminine in behaviour; I joined the National Cadet Corps (NCC Army Division; eleventh and twelfth standard at S.P. College, Pune) and enjoyed those two years very much. (I should note that I have a special attraction for handsome men in uniform.) Of course, I was closeted then. It would have been hell if I had been 'out'.

I enjoyed the touch of a rifle. We had very old 'retired' rifles with bayonets attached. There were some light machine guns (I don't remember the name) we used to practice setting up. It was fun. I wished they would take us to a firing range, where we would have done some real firing. But no luck. So, you see we all have some traits that are stereotypical and some traits that are not.

Editors: In America, did you benefit from the queer movement in general or from the South Asian queer movement in particular?

Khire: Well, Trikone benefited from the American Queer Movement and I benefited from Trikone. In fact, when I was going through the divorce, I contacted Trikone. I attended the magazine's mail processing meeting at San Jose (Bay Area) at the house of Ashok Jethanandani and Arvind Kumar. (Sandip was the editor of the magazine. I have a lot of admiration for his work in Trikone.)

At Trikone, I met a dozen or more gay Indian men and women at the mailing events. And, surprise surprise, a lot of them were Maharashtrians. That was the turning point in my life. My internalised homophobia disappeared. Over the next year, I became comfortable with who I was, went to movies with my gay friends, jabbered away in Marathi (I think I have spoken more Marathi in the US than I speak in Pune. In Pune, more often than not, I need to talk in English or Hindi, as many are not comfortable speaking Marathi). This cultural affinity with Indians and the Marathi language in particular went a long way in my becoming comfortable with my sexuality. I owe so much to Trikone.

Editors: You had a plum job in San Francisco, which some would call the gay capital of the world. What prompted you to chuck all that and return to India?

Khire: Well, I had started coming out to my friends in the US. I felt proud of who I was and felt that this is something I had to tell my parents in person. I also wanted to be close to my parents. There was a wish at the back of my mind that I wanted to start an organisation like Trikone in Pune, but at that time I was too worried about my coming out to my parents to seriously have pondered that issue.

Editors: On returning to India, there were two roads before you—taking up a job and plunging into activism. Why did you choose the latter course?

Khire: I did work at a couple of jobs in Mumbai and Pune for a year and a half or so. During that time, I had come out to my parents and dealt with their reactions. My being gay pained both my parents. They felt guilty. My mom felt that she did not bring me up properly; otherwise, I would have told her I was gay a long time ago. She and I went to a psychiatrist. By great luck, he turned out to be gay-friendly. He explained to her that there is nothing wrong with me. Ninety-five per cent people like oranges and 5 per cent like apples. If I don't like oranges, it does not mean that my liking/desire is bad or wrong. It's just like right and left-handedness. He mentioned that my parents should accept me as I am. My mom has, but my father still hasn't. He thinks it's a perversion. (We are on good terms but on this topic, he is not open to discussion.)

Editors: You have made the city of Pune your base. Any specific reason for doing so?

Khire: I was born and brought up in Pune. My parents stay in Pune. So what better place to set base?

Editors: When you set up the Samapathik Trust, you worked in collaboration with Ashok Row Kavi and the Humsafar Trust. Do you regard their work as important? Younger gay activists seem to have a problem with Row Kavi, but not you.

Khire: When I came back to India and started working in Mumbai, I went to the Humsafar Trust and met Ashok Row Kavi. I was very impressed with the trust's work. Ashok told me that he is looking for someone to start work in Pune and would I be willing? He mentioned that he would help me in every way possible. I gave it a lot of thought and decided that I should start a trust. He gave me a lot of support, financial backing, and technical know-how. There are no words in which I can express my gratitude to Ashok Row Kavi and the Humsafar Trust. I have certain differences with Ashok, but any two intelligent, thinking individuals are bound to differ in at least some of their views. It's okay to differ. We are very good friends and colleagues and I love and respect him very much.

Editors: How did you manage the funding for the Samapathik Trust?

Khire: Ashok Row Kavi gave me a grant to start the trust. He also helped me find trustees. Currently, we are not doing well because the HIV-targeted intervention funding is getting to be a very dirty business.

Editors: Like the Humsafar Trust in Bombay, the Samapathik Trust seems to have restricted its outreach work mainly to HIV and AIDS. Is the gay movement in India being hijacked by the AIDS endemic?

Khire: There are two sides to this issue—physical and mental health. There is no denying the fact that Men who have Sex with Men (MSMs) are a very vulnerable population. If we don't have Sexually Transmitted Infection (STI) intervention programmes, a lot of them will continue to become infected. So, this is definitely an important issue. Most of those who fund these programmes focus on physical health. (Unfortunately, the focus is only on 'quantity' parameters; very little focus is on 'quality' parameters. The quality of counsellors, outreach workers, and field officers working in the field of HIV is generally very poor.)

Most funding agencies do not seem to understand (or care) about the importance of mental health. Hence, sadly, very little money is being spent on mental health. (In this case, in some aspects, their hands are tied because of IPC 377. They don't want to be seen to be supporting gay relationships.) If we look at the amount of resources spent on HIV-related issues and the amount of resources spent on gay mental health, sensitisation, and advocacy, there is a huge difference. I hope more funders spend money on mental health, sensitisation and advocacy.

Editors: NACO has recently startled the nation by claiming that the earlier AIDS figures were exaggerated. Do you agree with their view? If so, is it going to make all of us complacent?

Khire: My gut feeling and my experience of working in this field tell me that those figures don't seem right. I have not studied the report and the processes followed for the research, the documentation done, ethical aspects of study, etc. So, I cannot comment on its reliability. Whatever the numbers, there is no denying the fact that the MSM population continues to be a very vulnerable population. I hope the government does not become complacent (especially with reference to MSMs).

Editors: Do you have a personal life at all, or does activism take up all your time?

Khire: For an activist, there is no such a thing as a personal life. I try to separate my personal and my professional life, but it's near impossible. (Personally, I find that activism adversely affects the chance of my finding a soul mate.)

Editors: How supportive are your parents of your activism and your sexual orientation now?

Khire: My mother and father support me in different ways. My mom is a huge support. She even asks me whether she can do some of my work to reduce my load. Although my father is very uncomfortable with my sexuality, he does not shy away from helping me. For example, when I wanted to buy a place for the trust, both my mother and father helped me financially. It sounds odd that my father, who is homophobic, can also be supportive. But it is so. So, despite our differences, my parents continue to be my greatest support.

In addition to my parents, I have some friends, colleagues, counsellors, doctors and psychiatrists who are extremely supportive and have helped me in innumerable ways.

Editors: As an activist, you address the Marathi-speaking middle class (which is conservative in its values), rather than the English-speaking intelligentsia. Does this have a backlash?

Khire: It is a big misunderstanding that the English-speaking intelligentsia is liberal. All classes are conservative. It's just that the English-speaking intelligentsia/socialists/secularists are more hypocritical than the rest. They will pretend to be liberal and accepting a lot of things (including alternative sexualities), but if their son or daughter tells them that he or she is gay (or say transgender) they will take their child to the nearest psychiatrist for a 'cure'. Oh! If only I had a penny for every publicly 'liberal' person I know, who is homophobic in private… (including a lot of 'liberal' psychiatrists). So far, there has been no backlash. I tell my audience my own experiences of growing up as a gay in a conservative environment. I try to make them think of whether they would want their children to suffer as much as I did if their children were gay. I try to sensitise them. As far as possible, I try not to dwell on religion. To speak on human rights and human dignity, you don't need it.

Editors: Are young people sufficiently aware of AIDS today? Is there a genuine increase in things like condom use and so on?

Khire: Nope. We have a very long way to go. Knowledge does not necessarily translate into safe-sex behaviour. Condom use is still very low. It is also a fact that many MSM organisations and funding agencies are doing such a shoddy job that sometimes I get depressed and frustrated. It's disgusting how some of these organisations are exploiting the queer community.

Editors: You have made your debut as a fiction writer in Marathi, tackling gay themes. What connection do you see between activism and writing?

Khire: Two connections. One, my passion, frustration and anger need an outlet. The only way to do that constructively is to write. It keeps me sane, which in turn enables me to work better. Two, you have to reach out to people. Whether it be writing books, writing articles (in Marathi) or participating in talk shows on TV (in Marathi), it helps me reach people who don't know English at all (or very little).

I think it is important to write and communicate in local languages. There is a lot being done in English, but very little percolates to the grassroots because of the language barrier. And unless we reach out to the masses, there can be no gay movement.

Editors: What is your vision of a gay utopia?

Khire: A world where each person has the right to his/her sexuality. A world where Lesbian, Gay, Bisexual, Transgender, Queer, Intersex (LGBTQI) people have the right to marry any human being, work in any profession and have/adopt children. A world where there will be no discrimination towards any individual of any sexuality. A world where there is no need for safe spaces for alternative sexualities. The world becomes their safe space.

Editors: Bindumadhav Khire, is there anything else you would like to say to readers by way of conclusion?

Khire: If you are straight, help us achieve our utopia. If you are gay, first become comfortable with your sexuality, then come out and help fight for LGBTQI rights. Don't shrink away from your activist responsibilities.

Bindumadhav Khire is the president of the Samapathik Trust, Pune.

ABOUT THE EDITORS

R. Raj Rao is professor in the Department of English at University of Pune, India. He is the author of the cult novel *The Boyfriend*, translated into French and Italian, the cult film *BomGay* (based on six of his poems) and a forthcoming novel, *Engineering College Hostel*. Rao is the public face of Indian gay writing all over the world.

Dibyajyoti Sarma wrote his M. Phil thesis on Western Queer Theory and how it differs from Indian queer experience. His book of poems *Glimpses of a Personal History* was published in 2004. He is currently working on his first novel.